T0375010

FIRE IN THE BIG HOUSE

FIRE IN THE

BIG HOUSE
America's Deadliest Prison Disaster

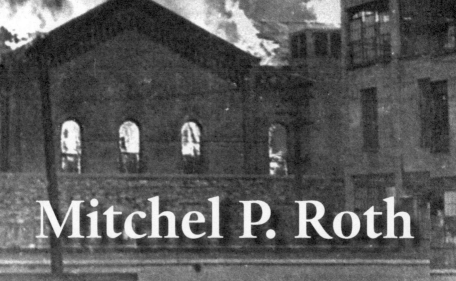

Mitchel P. Roth

Swallow Press / Ohio University Press

Athens

Swallow Press
An imprint of Ohio University Press, Athens, Ohio 45701
ohioswallow.com

© 2019 by Mitchel P. Roth
All rights reserved

To obtain permission to quote, reprint, or otherwise reproduce or distribute material
from Swallow Press / Ohio University Press publications, please contact our rights and
permissions department at (740) 593-1154 or (740) 593-4536 (fax).

Printed in the United States of America
Swallow Press / Ohio University Press books are printed on acid-free paper ∞ ™

29 28 27 26 25 24 23 22 21 20 19   5 4 3 2 1

Hardcover ISBN: 978-0-8214-2383-7
Electronic ISBN: 978-0-8214-4682-9

Library of Congress Cataloging-in-Publication Data available upon request.

This book is dedicated to the victims
of the 1930 Ohio Penitentiary fire
and their families.

CONTENTS

ILLUSTRATIONS

Map

Plates
Following page 127

ACKNOWLEDGMENTS

This book had a rather long gestation period, during which I wrote four other books as I continued to research *Fire in the Big House*. I am indebted to a number of individuals for their research assistance on the project over the years. Several of my teaching assistants helped find articles and teach me the intricacies of the Excel spreadsheet. I especially want to thank (now) Dr. Robin Jackson, who helped organize the appendix detailing the backgrounds of the victims of the fire. Duncan McCallum and Kathryn Perez have contributed at one time or another as well. I thank you for your assistance. While conducting research in Columbus, archivists at the Public Library and the Ohio History Center were particularly helpful. Lily Berkhimer at the OHC was especially helpful in reproducing images for the book.

Having written numerous books for a variety of presses over the years, I can say that the Ohio University Press has made this journey from prospectus to book as stress-free as writing a book and going through the review process can be. I would like to thank the three reviewers for their helpful suggestions that made this a much better book than it would otherwise have been.

At the Ohio University Press, acquisitions editor Rick Huard played a seminal role in bringing the book to print. I would also like to thank director Gill Berchowitz for bringing my prospectus to Rick's attention for ultimately approving its publication. Sally Welch deserves a shout-out as well for shepherding the manuscript to publication.

Finally, I would like to thank several Columbus prison historians whose work has been played an important role in contextualizing the fire within the larger history of the Ohio penal system. James Dailey III and his archival collection were always there when I had a confounding question. I would like to thank David Meyers for his contributions as well. I also cannot adequately thank enough Texas penal expert Professor Chad Trulson for reading each chapter and sending back thoughtful analysis. I also want to thank the imaginative Sam Kuzel for creating a map of the Ohio Penitentiary at the time of the fire.

Last but not least, I want to thank my wife, Ines, and son, Eric for their support of my many book projects. I am especially grateful that my mom, Leila, was able to accompany me on a road trip from Annapolis to Columbus, where I conducted research for a week. I don't think I would have ever written a book or fallen under the spell of the printed word if not for her weekly outings to the Annapolis public library as a wee lad. I love you all.

INTRODUCTION

But the public is not interested in the situation. It is only interested
after a tragedy has occurred, and not before.

—World's Work, *1930*

On April 21, 1930, having just finished their Easter Monday dinner,
eight hundred inmates returned to cellblocks G&H at Columbus's Ohio State
Penitentiary. Shortly after they were locked in, a number of convicts noticed the
first wafts of smoke. At 5:21 a shrill cry announced, "Fire!" Within less than an
hour 320 prisoners would perish in America's deadliest prison disaster (two more
would die later from gunshot wounds indirectly related to the fire).

The tragedy captured front-page headlines around the world. Within twenty-
four hours New York moviegoers were watching the Pathé News recording of the
disaster, the first live sound newsreel account of an American disaster. Theater
patrons not only witnessed some of the harrowing sights, but heard "the shrieking
of the prison siren, the hissing as water hit the flames, the howling of desperate
prisoners, the crackling of burning logs, the thud of falling beams, the commands
of Army officers and jail officers." It was a production tailor-made for the nascent
talking-film industry. Just three days after the inferno, Charlotte and Bob Miller
released the first of four recordings of the weepy ballad "Ohio Prison Fire."[1]
Commemorated in song, film, and newspaper reportage, the Ohio Penitentiary
fire and its aftermath, except for two self-published books[2] and several articles and
book chapters,[3] has since largely been forgotten.

I first came across references to the Ohio Penitentiary fire while researching
a previous book related to the history of American criminal justice. My curiosity
piqued, I sought a scholarly book on the topic and was astounded to find it had
never received the attention it deserved. As I began conducting research on it in
Ohio archives, I was surprised that outside of a coterie of local Columbus history
buffs and genealogists, most of the residents I came in contact with were unfamiliar
with what one would have thought had been a seminal event in the history of
Columbus, Ohio (let alone the United States).

The Ohio Penitentiary fire was the deadliest prison disaster in U.S. history, and the worst in the world until the horrific Honduran Comayagua Prison Farm fire in February 14, 2012, in which 361 prisoners lost their lives. It still ranks as America's most lethal prison fire and third-worst building fire (excluding 9/11), just behind Chicago's Iroquois Theater fire in December 1903, which claimed 602 victims, and the November 1942 Cocoanut Grove Nightclub fire, which took 492 lives in Boston. These disasters, as well as many others with lower body counts than the 1930 Easter Monday fire, including the 1911 Triangle Shirtwaist fire (146), the 1871 Chicago fire (200–300), the 1944 Hartford, Ringling Brothers Circus fire (167), and Chicago's 1958 Our Lady of the Angels School fire (95), have all been well documented.[4]

Although it caused only $11,000 in damage to the Columbus institution, 320 inmates perished from toxic smoke and flames in a little less time than it took to eat dinner. It was the quickest-acting building fire in American history until February 20, 2003, when, in less than ten minutes, 96 patrons died and 200 were injured at the Great White concert held at The Station in West Warwick, Rhode Island. (As in the Ohio fire, two more would die in the following days.)[5]

The dead came from many corners of Depression- and Prohibition-era America; among their numbers were shoemakers, mechanics, laborers and truck drivers, carpenters, butchers, tailors, electricians, motion picture operators, mill and iron workers, toolmakers, chauffeurs, blacksmiths, plumbers, painters and molders, bakers and marine engineers. Reflecting the punitive criminal justice system of the era, most were serving long stints for crimes ranging from robbery, larceny, and burglary to murder and rape. Still others were serving raps for violating Prohibition laws by making liquor. One victim was a former guard who was doing time for helping an inmate escape, while another had just been brought in for nonsupport of children hours before the inferno broke out. While most of the victims were sons of Ohio, others came from Pennsylvania, Tennessee, and West Virginia, still others from Mexico, Hungary, Austria, Ireland, Italy, and Russia. Of those who died, only eighteen were African American, in stark contrast to the ratio that one would expect to find in a modern-day prison facility.

By 1930 there were more Americans behind bars than in the military services. The Ohio State Penitentiary in Columbus was the biggest of America's big houses, housing more than forty-three hundred prisoners in a facility designed for fifteen hundred. The prison disaster climaxed a series of violent prison disorders that had occurred over the past ten months. The violence was attributed by some to myriad influences including recent legislation that demanded longer prison sentences, the elimination of good-conduct time, rampant idleness, and the granting of fewer paroles. Others blamed the brutality of the guards, or "screws" in convict jargon, a poorly paid and trained lot with few chances for advancement. They spent long hours watching their charges and probably often felt as locked up as the convicts. Add in unsanitary conditions, underfeeding, and overcrowding, and all the requisite elements were in place to ensure that some form of prison mutiny was always brewing. The disaster in Columbus would focus the attention of government and state officials on the condition of American prisons like never before.

At various times in its tragic and colorful history the Ohio Pen had been home to a number of celebrity convicts, including members of the John Dillinger Gang; Confederate raiders; Dr. Sam Sheppard, who inspired the TV show and motion picture *The Fugitive*; novelist Chester B. Himes; and William Sidney Porter, who would go on to become the acclaimed short-story writer O. Henry. While all of these temporary members of the prison demimonde have been the subjects of multiple books, no comprehensive examination of America's worst prison disaster and its aftermath has been published until now.

One of the most perplexing questions this book addresses is "Why has it taken so long for the complete story to be told?" Central to any answer has to be the fact that the fire's victims were convicts. They weren't blameless immigrant women working in a sweatshop, nor innocent patrons at the theater or at a crowded nightspot. Nor were they families with children settling down to watch a circus show. The victims were killers, rapists, robbers, and society's castoffs. But as what follows demonstrates, many were capable of heroic action when least expected.

Fire in the Big House, with the fire as its centerpiece, explores the lives of convicts, guards, and the warden, the rise of the big-house prison, political patronage, prison violence, as well as penal history and reform in Ohio and America. It is also about much more: about the fire's causes and its human aftermath, about stories of lives put at risk because of tightfisted economic and political decisions. A reconsideration of this tragedy still resonates almost ninety years later, as the United States continues to lock up more people than any other country in the world. An article in the *London Daily Telegraph* published several months after the fire asserted in no uncertain terms that "the prison system of the United States is an unendurable disgrace to a civilized country" and that "while convicts are decreasing in other countries," American citizens were "clamoring for bigger and better jails to accommodate criminals." Sounds familiar. Today a prison disaster of this magnitude would instigate a fierce outcry in the press and beyond. But in 1930 the fire kept the attention of society for a relatively short time, as darkening world geopolitics and the most recent lurid events overshadowed the horror in Ohio.

In his account of a tragic blizzard on January 12, 1888, that suddenly left five hundred dead on the prairie across Nebraska, the Dakotas, and Minnesota, author David Laskin wrote, "Chance is always a silent partner in disaster. Bad luck, bad timing, the wrong choice at a crucial moment, and the door is inexorably shut and barred."[6] The same could be said about the events of Easter Monday 1930, when everything that could go wrong did go wrong.

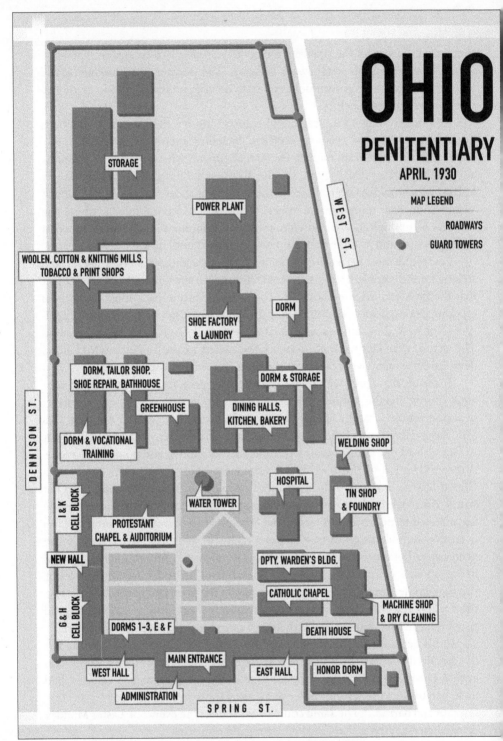

Layout of the Ohio Penitentiary in April 1930. Map by Sam Kužel.

1 FIRE IN THE BIG HOUSE

I hope I never go to Hell if it's this hot!
—Inmate Charles Oliver, 4H, April 21, 1930

My God what is going to happen next?
—Warden Preston Thomas, April 21, 1930

Sundown on Easter Monday 1930. The nightly lockup at the Ohio State Penitentiary had just ended. Although it was April 21, it was unseasonably cold outside, and within the forbidding thirty-foot walls of the aging and overcrowded Ohio State Penitentiary it probably wasn't much warmer. Located less than a mile from the Columbus state capitol complex, the gray edifice was the most crowded big house in America, bulging at the seams with triple the capacity it was designed for.

While there has always been some debate over the exact time the fire broke out, all agreed that it occurred sometime after the second dinner shift, which began at 4:20. Given barely twenty minutes to consume their prison victuals, the eight hundred inmates assigned to the aging G&H cellblocks were marched back to their cells and methodically locked up for the night, four to a cell, each cell locked separately. This was rarely accomplished before 4:45. It was then customary for a cellblock officer to telephone the stockade to affirm that the night count was spot-on (that is, that the same number that left their cells for dinner had been counted on their return).

None of the inmates in the G&H blocks could have predicted, as they contemplated their well-practiced routine of winding down for the long night ahead, that by 8 p.m. more than one-third of them would be dead. Whiling away their last hours, some read or wrote letters, others played chess and checkers, and others surely dwelled on upcoming court cases and parole dates.

Although estimates as to the exact time the fire began vary by only several minutes, those minutes were enough time to mean the difference between life and death. Some convicts testified smelling smoke in the cellblock as early as 5 p.m. However, most accounts suggest that the fire became obvious sometime after 5:20 pm. Inmate trustee Liston G. Schooley was covering Deputy Warden James C. Woodard's office by himself, just east of G&H, some 500–750 feet across the prison yard, when he first noticed smoke at 5:20 coming from the direction of the New Hall cellhouse. He had just returned from the last dinner shift and was getting ready to sit down and read a newspaper when he looked west and saw "smoke emitting from the roof or the upper windows of the cell block," but partly hidden from view behind the chapel.

Schooley would later recount that at virtually the same time he spotted the fire from the office window, an inmate nurse was exercising, walking back and forth on the walkway in front of the deputy warden's office. He turned and caught Schooley's attention at the window and yelled, "The G and H cell block is on fire." In his testimony before the fire inquiry, convened the day after the fire, Schooley noted that he called the central station in the guardroom and alerted the operator, a friend of his, who responded, "I know it, I got it." Schooley told the operator to notify the fire department. Later he expressed certainty that this had been done in a "most efficient manner." Predicting they would be needed elsewhere, Schooley went out on the front steps of the deputy's office and told the exercising nurses to go to the hospital at once. By this time the yard was filling up with smoke and he found breathing already "rather difficult."[1]

Inside the cell-house building itself, survivors would mostly agree that someone screamed "Fire!" around 5:21 p.m., but certainly no later than 5:35. Many sources asserted that if it had been anyone else but the convict prankster Barry Sholkey who first raised the hue and cry inside the G&H blocks at 5:20, things might have turned out differently.[2] Housed on the second tier of the doomed six-tier cellblock, inmate Leo Lyon later testified that Sholkey always played the "jester or joker." Lyon was playing cards in the cell above when he heard the fire warning and recalled telling his cellmates, "Oh, he is full of shit."[3] When nearby guards heard Sholkey's warning, they refused to take the bait as well and simply scoffed at the alarm. Not surprisingly, when the first signs of smoke were detected, most guards played down the potential peril. They were used to small fires being set by prisoners from time to time, mostly to get attention or out of boredom. Some thought it was probably a mattress fire, since that was about the only item in a cell that could burn, and it was not uncommon for convicts to burn parts of their mattresses to smoke out bedbugs.

Nonetheless, Leo Lyon was curious enough to check it out. Getting up from his card game, he "flashed the range," common prison parlance for the technique of taking a small mirror and sticking it through the bars to get a better look. It also allowed him to look over the wall in the building. That was when he first spotted "sparks between the blocks." He called to his partners and told them that there was indeed a fire. He too said that Sholkey was the "first man to give the alarm."[4]

A few minutes later, flames and dense smoke convinced the convicts and prison keepers that a fire was indeed threatening the prison building. Stiff winds from the northern part of the building fanned toxic smoke south into the blocks, and mayhem ensued as inmates closest to a now-billowing cloud of smoke began yelling and rapping the bars with their tin cups, like actors in some B-grade prison movie.

Many survivors pegged the time of day by their cheap dollar alarm clocks, while others depended on a centrally located wall clock to determine what time the fire began. Still others, serving relatively long prison sentences, had timed their daily routines to the minute and claimed they had little need for a clock. Edward Dolan, a prisoner out of Hamilton County, later testified that he was sitting in his cell on the first tier, reading a magazine, as three cellmates played cards, between 5:20 and 5:25 when he heard the shout of "Fire!" Asked how he was so sure about the time, he said it was because he was "waiting for the baseball man to bring the baseball extra [on the radio]."[5]

Six years into a ten-to-twenty-five-year stretch, Robert Farr was on the second tier playing checkers. He remembered the time because "it was customary like clockwork to play checkers from five to seven." After just a couple of games he heard screams and shouts and the rattling of bars from prisoners on the upper ranges of the cellblock. Prisons get used to the almost nonstop noise and clamor that comes with caging up thousands of young men with nothing much to do. Like others, Farr first thought there was "nothing to it," probably a cell fire, and no reason to get overly excited. So the checkers games continued. Farr remembered that he and his partner, whom he described as "rapid players," had been playing long enough to have finished a game and started another one when the yelling became more intense. They finished another game and had started again when the "smoke began to roll in" and his partner insisted they had to quit.[6]

Inmate Roy Williams was "just getting ready to play a game of hearts" on the bottom range of cells when he smelled smoke coming from the direction of the cotton mill. He would later report, "We heard a couple of shots and smelled smoke, and we figured it was the cotton mill, the wind being from that direction, blowing the smoke into the cellblock."[7] Williams hoped that it wasn't the cotton mill because he had already "rebuilt the place twice over" and "didn't want that job again." But if it was, he hoped "they burn[ed] it to the ground." In moments, one of the boys looked out and spotted a big cloud of smoke and said, "Hell that is right out here." On the same tier of cells, James Waltham asked a guard what was going on and was told by the nonchalant keeper that there "was some timber burning, nothing to get worried about."

Two tiers up, Edward Saas was engrossed in a game of pinochle with his cell partner. He didn't smell the smoke right away or become aware of the brewing disaster until he heard some hollering from tier two, just below him. He didn't pay it much mind at first, thinking it was a joke: "they were hollering, but that whole bunch is mostly half-wits and always raising hell."[8] But the smoke "got bad quickly." Saas and his cellmate were among the many convicts who took blankets and put them up on the cell bars to combat the smoke, but to little effect, as the smoke was now as low as their range on the third tier. Innovating moment by moment, they next soaked towels in water and wrapped them around their heads. It was only ten minutes since the first hint of fire.

George W. Johnson, better known by his hometown nickname "Cleveland," was serving a five-to-ten-year bit for perjury. He had been paroled after five years but twenty-nine months later was back in stir for a parole violation to finish out his sentence. He was working in the chapel as a porter close to the G&H blocks, mopping up, dusting off erasers, and cleaning windows, when he first noticed some smoke between 5:20 and 5:25. Fellow Cleveland native Roy "Whitey" Steele was on the bottom tier when he heard some screams and saw a little smoke on the upper ranges. He didn't think much of it at the moment, but curiosity got the better of him. He flashed the range with "a piece of mirror about an inch square" and "pushed it out in the block," where he could see "flames and a lot of smoke and we got scared and tried to break down the cell, a one-armed man and myself."[9]

Cincinnati-raised Edward J. Gallagher, a self-described "orphan asylum boy," was housed on the fourth tier. Gallagher and his cellies had come back from the first mess about 4:10, "rolled a smoke," and were waiting for the mailman. For Gallagher, the hand-rolled smoke was much more important; mail service didn't mean much to him, since "I never get any mail, I ain't got any family, but I like to see my partners get letters." Gallagher dozed off, but woke up again between 5:20 and 5:30 to find that his cellmates had covered their faces with towels and handker-chiefs. In prison jargon he asked them, "What's the come? What's the kid?" They pointed to the outside, where he saw the smoke.[10]

Murray Wolfe, in the first cell on the first tier, had returned to his cell after the first mess sometime between 4 and 4:10. He proceeded to wash up and clean his teeth before hopping on his bunk to read the latest copy of the *Saturday Evening Post*. Following prison rules, which prohibited smoking in his bunk, Wolfe sat on the side of his bunk with his feet dangling over the side, "smoking and reading at the same time, making myself comfortable" until the evening papers were delivered: "just a procedure for myself in the evening. I try to keep my mind occupied while I am in here reading. That is the only way I can keep it occupied." He later testified that he heard shouts of "Fire!" around 5:20. A former newspaper reporter, he had a good eye and ear for detail. He remembered that most of the inmates were talking, paying attention to each other, killing time, waiting for the papers. Like others, at first Wolfe thought it was typical mattress fire, having "no idea of the immensity" of the fire until "smoke began curling" up through the bottom ventilators."[11]

Wolfe's location in the first cell of the lowest tier placed him closest to the chief day guard's desk, situated in front of the cell, so he was well tuned to the rhythms of the guards night and day. From his vantage point he could see fifty-five-year old head day guard Thomas Watkinson washing his face and hands in the guardroom basin just outside his cell. Known as "the Englishman" for his na-tivity, he would probably have had his coat and hat off as he prepped to go home. Although he should have been on duty until his shift ended at 6 p.m., following his usual routine he began getting ready to end his day shift at 5:15 and then headed down to the guard room, where by 5:45 he would meet with the incoming night-shift guards, who went on duty at 6 p.m. This transition rarely took place later than 6:15. The fact that the fire occurred between shifts contributed mightily to the chaos and confusion that followed.

It had been a rough patch of days for the Englishman. The inmates had been "pestering" him because he had locked up the cons on the second tier on Easter Sunday, forcing them to miss their Easter dinner and the opportunity to attend Easter church services. As Watkinson dried off his hands and face, inmate Wolfe noticed that his "face changed terribly. I think the man was stupefied. I think he was frightened to death." Another inmate claimed, "He just stood there like a damned fool."[12]

During the day Watkinson was partnered with guard Hubert Richardson, whose recollections somewhat contradicted Wolfe's testimony. Richardson claimed the Englishman was actually in the process of getting a convict shoeshine in the guardroom when Richardson alerted him to the fire. Richardson was posted on the sixth range when he spotted the fire in the north end of the cellhouse. A former decorator by trade, he blamed current health issues on his prior profession, admitting, "I can't hold my water"; that is, the paint-related lead in his system from his previous occupation necessitated his constant urination. He had just returned from another run to the bathroom and was walking his range to make sure all was well when he looked to the north and saw "blazes" about 5:40.

The cantankerous "Englishman," Thomas Watkinson, would later explain to a Board of Inquiry that Richardson was "kind of new." Since there was "no place to take a leak there," the rookie guard walked down the stairs and up to the neighboring E&F dormitory, "where there is a toilet and leaked up there." He came back about seven to eight minutes later, went into the block, and then reported to Watkinson, "There is a Fire."[13] Richardson's version varied somewhat from Watkinson's. Richardson claimed that he hollered to the elderly guard, whom he referred to as "Shorty," on the first floor from his vantage point above the fifth tier.[14] Getting no response, he rushed down to deliver the alarm in person. He estimated it took him no more than a minute to do so.

Ohio Penitentiary warden Preston Elmer Thomas usually ended his workday around 5 p.m., but just happened to stay another twenty minutes on Easter Monday, before heading upstairs from his offices to his living quarters. He would remember being on his porch around 5:35 when he was told of the fire.[15] Thomas, "affectionately known as the Pig" by some inmates,[16] had been appointed warden in 1913 and by 1930 had a well-deserved reputation as a hardliner. Having personally helped stop past escape attempts, he was always fretful about the next one, lest it blot his résumé. He would come under withering criticism for not overseeing the immediate release of trapped prisoners from their cells as well as for not being in the prison yard directing rescue efforts, choosing instead to wait for the National Guard.

Warden Thomas would later claim he had a touch of asthma and could not smell the smoke, unlike almost everyone else, who smelled the fire before they saw it. He told the subsequent fire inquiry, "I can't smell. I lost my smeller several years ago. . . . I can't smell a skunk—I am not kidding. . . . I have had a good many operations for olfactory trouble."[17] His handicap might have been overlooked in the subsequent investigations if he had not consistently refused to institute safety devices, drills, or regulations to prevent fires. His main concern was preventing escapes at any cost. In his defense, in 1930, on the heels of a series of bloody prison riots the previous year, the primary focus of any prison warden was on keeping inmates in their cells, not necessarily preparing to get them out safely in the event of an emergency.

Looking out into the prison courtyard for a moment, Thomas saw the intensifying smoke to the west. He exclaimed something to the effect of "My God what is going to happen next." He asked several guards whether an alarm had already been sent to the Columbus Fire Department and was told that it had. At this point he made a decision that he probably regretted in the days to come. Rather than lead the growing rescue efforts within the prison yard, he decided to station himself outside the prison walls to supervise efforts to prevent any convicts from breaking out. Profoundly disliked by many of his charges, the warden was usually hesitant to spend too much time in the yard without sufficient protection. He would not make an appearance within the prison walls until two days after the fire. The "hero priest," Father Albert O'Brien, would later report that the convicts were indeed ready to kill the warden if he stepped inside the prison during the pandemonium.

Night guards Thomas Little and William Baldwin, as well as seventy-two-year-old Captain John Hall, had all arrived at the guardroom separately on Easter Monday, a half hour early for their shifts. It was customary for Baldwin to get to the guardroom before 6. His explanation was that he had an old car and "sometimes it don't just jump as it should," so he always liked to get a head start so he wouldn't miss his shift.[18] That day he stopped to speak briefly with Captain Hall, who was perusing a newspaper outside, before entering the guardroom. Following protocol, he signed in on two sign-in sheets and sat down. He recalled that he was sitting against the wall making small talk with night guard Thomas F. Little until about 5:45, when a prisoner ran into the guardroom yelling, "Fire."[19] As will be seen, the early arrivals of Baldwin and Little would prove serendipitous.

Leaving the prison yard, Warden Thomas made a beeline for the guardroom door and told Little and Baldwin rather cryptically to "get down there" on his way out of the building. The guards would later admit that no one was really sure which of them he was speaking to since there were others in the room as well, but they made off for the endangered cellblocks just the same.[20] Baldwin and Little hurried from the guardhouse through the E&F dormitory toward G&H, with the geriatric Captain Hall trying to keep up. Not surprisingly, the decrepit captain lagged behind the two younger guards. Reaching the cellblock, they found that Watkinson had stationed himself at the cage gate leading into the upper ranges. The cell house was rapidly filling with dangerous smoke, and flames could be seen in the upper reaches of the northern cellblocks (I&K). The guards intended, once Watkinson had opened the gate, to reach the men in the upper ranges. But this would have to wait, as some type of verbal altercation took place between the two night guards and the day guard Watkinson.

Watkinson, Baldwin, and Little all held the same rank, but since it was still before 6 p.m., the Englishman was in control of the cellblock, which he zealously protected. At this point Little and Baldwin had to overcome their first major challenge, which was to convince Watkinson to open the cage gate leading up to tiers two to six. The day guards had the cell keys to the upper tiers, but those would be worthless without access to the upper ranges. But Watkinson refused to cooperate, telling them, "I got no orders to unlock those men."[21] Even after they told the Englishman that he had verbal orders from the warden to release the convicts, Watkinson held firm, replying, "I have no order to open the door."[22] Little said, "We have to get it open and get up in there and get fellows out." Watkinson adamantly responded, "Well I can't open it without orders." Outranked before 6 p.m., Little recognized he needed to act quickly. He ran around to the west side of the block, looking for any opportunity to get the men out, but the smoke was so dense he had to run back around to haggle once more with Watkinson, wasting at least five to six valuable minutes.

After being refused entry into the cage door leading up to the top five tiers, Baldwin and Little returned to the adjacent ground-level cells on the first tier, the only ones they had access to without passing through the cage first, and began releasing the convicts. They were the first guards to actually release any convicts from the cellblocks. Little told Baldwin that they had to "get this goddamn door [cage gate] open or those fellows are all going to die." He could not know that they were already dying by the dozens. It was at this point that Watkinson finally came to his senses and decided to cooperate. He approached Little with the key, "but not fast enough." Little grabbed it out of his hand, opened the cage door, and started upstairs. He is credited with leading the first rescuers up to higher tiers, but not without making sure that others followed him in case he was over-come with smoke and needed rescuing himself. Initially, when he turned around he only saw Baldwin.[23] Five to eight crucial minutes had been wasted by the time the rescue could begin.

Watkinson's account conflicts sharply with that of the guards Little and Baldwin, as it did with Captain Hall's. The Englishman later claimed that he was just sticking his key into the cage lock to let the guards in when Captain Hall intervened and told him, "Don't open that yet, don't do that." Since Hall was the captain, the Englishman would argue, "he had to follow superiors or he would be suspended for disobeying rules and order." As to why Hall wouldn't permit it, perhaps Hall thought it "didn't look so dangerous in G&H." At one point during the exchange over the keys, Baldwin commented, "Isn't this hell?"[24]

Contrary to Watkinson's assertion that Hall had personally ordered him to keep the cells locked, both Little and Baldwin later testified under oath that Hall never even made it to the gate to prevent them from entering the tiers. In fact, they never saw Hall at the cage door. But they could definitely hear him hollering behind them for inmates to knock windows out to let in some air and the sounds of shattering glass. In fact, Hall could not possibly have reached the cage before them. Furthermore, if he had verbally directed Watkinson not to open the gate, he would have to have done this after the two guards got there, which simply never happened. Buttressing the guards' claims was Captain Hall's testimony that he "did not tell Watkinson anything.[25]

By the time Baldwin and Little had retrieved the keys from Watkinson, it was clear that the source of the fire was in the wooden form work in the adjacent I&K blocks, which were undergoing construction. When they got through the gate, the guards parceled out the keys to convicts taking part in the rescue efforts, many of whom had come from the E&F dorms. Baldwin and Little reached the third tier and were soon joined by a prisoner, but they couldn't make it farther than the fourth tier and had to retreat to the second range. Against his better judgment, instead of running outside for air, Little decided to keep up his rescue efforts and began unlocking the second range. As he ran up the second range, he could see the flames above but "couldn't tell whether they were in the ceiling or in the lumber on top." It was impossible at that point to ascertain whether the fire was actually in the roof or on top of it because there was only one story separating the roof from the fifth tier under construction in I&K.

Little was able to get everyone out on one side of the second tier. When a "colored" inmate came around, he told him to "get these fellows" out on the other side of the second tier. He went back up to the fourth tier, where he passed out from smoke inhalation and was carried out by Baldwin and three or four inmates. He later lamented, "I was so damned near all in I couldn't remember. . . . There was no man in the world who could have got up there at the time we got in the cage, no man, I don't care who it was."[26] Within five minutes the fire made a decided change. "Oh, it was fast, yes, it come down there, the smoke seemed to come all at once, just come down there in a big billow." In retrospect, Little and other rescuers regretted not starting at the top and working their way down. This was a moot point, though, since by the time the keys were turned over to Little most of the convicts in the top two tiers were at death's door.[27]

It was well documented that none of the G&H cells were opened before 5:45, six minutes after the fire department was officially contacted. Little would later note that by the time he and fellow officer Baldwin began opening cells the smoke was already too intense on the top range to save anyone on tier six. Little and Baldwin were quickly overcome by the dense smoke as they opened the first two tiers of G&H. One convict reported noticing blood trickling out of Little's nose. Abandoning their efforts for the moment, they passed on cell keys to other convicts, including William Robert Noel from the F Dormitory, who opened the third-range cells.

Baldwin and Little recovered after getting some fresh air out in the yard and returned to aid the rescue efforts in the doomed cellblock. But in the meantime the dense smoke had become even more suffocating. The valiant keepers could go no higher than the fifth tier before retreating. Curiously, some witnesses later reported seeing the two guards on the fourth tier and as high as the sixth, but as with so many other observations, the tumult of the night's events prevented the substantiation of many statements.

Guards Baldwin and Little, whose presence the warden regarded as a "godsend," would later testify, as mentioned above, that the warden only took time to shout several cryptic orders to them in the guardroom before disappearing outside. However, as the warden told it, "I told guards to take those keys and go down there." His badinage with the inquisitors the following day sounded like part of the Abbott and Costello "Who's on First" sketch. When the warden was asked if he had specifically told them what to do when they got down to G&H with the keys, Thomas, obviously losing patience, responded, "Unlock the prisoners; wouldn't take the keys down there and play with them." However, both sides would eventually agree that he probably only said, "Get the keys down quickly."[28]

While it is uncertain who was actually the first to observe the fire, "it was presumably seen by several at about the same time." By some accounts "a guard in the tower on the outside wall," a short distance beyond the north end of the building where the fire originated, was among the first and "called someone at street level who pulled fire alarm box 261, at the head of Dublin St."[29] A day guard named Porter, working near the wagon stockade, testified that he had turned in the fire alarm three times beginning around 5:40 before firing his rifle to get someone's attention.

It is also conceivable that the fire was first observed by a trustee who was driving back from town to the prison, after running an errand for the warden's wife, sometime between 5:30 and 5:35. When he noticed smoke outside the cellhouse structure, he went to a fire-alarm box and turned in the first fire alarm at exactly 5:39, the time when Columbus fire chief A. R. Nice claimed he received the first alarm from box 261, outside the penitentiary on the corner of Dennison and Dublin Avenues. This clearly contradicted the claim of Liston Schooley in the deputy warden's office that his friend had notified the fire department around 5:20. Times were logged immediately at the firehouse, making the fire company's reported times the most reliable. But the time of this first fire alarm was almost twenty minutes later than the times reported by convicts and guards inside the walls. By 5:39 the fire already had an almost half-hour head start. During the subsequent Board of Inquiry that began the day after the fire, Nice declared that all could have been saved if they had been released from cells as soon as fire was discovered. He told the board that "there must have been undue delay because the first alarms came from a box outside the prison walls," rather than from inside the facility when smoke was first spotted.[30]

At 5:40 another alarm was received from the box closest to the penitentiary. After another alarm at 5:42, the fire chief left his home on Gilbert Street and arrived at the Spring Street gate on the corner of Spring and Dennison Streets within seven minutes, where he was met by assistant fire chief Ogburn, who had responded with Company #1. Seeing the fire burning at the north end of the building, Nice, he later testified, turned in the fourth alarm at 6:03, summoning more fire companies to the scene.

Deputy Warden James C. Woodard, who had been on a brief hiatus and was on his way back to the prison when he was alerted to the brewing disaster, arrived close to the same time the fire department did. The warden recalled telling Woodard to "hustle right inside, you take care of the inside and I will take care of the outside."[31] After making sure that prisoners were being released from their cells in

G&H, Woodard ordered prisoners from the adjoining E&F dorm to be released as well. As smoke threatened the upper blocks of A&B and C&D, the infamous White City (so named because the interior was painted white), Woodard, fearing that flames might follow, returned to the guardroom, grabbed keys for those blocks and released its inmates into the prison yard.

Woodard was careful to prevent convicts in the so-called Bad Boy Company, Company K, from also being released. To assuage their fears, he told Company K convicts that the fire did not yet pose a threat to them and promised to return and release them if it did.[32] Woodard was quite sensitive to claims made later on that some of the K Company convicts actually had been let out of their cells. "While it is said some of them was in the yard, but there wasn't," he testified later, explaining that this rumor got started "when a man without clothes went to the commissary and got whatever he could," which turned out to be the same "striped shirts and striped coats" worn by K Company.[33] For good measure he placed death row prisoners in solitary cells for safety as well.

In the fire's immediate aftermath, much of the blame for the tragedy would be directed at Warden Thomas, in no small part due to his decision to station himself where he did "to prevent escapes." To be fair, the warden's main concern, like that of other big house wardens of the era, was to prevent inmates from escaping at any cost. It was an era when keeping inmates behind bars always took precedence over getting them out of their cells safely in an emergency. The warden later admitted that "he considered the menace of a possible break for liberty by the prisoners as more pressing than the fire itself." He also assumed that the proximity of the prison to the fire department, just blocks away, was his ace in the hole. But he placed too much faith in the firefighters' response time.

Convinced that the fire was part of a larger escape attempt, the warden phoned the headquarters of the 166th Infantry Regiment of the Ohio Militia for support and went out to the street to await their arrival. As he left, he issued orders to shoot any escapees.[34] When Columbus city police officers and federal troops from Fort Hayes arrived before the guardsmen, the warden, some ten minutes after positioning himself outside the walls, put his defensive strategy into practice, ordering the troops to facilitate the entry of the fire department through the stockade gate. By 6 p.m., Columbus city police had been ordered into the prison yard to restore a semblance of order. They were soon joined by other day guards. Unaware of the scale of the pending disaster, guards rushed to and fro, adding to the general disorder, picking up machine guns and shotguns, shouting for ammo, and preparing for a prison riot, while outside, grim-faced guards, police, and members of the arriving military units trained their gimlet eyes and weapons on the walls.

As the subsequent Board of Inquiry would prove, the warden had plenty of reasons to keep himself scarce within the prison walls. Father Albert O'Brien, who had reported that the convicts were probably ready to kill the warden if he stepped inside the prison courtyard during the pandemonium, added, "Those men had no thought of escape. They were thinking of those men perishing in the flames like moths. They were enraged because of the utter helplessness; because they were beyond the help of those gathered outside the wall." When the warden finally entered the walls on Wednesday, two days after the fire, hundreds of convicts "let loose a crescendo of jeers and catcalls."

There is some controversy over when Little and Baldwin retrieved the keys for the endangered cellblocks. Most accounts agree with their claim that Little already had the range keys in his pocket before he had heard anything about a fire.[35] The two guards had established a well-rehearsed routine and had an understanding that Little would always open the small door in the guardroom containing the keys when they got ready to go on shift, take one set of keys, and carry it on to the cellblock. As night guards on G&H, either Baldwin or Little would work on the bottom range and hold on to the bottom range key while the other took the keys to the higher ranges. They would then switch range watch and keys each hour.

Whoever was manning the first tier was also responsible for the second tier and would stay at the desk located near the first tier, answering phone calls and the like. Unlike the other five tiers, the first floor was not enclosed, but the guard on the range was responsible for that floor and held the key to the cage as well as the first-tier range key, just in case incoming prisoners came in too late to be assigned a new cell. So, in effect, one guard would have two keys and the other would have five keys for the other five double ranges.[36]

Little was later queried why the keys were not returned to the safekeeping of the administrative offices after each count and why it was necessary for guards to hold onto the keys while on duty, since they were not really necessary for the count. Moreover, this strategy brought up serious security concerns in the event one of the guards was overpowered. Little explained that it was convenient to have them since the G&H guards were stationed "quite a distance" from the guardroom, and almost every evening packages were delivered, including new shoes and other items that could not be slid under the cell door like mail. Little also noted that the cellblock housed the machine shop company and all of the construction companies, and almost every day there were a few prisoners on special detail, so the keys were needed to let them back into their cells.[37]

Between 5:30 and 6, Ray W. Humphries, the editor of the popular civic publication *Columbus This Week*, returned to Columbus from Grove City. While taking a shortcut home that took him by the corner of West Spring and Dennison Avenue, he "noticed under the viaduct west of the penitentiary" members of the fire department and a lot of commotion. His journalistic instincts were strong, and he proceeded closer to the prison. "Some chap yelled at me from the filling station on the corner" and told him, "There is a Fire in the Penitentiary."[38]

Humphries continued driving north on Dublin Avenue when he realized he had his Graflex camera with him. He got out of his car and looked for a good spot to take pictures from. He quickly spotted clouds of smoke coming from the cellblock. He then ran over to the Paragon Oil Co., where he took five pictures. He remembered an old newspaper adage: "When you get through taking pictures that are 'unusual,' you usually look at your watch." He did; the time was 5:47. He went back to the corner of Spring and Dennison to get closer to the action but was forced back each time by a police cordon. He lamented that he "didn't have a badge like a news photographer would."[39]

Other locals took note as well. The operator of a nearby filling station near the southwest corner of the penitentiary remembered seeing flames and hearing cries as he rushed to the prison gate. "It seemed like a thousand men were yelling and beating on the bars." He made out a lone voice screaming, "For God's Sake let me out. I'm burning—I'm burning." This proved too much for the attendant, and he reversed course away from the fire. When he came back about fifteen minutes later, "most of the cries had stopped" by then. One reporter would describe how the prisoners screamed in terror as a "snakelike coil of heavy black smoke crawled into the cells through ventilators."[40]

The fire seemed to draw spectators like moths to a flame. Indeed, "The blazes leaping into the sky acted as a beacon for the curious from all over the city. . . . Rooftops were crowded in the vicinity, and thousands clambered upon every available point of vantage to see something." Radio broadcasts also contributed to the growing crowds, especially since the late newspapers had not been delivered yet. "Even the radio, broadcasting its appeal [for help], struck alarm into the homes of thousands," who would drive, walk, and run to Spring Street. Police were faced with the task of controlling the area so that rescue workers, doctors, guards, soldiers, and others could make their way into the burning Ohio Penitentiary.[41]

Radio transmissions might have brought legions of curious citizens, but the broadcasts' ability to summon emergency personnel was inestimable. "Radio played one of the principal roles when Old Man Terror staged his recent thrilling two week melodrama. . . . Almost as the curtain rose on that spectacle of fire and disorder, radio was on the stage, and it stayed there until the show, from spot news standpoint, was over."[42]

The blaze flashed along oil-soaked forms and dry timbers from I&K, undergoing reconstruction, southward into the ill-fated cellblocks, igniting the ancient wooden roof, which was overdue to be replaced. Clouds of smoke billowed out, filling not just the cellblocks but the prison quadrangle as well. Assistant Fire Chief Osborn would later suggest that the guards "seemed a little slow getting cells open," but followed up by diplomatically commenting that he could "understand" their lack of progress "in the face of terrific heat, dense smoke and so many cells."[43] As the heat grew more intense, some prisoners still locked in the G&H tiers ran water in their sinks and dashed water on their faces and each other; others soaked blankets and hung them in front of their cells to keep smoke out; still others dipped their heads into their water-filled toilet bowls (some of the dead were found in this position). Several reportedly slit their own throats rather than burn alive, while others pleaded with guards to shoot them, forgetting that guards, even if they wanted to oblige the desperate men, were prohibited from carrying guns inside the cellblocks.

The convicts responded to the fire in a variety of ways. One of the more curious responses was a submissiveness that took over certain prisoners, not unlike death row inmates who had already made their peace with walking down the long "green mile" to the death chamber. Chester Himes, who would later gain fame as the author of a series of detective novels set in Harlem featuring the black detectives Coffin Ed Johnson and Grave Digger Jones, was a witness to this behavior, which he called "that queer docility common to prisoners."[44] He would draw on his experience as a survivor of the prison fire in his short story "To What Red Hell?," in which a prisoner finds himself utterly incapable of functioning during the Ohio inferno. Prison conditioning has so diminished the protagonist that when he hears a voice tell him, "Get a blanket, and give a hand here," he can only say, "'No can do,' in a low choky whisper. . . . He really wanted to go up in that smoking inferno where heroes were being made. . . . But he couldn't, just couldn't, that's all."[45]

But other convicts utilized their ingenuity and survival skills, honed during long hours of idleness and contemplation, and managed to live to tell their tales. Many improvised as the smoke poured into their cellblock. Inmate Wolfe advised his cellies to wet their handkerchiefs at the water fountain inside their cell and place them over their faces. Several convicts picked up chairs and started banging on doors for attention. Meanwhile, "bedlam was raring in the building" as the rest of the inmates began pounding on their doors to be let out.[46]

Charles Oliver of Toledo was trapped in his cell on the fourth tier. "Almost before we realized it the flames were sweeping along the cellblock and it began to get hot." Together with his three cellmates, "We yelled and yelled for them to open the cell but they wouldn't. When it seemed that we would be roasted alive we started the water running in the faucets of our cell and as the floor became flooded we lay down in the water," putting their faces in it and splashing each other. "We were scared. I'll admit it, scared to death . . . seemed we would be roasted alive. It got hotter and hotter. I hope I never go to hell if it's this hot." They had fully "expected to die, lying there in the water with flames all around us," until miraculously some convicts came and knocked the cell locks off with sledgehammers. Oliver and his two companions got safely out of the cell, but not before they had a good bit of hair "singed off" their heads. It was a small price to pay for rescue. Once freed, rather than make a mad rush to freedom, Oliver and his partners joined others, dashing through a wall of flames to help free the inmates on the next range of cells.[47] The scorching heat forced the rescuers to beat a hasty retreat after knocking the locks off just three cell doors.

Columbus residents, inmates, and guards survived with indelible images etched into their memories. One recalled a "negro clutching at the iron grilling of a window" on the fourth tier, pulling frantically at bars that wouldn't budge. "Delirious with fear . . . he shouted at the guards, firemen and police below," but no one could understand him as "he gibbered high up behind the grilling" of a solid window.[48] A guard looked up at the caged convicts and "saw faces at the windows wreathed in smoke that poured through broken glass." A United Press reporter observed a fellow being lowered down with a rope until it slipped and tightened around his neck, strangling him to death—a public hanging.[49]

Convicts on the fifth and sixth tiers, closest to the blazing roof, cursed and prayed, others broke down and cried, while others uttered "blasphemies, too horrible to repeat." Some early accounts described men scratching at the doors to their cells "with bleeding hands." Others "ripped at their hair" or "chewed at the steel barriers with their teeth like caged animals." One report had a prisoner slashing his own throat with an improvised knife. One of the heroes of the evening, later confined in the hospital with severe burns, remembered passing one cell as he held an unconscious victim in his arms, where he saw a fellow convict "dangling at the end of a twisted shirt in the last throes of death by strangulation."[50]

Few prisoners chronicled their Easter Monday fire experiences, and those who did often recorded their memories decades later, when they were liable to be distorted by the passage of time. Sugar Bill Baliff, a bank robber doing fifty years, was interviewed about the fire almost twenty years later. He was housed in a nearby cellblock, and it wasn't long before the smoke was being pushed into his quarters. He recalled shouting for help until he was rescued by two men bearing sledgehammers, who helped break him out of the cell. Baliff claimed to have joined others from his block who headed to the burning cellblock to help in the rescue. He said, "We started to move the men. We didn't have enough stretchers, so we used blankets. Some of the boys died locked together. After we [delivered] them out in the yard, we counted them—322."[51]

Sonny Hanovich shared some of his memories over a half century later, offering some of the most detailed and insightful comments on the event. He remembered that it had been "a beautiful spring day. The sun was shining. The shadows were slowly creeping over the huge quadrangle and I noticed this sort of haze or mist." He didn't pay attention to it until it got darker and "began to sort of roll, like a fog. The next thing I know someone says that's smoke, dammit, that's smoke." One of his cellmates asked him, "Sonny, do you hear anything?" He responded, "Yeah, the last few minutes I've been hearing something like screams, or something like that," and in the next moments he heard someone shout "Fire."

Fifty years later, Sonny still vividly remembered the bodies: "[I] thought . . . these were all colored men in there, because when we started carrying them out, stretching them out on the grass there, I thought they was all colored, that's how charred they were." Sonny was among the observers who were under the impression that "no one burned to death," and that the burns must have been received after suffocating to death.

Although Hanovich was not housed in the threatened cellblocks, he recounted that many of the convicts in his block feared the whole pen was going to go up in flames, while others took "any opportunity at all" to "join in the melee and make as much racket as they could." Sonny considered himself lucky for having been recently transferred from the fatal 6G tier to the A&B blocks in another building.

Like many other rescuers, Sonny could only make it up to the fourth range before being forced back by smoke. He backtracked to the third tier. By then "the smoke there was already down to a couple of feet from the top of range. . . .

We walked along the cells there peering in to see whether or not we could see any signs of life. . . . This one man ahead of me, he passed one cell, and just as I approached it, I thought I see a man make a movement. Now there was inmates lying in all positions, some on the bed, some on the floor, and one guy had his head in the toilet, see. This one particular body, he had his fingers entwined in the cell grating and was just hanging there." As he and another inmate tried to pull him away from the cell bars, "it just left most of the right hand there." Thinking he saw one body move, Hanovich "hollered to this guy, 'Hey get back here.' He came back and I said 'I think I saw that guy move.' We stood there watching for a couple of seconds and he said, 'No hell, all these guys along here are gone. Let's go down to the next range, maybe we can help them.'" On their way down they could hear men battering with hammers, sledgehammers—but "there was no order. . . . There was no one there to take command, no guard or anything." Sonny would later help remove the bodies. He and the other rescuers were instructed to use regular stretchers, instead of the makeshift alternatives they had assembled from blankets and other materials, "to make sure bodies didn't fall apart."[52]

One guard recounted "the heart rending" screams of the dying and those helpless before the searing flames. Agonized screams echoed through the cellblocks, probably not unlike how caged animals in a zoo respond in similar circumstances. Meanwhile, terrified guards, who had been conditioned against liberating their charges, saw the flames but hesitated to immediately unlock the cells, thus losing the brief window of opportunity. This delay doomed hundreds of prisoners.

When rescuers reached the top two tiers, they found that the keys would not unlock the cells. Due to the intensity of the heat, some locks had been melted shut or were too warped to open. Guards, firemen, and inmates resorted to axes and sledgehammers to smash the locks. Of the 262 prisoners housed on the top two tiers, only 13 survived. By the time Fire Chief Nice entered the blocks at 6:16, most of the men were dead. At 6:40 the roof over G&H collapsed, preceded by bits of burned timber that ignited anything that would burn, including bedding and mattresses.

One of the more remarkable aspects of the disaster was how guards and convicts forgot their mutual antagonism, at least for the moment, in order to save their brethren. Indeed, for probably the first time in the history of the Ohio penitentiary system, convicts were entrusted with ropes, axes and hammers, and other rescue equipment, items that in quieter times might have been turned into deadly weapons to be used against each other or the guards. In the bedlam, "a Negro convict [ran] with a piece of white cloth over his nose," carrying a rope and hook, which he made "valiant efforts to throw into a barred window." He finally succeeded and proceeded to shinny up the rope in an effort to gain entrance to the burning block. At the same moment others were assaulting locked doors with sledgehammers.[53] Once freed from their cells, most inmates headed to the safety of the prison yard, while others returned to the cellblocks to help in the rescue efforts.

Inmate survivor Chester Himes featured the fire and the heroism of the convicts in several of his early stories. In one of them, his fictitious alter ego Jimmy Monroe was most impressed by the gallantry of the convicts as they rushed into the burning G&H block. He tried hard to fathom the binary lives of these men "who were in for murder and rape and arson, who had shot down policemen in dark alleys, who had snatched pocket books and run, who had stolen automobiles and forged checks, who had mutilated women and carved their torso into separate arms and legs and heads and packed them into trunks." How could you explain these men now "working overtime at their jobs of being heroes, moving through the smoke with reckless haste to save some other bastard's worthless life. . . . All working like mad at being heroes, some laughing, some solemn, some hysterical—drunk from their momentary freedom, drunk from being brave for once in a cowardly life." Monroe figured it out: "It was exciting. The fire was exciting. The live ones and the dead ones were exciting. It gave them something to do . . . something to break the galling monotony of serving time."[54]

People die in fires for two reasons: they are burned to death or asphyxiated. Smoke and hot gases produced by a conflagration unite as "deadly enemies." When fire reaches a certain stage, it creates its own draft and carries itself along. The heat mushrooms up and settles down and suffocates, as it did in the upper tiers of G&H blocks. Making matters worse were the ancient timbers and sheeting exposed on the interior side of the roof in the cellblock under construction. As fumes meet an obstruction like a ceiling or a roof, they spread out laterally until they reach the wall. In this case the wind and the flames conspired to spread death, trapping many convicts in their cells, beyond human aid and fearing what was to come. Their voices joined in a mighty crescendo of screams.

One of the best-chronicled building fires in the history of the United States, the 1942 Cocoanut Grove fire in Boston, offers insight into how victims often die in fires. The patrons were of course not locked in cells like the Ohio inmates, but they might as well have been. One account described nightclub victims who "seemed to be falling down without even trying to run or to push. They were suffocating. Some were falling victim to carbon monoxide in the thick smoke that was already replacing the oxygen in their bloodstream. Others were burning up inside as they inhaled the superheated air—burning wood and fabric that can generate temperatures . . . that seared shut their throat and lungs."[55]

There were a number of other parallels between these two fires. Both were first reported at 5:20, and both moved with "astonishing speed." Both were short-lived but resulted in high mortality. At Cocoanut Grove, firefighters not only had to battle flames quickly but had to cope with a frenzied dinner crowd running helter-skelter in the dense black smoke. Similarly to the Ohio Penitentiary event, where guards failed to take charge and use common sense, at the Grove a waiter asked one of the employees for keys to the locked service door, which he knew were kept in the kitchen, and was told, "Not until the boss tells me."[56]

The almost twenty-minute gap between when the fire was first discovered and 5:39, when the Columbus Fire Department received its first alarm, meant the difference between rescue and mass death. It took about two minutes for one fire truck and three engine companies under the command of Assistant Fire Chief Osborn to reach the pen from the No. 1 firehouse on Front and Elm Streets. By the time they arrived the fire had already spread through two-thirds of the cell house containing the four blocks. Despite their best efforts, the strong northerly wind continued to push the fire and smoke into the occupied G&H block.[57] By 5:45 the firefighters had brought their equipment into the prison. Two minutes later, the first photograph of the fire, taken at 5:47, "showed the north quarter of the roof of cell building already burned down and all the remainder of the roof visible in the picture gutted or in full flame."[58]

Upon their arrival the firemen connected a hydrant at the northwest corner of the new auditorium (across the yard from the E&F dormitories and the closest building to I&K) and directed a stream of water into a notch window in the I&K cellblocks. Unfortunately, the heavy iron grilling on the windows caused the stream of water to become "so broken up as to be rendered ineffective," and the line was soon cut off.[59]

By the time all pumpers were operational and connected to hydrants, "the fire was burning fiercely and the entire roof over I and K had fallen in." Initially several convicts took the hose away from some firefighters they thought were not responding fast enough and attempted to carry it into the ranges themselves. They were quickly persuaded to let the firemen work unimpeded. Several more lines were hooked up to pumpers to extinguish the fires burning in bedding and cell furnishings in various cells.

It took the firefighters ten to fifteen minutes after arrival to ascend to the top range of cells, having first had to direct the laying of hose lines outside. Once there, they saw dead men in the cells.[60] The firefighters would spend most of their time that evening inside the walls, since they also assisted in the removal of bodies. According to a spokesman for the department on the scene, they believed the fire started from the north end and traveled south with the stiff wind.

Ohio has a legacy of firefighting knowhow. The nation's first paid fire department was inaugurated in 1853 in Cincinnati, just a hundred miles from Columbus. A year earlier, Boston had introduced a fire box system, making "telegraphy the servant of firefighting." The precursor to the call box used to summon firefighters to the Columbus fire, it was described as "a system of metal alarm boxes that when 'pulled' would immediately transmit their location to a central office. From here the location of the box would be tapped out to all firehouses in the vicinity, so that the nearest one knew to respond first.[61]

Unlike their modern-day counterparts, alarm boxes in the 1930s were purposely made so they would be difficult to pull. Authorities were concerned that "light-minded people would play with the fire alarm equipment and cause needless runs." In order to even open the box, an individual reporting a fire would have to retrieve the key, which was kept at a nearby house or business. Not surprisingly, this process often led to delayed alarms. Except for these devices there were surprisingly "few innovations in firefighting until the early twentieth century."[62]

The assistant fire chief, who would go on to help direct the removal of the bodies after the catastrophe, remained firmly of the opinion that the fire started in the north end and traveled south with the wind. Moreover, he was convinced that the fire must have started no more than half an hour before the alarm sounded.

The Columbus firefighters discovered multiple secondary fires, including a "burning pile of rubbish, rags and paper" under the steps leading to the chapel and fires in the cotton mill building and the E&F dormitory.[63] Fire officials testified later that these fires were of incendiary origin, not part of any prearranged prison escape but just convicts being convicts, taking advantage of the pandemonium to "add to the excitement and general confusion."

The chapel fire was controlled quickly with only slight damage to the exterior. The cotton mill fire, the largest of the secondary fires, was located on the first floor of the north end of the building. The chief engineer at the power house luckily discovered the blaze and was able to break through the building's door and spray the contents of a two-and-a-half-gallon chemical extinguisher. It would come out during the fire inquiry that extinguishers were only available in the factory buildings. (Since extinguishers were frequently targeted by incendiaries and there had never been a fire of any magnitude in the cellblocks, this was considered an appropriate strategy under the Thomas administration.) With the assistance of a hose line manned by firemen, this fire too was extinguished. Except for some water damage, the cotton mill building was little damaged.[64] The third of the incendiary fires was found in the bunkhouse housing black prisoners. It turned out that several beds had been torched, and when a fireman stepped in to put it out he was threatened by the occupants. He was soon joined by other firemen supported by prison guards, and this fire was extinguished as well.

One firefighter would later lament that "the prisoners expected us to do the impossible. Our line wouldn't reach to the second floor. We had hell. The prisoners took the line away from us. . . . If they had any leadership we would have been completely mobbed." They implied that the prisoners wanted them do something "we couldn't do." By some accounts there were an estimated 140 firemen on the scene at the height of the fire, working twenty-three lines, so as to direct twenty-three different streams on all sides of the burning cell house, and eight pumpers, each with a one-thousand-gallon capacity. However, an initial fire report suggested that the number of firefighters was actually higher, as it was "considerably" supplemented by members of the off shift.[65]

When the hoses didn't work, firemen resorted to acetylene torches to open cells. Unfortunately, their hoses did not reach the sixth tier, and they were soon surrounded by frantic convicts trying to wrest them away. One firefighter commented, "I don't think they were trying to be malicious—just crazy with the horror of seeing their fellows die like rats" on the upper tiers. But other cons did make deliberate attempts to stop them from doing their jobs, such as the madman who cut a hose line before being seen running away gripping a knife.

Prisoners and firemen were both adversaries and collaborators. At one point they spent almost three hours helping to loosen the No. 1 ladder truck, which had become stuck in mud in the prison yard. Conversely, convicts tried to set a gas tank attached to a fire truck on fire as the main blaze came under control. Some threw blankets under the gas tank as others threw matches at it. Firemen jumped on the trucks and drove them and the gasoline tank away.[66] Some prisoners tried to drain gasoline from the fire truck and as it was being driven away by firemen, others began throwing rocks at it, knocking out one of its headlights.[67] Assistant fire chief Norris J. Ijams was attempting to connect a hose to fight the fire in the cotton mill when he was attacked and slightly injured. Convicts also cut two sections of the hose.

The clergy was well represented on Easter Monday. None though were as prominent as the Rev. Albert O'Brien. Following an excited phone call to Aquinas College in Columbus beseeching its Dominican priests to rush to the dying men at the penitentiary, he was among the first to answer the call of duty. Born in a small town in Ireland on January 14, 1888, O'Brien left for America in 1908 after completing high school. He was ordained in Washington, DC, in 1915 and served the Dominican Order in a number of states before landing at the Ohio State Penitentiary in October 1926 as chaplain to the prison's Catholic inmates, a position he held until his death in 1933. His humor and kindness earned him well-deserved reverence among the prison population.[68]

O'Brien's former secretary, identified only as Ex-Convict 59968, chronicled the priest's heroism that night. He said that O'Brien was at home in his rectory at the St. Patrick's Parish on East Naghten Street "preparing for dinner after a busy day" when he was informed by phone that the prison was on fire. He left immediately and made it inside the prison within ten minutes. Garbed in his purple stole, O'Brien immediately took charge of the Catholic clergy there. Once fourteen of them had arrived, equally divided between Dominicans and diocesan priests, he sent several to the prison hospital, where he knew they would be needed "to give Extreme Unction to those of the faith, who seemed yet to be living." He positioned himself and the rest just outside the burning cellblock building, where they could give absolution to the convicts as they were brought out by fellow inmates and set down "among the long lines of the dead and dying" in the darkening yard. They were helped by a prisoner, who identified which were Catholics. O'Brien was standing so close to the cellblock that an inmate suggested that he move further away due to danger of the walls falling on him. The walls crumbled shortly after the inmate's admonition, "burying prisoners beneath the smoldering debris."[69] Once he was sure that all had been tended to, O'Brien went into the still-smoldering block to help with the rescue, but like so many others before him was unable to get beyond the third tier. He went back into the yard, where he was temporarily overcome by the smoke.[70]

In the fire's aftermath, Father O'Brien, the "hero priest," noted that eighty-five Catholics were on the list of victims being compiled and that "all had received Holy Communion on Easter," the day before the fire. He recounted a number of poignant scenes, including his walk "among the lines of the dying," many of whom "reached up their hands, and died as I imparted absolution." He was particularly struck by a young man who held a rosary in his hands and another who held "a tiny cross of palm on his coat."[71]

The G&H cellblocks were adjacent to the prison courtyard, sometimes referred to as a quadrangle or quad. At first glance the bucolic plot of green space could have been located on any college campus, until one peered up at the barred windows looking down from all sides. As soon as a lifeless or injured victim was brought out of the cell-house building, he was placed in the darkening prison yard. The bodies were often joined by groups of convict survivors, many crying hysterically, others wrapped in blankets and drenched in the water from the fire hoses or seeking treatment for burns suffered in their escape from the blaze. The green lawns of the prison yard were soon dotted with the hulks of men bleeding and gasping for air, many of whom were soon covered with blankets in the repose of death. As the acrid black smoke billowed into the cellblock tiers, it began to fill the quadrangle as well, sending panic through the already terrified inmates.[72]

Poignant scenes played out across the yard. A severely burned white inmate was tenderly administered to by a group of about twenty black convicts. According to lore, he would owe his life to them. They had come upon the injured man lying on a blanket near the west wall and after gathering around him pleaded with him in unison "not to die," telling him, "hang on friend, don't leave us." Witnesses reported them "bursting into strains of familiar plantation songs" as his life ebbed away. And then something miraculous occurred. "A grim smile appeared on his [burned] face" as "he clung to a meager thread of life" and appeared likely to recover.[73]

In another corner of the quadrangle ten convicts huddled in a circle around one of their buddies on the verge of death. They took turns working on him for two hours, one repeating over and over, "Come on Walter, don't give in! We're pulling for you!" As he succumbed to his injuries, one pal was crying into his ear, while another rubbed his arms and another pumped his lungs—all to no avail.[74]

One of the more embroidered accounts of the fire was published in the national edition of the *Chicago Defender*, among the country's leading African American newspapers. It cited the death toll as "the heaviest in the history of disastrous fires in America,"[75] noting the seventy-five "Race inmates," as it referred to African Americans, among the dead. Actually, a perusal of the death certificates from the Ohio Penitentiary reveals that fewer than twenty prisoners of color perished in the fire. The *Defender*'s editors were obviously proud of the heroism displayed by many black convicts that evening, as illustrated by the following account: "Our prisoners were the outstanding heroes of the disaster. They made quick decisions at the critical time. They were the first to dash from the comparative safety of the prison yard into the fiery inferno of the doomed cell block to rescue their fellow prisoners, the majority of whom were white."[76]

Other accounts offered by the *Defender* included the actions of a twenty-two-year-old inmate who carried a white inmate across his shoulders until he crumpled to the ground in front of the main gates. The white convict was already dead, and according to the paper's account the young rescuer's condition "was such as to give him slight chance to live. His clothing had been burned and his face was seared, but had a trace of a smile as a guard pumped air into his lungs." Also mentioned were brave men such as George Alkens of Cleveland, who broke inmates out of the fiery cellblocks, and Roy Buttle, also from Cleveland, who went through a burning cellblock with a hammer "smashing locks to liberate half-crazed prisoners." Another "unknown Race prisoner overpowered a guard who refused to open cells over which he had charge." He allegedly secured the guard's keys and saved men on the 5H tier.

Understandably, the African American paper tended to inflate some of the exploits of the black convicts, crediting them with herculean rescues that did not add up once the entire narrative of the disaster was in place. Their heroism was unquestionable, but the numbers saved by black prisoners do not jibe with the majority of the available accounts. For example, the claim that Howard Jones, who raced through the smoky tiers breaking locks with a sledgehammer, saved "the lives of 135 men" rests on shaky ground. Similar exploits were attributed to other convicts, such as Dan Evans, who rescued twenty-one men; Jack Wright, who carried seventeen prisoners to safety on his back; O. B. Hawkins, who saved seventy-five men "before he collapsed and was removed to the hospital"; and John Jackson of Columbus, who escaped the E Dormitory to help carry forty men from the top two tiers. This last claim is surely suspect, since all of the prisoners on the sixth tier perished, as did most of those on the fifth.

The *Defender* asserted that the "heroic trio" of Eddie Crawford, R. W. Mason, and George Thorpe were "the first men to gain entrance in the cell tier in which the flames were raging." They very well might have been involved in cutting the screen with wire cutters and sledges and rescuing more than twenty inmates, but the Board of Inquiry left it beyond dispute that guards Baldwin and Little were the first to gain admittance to the smoke-filled G&H cellblocks. Rescued inmates, prison officials, and guards recounted their actions in separate testimony.

Other black convicts mentioned included one named Tucker, who carried the bodies of six men before he died, and Henry Caldwell, a lifer, who almost paid with his life saving inmates.

Among the most celebrated actors on Easter Monday was the warden's daughter, Amanda, who has been credited in most contemporary accounts with giving the alarm that "brought every piece of fire apparatus in Columbus, every available policeman, a company of the National Guard and 600 soldiers, and every doctor and nurse from miles away."[77] One reporter described how she "worked frantically at a telephone hook and talked herself hoarse to a mechanic on the other end in an effort to get power turned on" from a different power station.[78] Some accounts had Amanda Thomas ordering guards to their posts while she "issued guns and ammunition, called doctors and nurses, summoned troops and performed many other duties."[79] Another described her as "one of the outstanding figures in maintaining peace and order among the convicts during the disaster." The account boasted that "throughout the fire and panic" she worked "untiring, helping her father place guards, directing the activities of physicians and nurses and broadcasting appeals for assistance."[80] The warden's daughter, for all of her spunk and courage, relinquished much of her gravitas when it was revealed that as the fire approached her family's residence in the penitentiary main building, she turned her attention from the unfolding prison holocaust to "ordering her valuables removed" from the house.[81]

In reality, Amanda Thomas was one of many women who pitched in Easter Monday. Elizabeth Sampson, director of the Physicians and Surgeons Bureau, "played an important part in the rescue work," calling all the area physicians to the prison after she was contacted to do so by Warden Thomas. For the time, the exchange represented a big stride toward more effective emergency response communications. Each doctor in the area called the exchange hourly and it was only through Sampson that the doctors could be quickly contacted. She was assisted by several young women in contacting doctors at their last reported locations.[82]

Caught up in the excitement of the moment, newspaper reporters went out of their way to create heroes in order to capture the fancy of readers in a newspaper-saturated era. Like those of the African American inmates chronicled in the *Defender*, Ms. Thomas's contributions were likely embroidered for public consumption. While initial reports cast her as a central figure, she was barely mentioned in the 722-page Board of Inquiry report. Indeed, early reports suggested that the "women members of the Thomas family [were] all panic stricken standing near the door to their home to watch guards and volunteers remove valuables from the warden's residence," fearing it was in the path of the fire.[83]

Monday night the warden's wife collapsed, but she was revived and placed under the care of a physician at 7:15. An African American newspaper correctly reported that a "Race" convict had come to her aid, supporting her on his arm and giving her a drink of water to revive her. However, his "race" was not reported in the local newspapers at the time. After some rest and the application of restoratives she declared herself fit to render aid.[84]

With darkness approaching on Easter Monday, it was obvious that more lighting would be required inside the prison walls. Floodlights were set up above the prison by the Superior Electric Company, allowing workers to more effectively administer first aid. Soon a large number of smaller lights, removed from the swimming pool at Olentangy Park, were brought to the pen.[85] By sundown soldiers had delivered a boxload of new flashlights as well. Meanwhile, electricians were feverishly attempting to hook up a power line so that wall lights and inside lights could be used.[86]

One story that continued to gain traction as it was passed around through the prison grapevine was that a guard had refused to let a convict out of his cell and a black inmate had tried to liberate him with the help of a chisel. In one version of the events, the guard supposedly shot both prisoners and ran away. Another account had a Cincinnati convict named Albert Johnson crying as he showed a reporter his hand, saying, "Mister, we pleaded and pleaded with that guard to let us out but he wouldn't. . . . He only said get back there you black ———— and forced us away from the door. Then he ran out and left us to die."[87]

The story was given significant attention by the African American press. An article in the *Chicago Defender* entitled "Guard Slays Two," based on the recollections of several survivors, reported that "two Race prisoners were killed by a guard when they attempted to escape from their cell." The paper preferred the sobriquet "Race prisoner" over other identifiers used by mainstream press.

The most graphic account of the shooting was provided by the *Ohio State Journal*, reported by a white lifer who refused to give his name.

> That guard was the worst coward I ever saw. I feel sorry for him if he ever shows his face inside the prison again. It wasn't so bad when he just refused to open the gates, but then I and another convict, who

had been freed by Guard Little, went to the coward and begged him to open the doors, and again he refused. My partner had a heavy chisel and he offered to the 2 boys locked in the cell. The guard tried to take it away from the men, but they refused and went to work on the lock fighting to get out. The guard said, 'Give me that chisel or I'll shoot you' at the same time cursing loudly. They refused and he fired twice. We saw both men fall and the guard run from the tier, taking the keys with him . . . we heard he had been placed under arrest by the warden.

Prison officials denied these charges but refused to report where the guard was.

One of the rare accounts of an inmate killed by gunshot wounds came from Sonny Hanovich, who claimed, more than a half century later, to have seen one body with a bullet hole in the back, and to have heard of another shot in his cell. Perhaps he was referring to the aforementioned account, but this incident is all but missing from every modern chronicle of the fatal fire and has never been satisfactorily substantiated.

Although there were several accounts of bullet wounds and shootings of inmates, no bullet wounds were ever authenticated. But the story gained credence the more times it was told. Tell a story enough times and it becomes fact. Although the shooting was quickly "corroborated by a group of twenty or more men," officials continued to deny it, saying there was nothing to it. To the credit of the officials, in order to put the rumors to rest, a careful check for bullet wounds was made of every corpse at the temporary morgue, as well as all bodies being taken away for burial.

Several inmates and guards later reported hearing gunshots right before the inferno moved into G&H. During the investigation in the days after the fire, it was revealed that day guard Harold Whetstone, on watch above the warden's residence (his perch consisted of a little walkway about fourteen or fifteen feet long that ran along the Spring Street wall), had heard several gunshots being fired over in the yard north of the chapel at about 5:40. Looking in the direction of the shots, he saw another guard named Porter around five hundred feet away, firing shots into the air. He deduced correctly that it was an attempt to grab his attention. Whetstone responded in kind, firing his 30-30 into the air. Porter, a day guard at the wagon stockade that ran through the cellblock, yelled back, "Turn in the fire alarm." Whetstone pointed to the guardroom and hollered back, "I did." In fact, he had done so three times before a shot had been fired.[88]

The night of the fire witnessed the actions of remarkable heroes, while others in the days to come would be given credit for actions they could *not* have taken. One inmate, "Wild" Bill Croninger, was credited with having saved twelve men before collapsing and dying. As some told it, he went into the dense smoke repeatedly until he could not go any further. Injured and overcome by smoke, he sank down, said, "I've done my part," and took his last breath. It made for a sensational story—but it wasn't true. According to several Columbus historians, Croninger was not listed among the dead. In reality he was arrested several years after the fire for a spree of petty thefts. His codefendant Don Ford, however, was the nineteen-year-old son of an inmate who did die in the fire. Croninger had been friends with his father, who perished while serving time for child abandonment.[89]

One "big burly negro convict" told three rescuers, "I can walk, leave me alone" after they dragged him to safety from the building ruins. Once they let him go, the convict "straightened up, brushed a brawny hand across a pathetically seared face and headed down the path to the hospital. Took several resolute steps then faltered and plunged face downward into a pool of water. He managed to roll over on his side. 'I can't walk,' he muttered, 'lay me down.' They did and he was dead."[90]

One of the most difficult challenges was bringing out the bodies of the dead from the top three tiers. A number of them were lowered to the ground with ropes and, once prostrate on the quadrangle, were covered with blankets, "where they lay in grotesque positions" until removed by National Guardsmen. The process began before the fire was out but after most victims had succumbed to smoke. Demonstrating the ingenuity shared by longtime inmates, bodies were lowered from tiers with ropes as "flames still licked at ruins" and lethal smoke filled the air. A score of convicts managed to find some ropes somewhere. "Tripping over the hot and smouldering [*sic*] embers they scrambled up the six tiers of the ruined prison. Howling, eager, unorganized, they managed to get into shape for the work. They distributed themselves, a few men on each level, and strung their ropes from one tier to another. The first body was dangled down and swayed a moment in midair," before one rescuer yelled from above, 'Here comes one! Here comes one!'" Another disembodied voice chimed in, "Here he comes, here he comes, ketch 'im, don't let him fall. . . . The bodies dangled down in an endless stream" as the prisoners got the hang of working together. Occasionally cries of alarm rent the air; in one case they indicated that "a body had fallen on the backs of laboring men on the third tier."[91]

Above the din inside the walls, parallel acts of boldness were taking place as volunteers from all walks of life volunteered to assist. Although gate regulations prohibited anyone except soldiers and law enforcement officers beyond the bullpen Monday night, "a Boy Scout of 'half-pint' size, his shoulders thrust back, trooped through the phalanx of guards to gain the inner sanctum." Joining the legions of volunteers, Bertillon identification system officers Homer Richter and Johnny Rings of the city police "donned a uniform Monday night for the first time in many years and acted as patrolmen."[92]

Sirens and ambulances could be heard speeding back and forth through the rubbernecking crowds interfering with traffic down Spring Street from High Street all the way to Front Street. Doctors and medical personnel responded in great numbers. As they drove up to the gate they were stopped by police and asked, "Are you a doctor?" Those who answered in the affirmative were told "Go on, hurry" and directed down to the railroad yards on the east side of the prison, where they got out of their cars and walked to the pen doors. They moved snakelike through the guardroom out into the prison yard and into the hospital, where they found the dead and dying crammed into every conceivable space "like sardines."

As a result of the overwhelming response, doctors soon had little space to navigate in. Others were told to go and sit in the front office until their colleagues needed relief. Likewise, nurses, described by one reporter as "calm, cool, and efficient looking," swarmed through the front doors.[93] They too waited until needed in the hospital, when they headed across the prison quad in small groups. Few had time to worry about walking through a gauntlet of hundreds of Ohio's most dangerous convicts, including Dr. Betty Morris, the first female physician at the scene of the fire. It was hard to miss her moving through the prison yard reviving men with "spirits of ammonia." Her bravery led one journalist to write, "The only woman among a crowd of workers and white and black prisoners, she was treated with utmost respect."[94]

In perhaps the oddest moment of the tragic evening, Ohio State University junior James F. Laughead, who happened to be driving past the prison as the fire was raging, tried to gain entrance by representing himself as a physician's assistant. When his ruse failed, he tried another plan. He signed the name of a prominent Columbus newspaper editor to gain entry and managed to make it as far as the prison yard just as casualties were being brought out from the cellblocks. However, he was soon mistaken for a convict and forced into a cell, as the fire was still blazing and a riot was on the verge of breaking out. He was kept behind bars for two hours until he could be properly identified.[95]

The Ohio Penitentiary fire was the first major American disaster to be covered *instantaneously* by sound motion picture crews, radio stations, and newspaper reporters, the three major arms of the mainstream media. After Fox Movietone covered Lindbergh taking off for his solo flight to Paris in May 1927, audiences had to wait several days to watch it in person, and only those in New York would have been able to see and hear the airplane take off, since the "sound equipment was still confined to" movie palaces in the Big Apple. Nonetheless, audiences would thrill to the hum of the iconic monoplane *Spirit of St. Louis* taking off and then "ris[ing] above Roosevelt Field."[96] Within a few years and by 1930, "sound newsreels" were issued twice weekly by Fox, Pathé, and Paramount and shown on almost twelve thousand screens across the United States.

Airplanes played a significant role in transporting news to the free world. During the first hours of the unfolding disaster, photographs and news articles were rushed to their home offices by plane. In fact, that evening airplanes were warmed up and on standby at the local Norton and Sullivan Fields, in case they were needed to transport photographs or other tasks.[97] The *Dallas Morning News* reported its photographers transmitting photos "by telephoto" over regular phone lines to Chicago. From there the photos were flown to Dallas.[98] Thanks to advances in newspaper technology, the world of news was rapidly changing, and editors wanted to tell stories in pictures whenever possible.

The penitentiary fire had burned itself out after about two hours, but by three o'clock the next afternoon, only twenty-one hours after the first alarm, theater patrons in moving-picture houses on Broadway, some six hundred miles away, "not only [saw] the harrowing sights; they also heard the shrieking of the prison siren, the hissing as water hits the flames, the howling of desperate prisoners, the crackling of burning logs, the thud of falling beams, the commands of Army officials and jail officials."[99] The short clips were accompanied by a "brief talkie lecture by an expert on prison conditions, explaining the causes of the tragedy and suggesting means of preventing its occurrence." One leading popular science journal declared that this should be "considered a world's record in the speedy gathering and presentation of audible photographic news." Except for a few photos transmitted by special wire, "the pictorial story was in the theaters before the New York dailies had their pictures in print." The 300 feet of Pathé film played in about two and a half minutes. The "sound newsreel" had come into its own in April 1930 as a "talking newspaper."[100]

It is worth noting that the sound men who were on their way to cover the fire "narrowly escaped death" when their "camion" or sound truck was hit "by a high tension electric wire during a wild night drive through a storm to the scene of the disaster." Beating their competition to record the fire in Columbus was made possible by the fact that they were already in Cleveland, 126 miles away, reporting the opening of the American League baseball season when the disaster took place.[101]

Every form of communication was utilized during the course of the disaster. *Ohio State Journal* staff reporter Ray Coon, besides contributing print coverage, also broadcast the details of the fire over WLW Cincinnati. He somehow managed to set up an emergency broadcasting station in the Department of Education building in the statehouse annex. From there he stayed in touch with his newspaper in order to offer descriptive details of the scene inside the prison.[102]

Also on the spot Easter Monday was Columbus station WAIU. It had its own remote-controlled equipment already inside the prison walls, making it possible to broadcast directly from the scene of the disaster. So, as the reporters for the city newspapers were sitting down for dinner, the conflagration was simultaneously broadcast by radio. It would be another several hours before all of the newspapers were fully staffed.[103]

The Ohio Penitentiary was so inundated with phone calls from Ohio and beyond that special telephones and switchboards had to be placed in its lobby.[104] Magnifying the confusion were an estimated five hundred telegrams sent from the penitentiary to the families of the deceased at midnight on Easter Monday, alerting them to the tragedies that had befallen their loved ones as well as where they could reclaim the bodies.[105] The telegrams and news dispatches about the fire challenged the "physical and human capacity" of the employees of the Western Union Telegraph Company and the Postal Telegraph Company. By the following morning Western Union had handled two hundred thousand words in seventy-five hundred different messages, while the Postal Telegraph Company had handled more than thirty-five thousand words during one six-hour period ending Tuesday at 1 a.m. Messages sent included special correspondent reports to their newspapers as well as convict messages to relatives and agencies involved in identifying the dead and the survivors.[106] (Prisoners had to pay for their own messages to be sent.)[107] More than one thousand telegrams had inundated the prison from the relatives of convicts from throughout the country. The entire workforce from the outer office, augmented by volunteers, worked to check prison records on individual inmates.

One of the few feel-good stories to be had in the direct aftermath of the prison catastrophe was that of Convict 46812, better known as Otto W. "Deacon" Gardner, a graduate of the Moody Bible Institute of Chicago, whose actions on Easter Monday earned him national acclaim. The thirty-five-year-old

Pennsylvanian, who had entered the Ohio Penitentiary in 1917, was doing life for the murder of his wife and another woman in Youngstown, Ohio. According to the African American newspaper the *Chicago Defender*, Gardner was one of the most popular and best-known inmates. The night of the fire he delivered "one of the epoch events in radio broadcasting."[108] As he vividly chronicled the fire on station WAIU, the prison radio station, "his voice was carried into thousands of homes throughout America over the Columbia Broadcasting System." (The prison radio station was a unit of the Columbia system.) CBS president William S. Paley rewarded him with a check for $500 (over $7,000 in 2017). "At a time when the entire country was anxiously awaiting news of the worst catastrophe in American prison history," Paley told him, "you willingly, in the face of great danger, gave a sympathetic and accurate word picture of the holocaust." From 7 to 12 p.m., Gardner, who was "only 30 feet from the blaze at the time," reached out for doctors, nurses, and "narcotics."[109]

Between 8 and 9 p.m. the fire might have been under control, but the prison yard was seething with anarchy as thousands of prisoners freely milled about, screaming, shouting, and menacing firefighters. Fire chiefs threatened to let the whole prison burn down unless guaranteed protection. The first reporters on the scene often embellished and exaggerated what they saw or heard, mostly the latter. Firefighters and guards may have testified seeing convicts drop in their tracks, but reporters' claims that they saw prisoners "literally burned alive before our eyes" is rather farfetched considering the totality of evidence and accounts of the fire. But it did sell papers. These reports would be dispelled in the days to come as the morticians and coroners did their jobs, finding that the overwhelming majority died from smoke inhalation, and that most burns had been postmortem. All the prisoners on the sixth tier, all but thirteen on the fifth tier, and a number on the fourth range were dead. Now it was up to a Board of Inquiry to begin the truth-seeking process.

2 THE FAIRGROUNDS

Those going in are alive; those going out, dead.

—*A physician at the prison hospital, April 21, 1930*

Once the fire danger had passed late Monday night, reporters and survivors in search of fellow convicts were curious as to the human consequences of what had just transpired. One intrepid reporter described scenes of carnage and the reactions of inmates as they searched the corpses in the penitentiary quadrangle before they were taken away to a temporary morgue at the fairgrounds. He saw "scores of closely cropped heads protruding from beneath water soaked blankets, pair after pair of roughly shod feet and here and there a seared hand . . . shapeless masses that lay row upon row." One of the survivors "searched tirelessly among the corpses for his cell buddy, throwing the beams of his lantern into one horrible face after another." One journalist on the scene as the identification process continued in the prison yard described "bobbing lanterns" throwing "ghastly circles of yellow light on the upturned faces as the men detailed to the job of identification made their rounds. They did not look at the features of the corpses" if possible, but focused their attention on the stenciled numbers on their prison uniforms.[1]

Paul Ferguson, the son of the Plain City, Ohio funeral director, recalled sixty years after the fire what he considered "the darkest memories in his career as mortician." The sixteen-year- old happened to answer the telephone at the family funeral home the night of the fire to find out one of the victims was the son of local residents who had just been notified by prison officials to come to Columbus to recover the body for burial. Ferguson and his brother Jay wasted no time heading out to retrieve the body. It is unclear where Ferguson's father was at this time or how long the teenager or his brother had been involved in the family business, but it seems Ferguson was familiar with the mortuary business. He recounted in 1990, "I wasn't even supposed to be in there, not at my age. But I sneaked in anyway because we had to get the boy." While in the prison courtyard he took the opportunity to look at some of the dead bodies. The body he was to bring back "wasn't burned nearly so bad as some were, but he was pretty bad. Some of these guys were pretty near cremated."[2]

Young Ferguson witnessed firemen still struggling to put the fire out as shaken prisoners carried out dead convicts from the cellblocks and laid them prone in the yard. Some of them were embalmed on the spot. Ferguson observed one embalmer using a long tube, known as a trocar, "[inserting it] through the victim's abdomen to shoot embalming fluid in." He explained "that was about all you could do with a lot of them. They were too badly burned." Ferguson recounted how, despite the frenetic aftermath of the disaster, the prison yard seemed "cloaked in sudden silence."[3]

On Tuesday morning, parole officer Dan Bonzo released the "first official account" of the dead, tallied at 276. Given the confusion at the scene, the count would fluctuate over the first twenty-four hours. One spokesman for the prison hospital put the figure at 336, while journalists who had free rein following the fire counted the "dead strewn around" the prison yard as 305.[4] Row after row of bodies were still lying on the water-soaked prison courtyard during the first body counts. Prison officials promised a more accurate death count once all of the bodies had been taken to the fairgrounds. Some 319 men would soon be laid out in long lines, "grim proof of the disaster." One observer described the bodies as "seared and blackened." The long horticulture building, "where flowers will be displayed next fall at the fair, was draped in black and blossoms from the state greenhouses."[5]

Not surprisingly, some witnesses to the aftermath compared the scene to a battlefield. Many inmates and rescuers had served in the armed forces during the

Great War, and would have been familiar with such scenes. According to Captain Tom W. Jones, who aided in the rescue attempt, the "scenes within were worse than anything he witnessed in the [battles of] Argonne or St. Mihiel." One inmate compared the fire to warfare as "he leaned against a tree for support while his swimming eyes surveyed the sodden corpses." A fellow convict shouted out, "The War! Don't try to tell me this was like the war! I seen both, brother, over there we had a chance for our lives. We had two legs and could run if we couldn't fight. But not here." One local doctor, a war veteran himself, agreed that the prison yard "resembled an overseas emergency camp in the world war" as he reflected on the many victims "lying there burned to a crisp, while others suffered from carbon monoxide poisoning fumes which affected them like gas attacks" in the late war.[6]

The bodies' repose in death offered a glimpse of the victims' last moments of life. Those with "seared backs revealed how they turned to face to the walls of their cells protecting eyes and faces in vain." Other victims were found in a crouched position, the so-called pugilist stance, "with arms outstretched in grotesque fighting poses,"[7] the result of the contraction of larger muscles from the heat of the fire. In other instances, dying inmates had enough wherewithal to recognize their minutes were numbered and managed to scrawl notes or some type of identification information that could be used in case their fingerprints and faces proved unidentifiable. One doomed convict, a reporter wrote, possessed enough clarity "to seize pencil and paper and scribble as flames crept close." Stopped midsentence, he only had time to write, "Dear Mother . . ." The note was found "scorched and water-soaked" as it was pried from "the stiffened fingers of a huge black man. He still held the pencil as he lay under a gray blanket in one of the rows upon the turf of the quadrangles. When the flares set off by the cameramen lighted his ebony countenance, there was not fear visible on it. Only resignation."[8]

Inmate Gus Socha must have assumed this was not going to turn out well for him. When found in his cell he had a note pinned to the back of his shirt that read, "Notify John Dee Armory Avenue, Cincinnati."[9] Former blacksmith Theodore Cottrell, doing life for murder, was found among the "blanket swathed victims on the courtyard." His intuition had been telling him he might die before his time, confiding to a friend the previous Christmas that it "will be my last Christmas here."[10] Of course he might have meant he hoped to escape or be paroled before then.

Much of the immediate postfire activity was centered at the prison hospital. Here the scene was chaotic at best, with doctors responding to emergency call broadcasts from the greater Columbus region. Their main task was to sort through the dead and wounded as each was laid down before them. As soon as a convict was declared dead, the identification number on his prison garb was taken off and matched with prison records to reveal his identity. The victim would then be declared "Checked out."[11]

One physician observed the "stream of pitiful forms, some gasping and shrieking, others horribly charred, pouring in and out" of the hospital, succinctly noting to one query, "Those going in are alive; those going out, dead." One convict was overheard shouting, "Gangway! We're bringing in my buddy." But it was obvious the injured man was not going to make it, as "his face in death distorted by his last frantic effort to get a breath of fresh air in the holocaust which took his life." As four men carried his blanket-wrapped body into the hospital, "onlookers fell away to make room." A doctor in the hospital corridor checked the victim's chest "gingerly" for a heartbeat. His stethoscope was silent, and all he could tell the man's buddy was, "He's dead." In prison parlance, the four convicts bawled that he had "gone west," screaming for vengeance as "another scorched human shell was placed alongside the endless rows of lifeless forms" in the prison courtyard just outside the hospital.[12]

Reporter Kenneth D. Tooill chronicled the tale of an inmate named "Pete" who was having his "good arm dressed" in the hospital. Pete noted that his other arm had been useless for years, "full of machine gun slugs." But the "good arm did heroic work last night. It pulled man after man from the blackened cells." Some were alive, others, such as his buddy, were not. Pete recounted that when he tried to pull his friend from the ruins of his cell "he came apart." As the reporter listened, Pete began "raving about it and trying to rub his eyes out," forcing a hospital assistant to "tie his good arm down."[13]

By 5:30 a.m., the morning after the fire, many of the surviving inmates were herded into the prison chapel, where some turned benches into beds. Other convicts were sent to buildings untouched by the fire. In the meantime the prison yard was cleared of inmates. One local reporter wrote, "More horrible than the dead were some of the injured who had been carried to the prison hospital, stark, or raving mad, a few of them blinded and maimed."[14] By then the prison hospital was, like the prison itself, well over capacity.

On Tuesday, surviving victims spoke "quietly among [them]selves," trying to find comfort on the "trim, white hospital cots" they were provided. Initial estimates placed 231 injured in hospital. A late check that day found only 5 of them in critical condition. The rough-hewn cons were attended to by prison nurses and inmates trained in the nursing arts. The inmate nurses were well respected by their comrades. Authorities recognized "their cool-headedness" and credited them with saving many lives and avoiding a near panic during the early hours of the catastrophe. They worked "systematically" as they "shunted case after case into the prison yard and administered oxygen under direction of a physician."[15] The hospital patients offered a variety of dispositions. One smoked "stoically and inquired about his pals." Another asked for permission to go out and get fresh air, and another was more interested in reading the newspaper.[16]

Among the most prominent caretakers was the Ohio Penitentiary's only physician, Dr. George Keil. On call twenty-four hours a day, he was at his post by 6 p.m. Easter Monday. As soon as he got to the hospital he called several local doctors, and after speaking with the warden was told to "call up all doctors you can get." Keil called his wife and told her to do likewise. The response was more than was expected; he remembered that there got to be "more doctors than patients," necessitating a directive to stop any more doctors from coming into the hospital.[17]

The hospital had bed capacity for 160, of which 147 were filled at the time of the fire. Anyone who was deemed ambulatory was asked to give up his bed to accommodate the avalanche of burn cases being brought in. By 8:30 p.m. the "National Guard or somebody" brought in a number of temporary cots, adding 150 more injured to the 160 already there.

During his testimony to the Board of Inquiry in the following days, Keil attested that a number of deaths both in the yard and hospital "just breathed and gasped and died. . . . They seemed to have inhaled either flame or gas and died." As soon as a victim was pronounced dead, the body was removed. With so little space, as soon as six dead victims were taken out, six live ones were brought in. He admitted there was no way of knowing for sure whether the deceased died from burns, but strongly believed, as did most other authorities, that the vast majority died from suffocation. Asked how many of the 150 in the hospital died there, he responded that "15 or 20 possibly died or were already dead when they were brought in," but recalled losing only one who had died since 10 p.m. on Monday evening, a victim who succumbed to bronchial pneumonia "from inhalation of smoke and possibly flames."[18]

Investigators were interested in whether any of the victims had shared any last words with the doctor before taking their last breaths. Keil responded that even if they did say something, he wouldn't have had time to listen with the ranks of the injured growing so quickly. Moreover, any who died in the hospital were already unconscious when they were brought in. Pressed further as to whether he heard any inmates speak about how the fire might have started, he told the authorities he was there "to take care of the sick" and was "not interested" in how it started.[19]

Badly burned convicts were at the mercy of contemporary medicine. Before World War II, surprisingly little was known about treating burn victims. Most advances would come too late for the Ohio Penitentiary fatalities. The go-to drug during the aftermath of the fire was opiates. It wasn't long after the fire was contained that the prison ran out of its supply. Opiates were noticeably scarce at the prison chapel next to the burnt-out cell house, where "nearly a score of men lay with severe flesh burns . . . but painless under the influence of opiates administered by scores of Columbus physicians." Fortunately, appeals to city physicians "brought more than enough" new supplies.[20]

Most fire victims, as in the case of the Ohio Penitentiary fire, die from carbon monoxide (CO) poisoning; indeed, it is rare for fire victims to die from burns. Most thermal damage to the body occurs post mortem. Carbon monoxide poisoning occurs when the deadly gas combines with the hemoglobin in the blood, preventing it from carrying oxygen. Blood cells loaded with CO are unable to transport the life-sustaining oxygen to the body, and consequently the body becomes starved of oxygen. But if the pathologist does not find CO in the blood, the victim was probably dead before the fire. In the case of the Easter Monday blaze, there were so many dead that it was impossible to perform more than cursory checks of the bodies before embalming them. Therefore, autopsies were out of the question. However, if autopsies had been performed, forensic pathologists would probably have found soot in the stomach or, if the victim had been alive during the fire, in the victim's airway (nose, throat, larynx, trachea, and bronchi).[21]

The disposal of the more than three hundred bodies "was the most solemn task" confronting officials on Tuesday and Wednesday, as wives, mothers, fathers, sisters, brothers, children, and friends of the deceased continued to mass against "the iron bars of the main prison gate," hoping and demanding to be admitted into the still-smoldering pen. Although an officer read off the names of survivors and those who had escaped injury, many in the throng refused to believe it until they could see them in person. "They stood in dazed groups after a night of horror splashed with acts of heroism by some of those who had been considered the most desperate inside the walls."

As soon as the mother and wife of Herbert Ross of Cleveland, serving time for carrying a concealed weapon, heard of the fire, they "departed so quickly" from the dinner table that they were still "attired in house dresses and aprons." Newspapers lavished ink on them for making the drive to Columbus in two and a half hours, considered a "record" time for the era. Upon arrival they found to their great relief that Ross had been housed in another section, "serving as a waiter in the dining room," and was unharmed.[22]

Once family members arrived and a protocol for collecting bodies had been established, they were instructed to pass through the outer gate and were handed pencils to fill out a reference book. Then they were taken in charge by the warden's daughter, Amanda Thomas, and parole officer Dan Bonzo. Many stood around the main gate for hours until they received a burial permit that allowed them to reclaim the body once it was conveyed to the temporary morgue in the Horticulture Building at the Ohio State Fairgrounds.[23] This would serve as the staging area for medical response personnel, including doctors, embalmers, nurses, and other volunteers.

The Horticulture Building, described by one reporter as a cattle barn, would serve as a combination morgue and hospital until the end of the week. Among the first on duty was the Red Cross, which set up a canteen at the fairgrounds. The Red Cross had charge of the fairgrounds and was assisted by members of the Columbus Junior League. As pleas for assistance continued to resonate throughout central Ohio, volunteers began arriving en masse. Among them was a delegation of physicians and students, led by Dr. J. C. McNamara from Marion. The Salvation Army, the Volunteers of America, and St. Francis Hospital offered their services as well. The Salvation Army set up a canteen in front of the prison to pass out food, coffee, and succor to exhausted firemen, rescuers, and inmates who aided in the rescue.

Every available physician was called to the disaster site, soon to be followed by an army of undertakers and coroners. They sped to the prison yard in trucks and private autos laden with spirits of ammonia, hoping to revive victims. But upon arrival they could do little to save the injured and dying in the prison yard, so they headed over to the state fairgrounds.

The work of transferring the deceased to the fairgrounds went more slowly than expected. There were only eighteen regulation-sized stretchers available. Using any other type of makeshift conveyance, such as blankets and quilts, could not prevent "bodies from falling apart."[24] As the convicts carried the dead bodies to the trucks from the prison yard, one observer was struck by their "Cries of Gangway," repeated with "monotonous regularity." A prisoner who soon after the fire wrote a novel based on his experiences at the Ohio Penitentiary had one of his fictional characters take exception to the way the bodies were handled during transport. "There is nothing nice about the way they are handled. They are hoisted, carried to a truck which has high sides, then flung on the floor in the manner, possibly, that a dealer in hogs would throw his dead purchases into a lorry. One atop another, legs and arms in a jumbled batch, the dead are piled into the truck." Taking one last look at the trucks as they headed to the fairgrounds, he watched a "receding view of a mass of legs and arms, of blackened faces and tousled hair."[25]

It was understood that the transporting of the bodies was supposed to be completed before dawn on Tuesday. Trucks and ambulances carried the lifeless bodies into the fairgrounds under heavy guard, in a process that to some observers resembled the ferrying of casualties from a battlefield. The large army trucks used for transporting the dead had been turned over to the state militia by the federal government shortly after World War I to be utilized as hearses. Few could have imagined they would be used for such a mass casualty event. One local reporter observed that "a caravan of death . . . rumbled in its grim way through the almost deserted streets of North Columbus early Tuesday morning." Onlookers were struck by the "olive-drab army trucks looming gray under the garish light of street lamps" as they transported "their gruesome load of freight" from the penitentiary to the fairgrounds, where grieving relatives "braved the chill damp of the night to stand for hours waiting for the dreaded news."[26] The first three trucks, driven by militiamen, delivered their "silent loads" at 1:35 a.m. Each truck transported six bodies. The grim task continued through the small hours before dawn, arriving on what one reporter dubbed "military schedule," twenty minutes apart. The last of the bodies was removed from the Ohio Penitentiary by 4:14 a.m., making the dawn deadline.[27]

By Tuesday morning one hundred embalmers and assistants were on duty. Before them were 230 operating tables covered with white sheets, all set up to await the arrival of the motor transport unit transferring the bodies from the prison yard. Several hours before the bodies arrived, a "small army of state employees" had dusted off the tables, all "arranged in orderly rows," in preparation. A pad of absorbent cotton and other supplies were placed on each table. At the head of each table was a headrest, "a small box, a foot long, a foot wide and about three feet deep." A reporter noted that "in happier times these little boxes had housed prize apples."[28]

Among the embalmers was the All-American Notre Dame football star Jack Cannon, one of the last "bareheaded" college football players, whom the noted sportswriter Grantland Rice would later call the best guard in Notre Dame's history. A resident of Columbus, Cannon volunteered his services after letting it be known that he had studied embalming in college. He went directly to the

Horticulture Building at the state fairgrounds soon after the first body was carried in, helped bring the second victim into the improvised morgue, and immediately set to work.[29]

Once the bodies arrived, they were rigorously inspected for identification before they were allowed to remain at the fairgrounds. An elaborate checking system was required before bodies could be turned over to relatives. All of the records for the convicts in the G&H cellblocks were relocated from the prison records office to the fairgrounds. To prevent mistakes, Bertillon measurements, prison numbers, and other forms of identification were checked. The potential for misidentification was brought home on Wednesday, when three men previously listed as dead turned up alive, including William Law and Andrew Jackson from Cleveland and one of two Cincinnati brothers.[30] One final step was to require all convicts to return to the very cells they had cried to be released from less than forty-eight hours earlier. With close to fifty bodies so charred and disfigured that no forensic tools at the time could identify them, a process of elimination was used. Each of the cells where the fire took place contained the prison numbers of its occupants. Numbers were then checked to see who was unaccounted for. Once this task was completed, the convicts were allowed back out.

Fire survivor "James R. Winning,"[31] the anonymous convict turned novelist, claimed in his 1933 roman à clef *Behind These Walls* that he had been talked into helping with the identification process. His contribution was taking shipping tags from the deputy warden and helping mark the dead in the cells and prison yard. In order to be sure, he needed access to the prisoners' shirts, which had the numbers written on them. Many were without shirts, however. For those victims who could not be identified he was told to leave behind a blank card. Other victims were so charred they had to be rolled over to pull the shirttail from underneath them. By this time many of the bodies were growing stiff from rigor mortis. Their arms were often sticking straight out, "with the forearm and shoulder forming a pivot so it is impossible, almost, to roll them over." When he was able to recognize a body, a helper held a flashlight while he wrote down the convict's number on the tag. "As fast as we tag a group they are carried away."[32]

A number of physicians with stethoscopes made sure "life was extinct" before bodies were prepared for burial. Once they were satisfied with the identification, the bodies were turned over to morticians and undertakers, who were busy "working with their fluids and instruments." Captain C. B. Weir, representing Edward E. Fisher Undertakers, was selected by the state to take charge of the bodies. Weir noted that three hundred suits had been ordered from different stores to clothe the dead for burial. In addition, he mentioned to one reporter that "300 conservative caskets and 300 rough boxes in which caskets will be placed when bodies are buried" had been ordered. Ohio state authorities not only made sure that bodies were properly prepared for burial, but also paid for bodies to be sheathed in black shrouds, white collars, and wing ties,[33] placed in plain coffins, and provided transport to their hometowns. Relatives who could not make the trip were permitted to telegraph instructions to the warden.[34] After the dead were identified and placed inside their caskets, "some were covered by flowers placed there by friends or relatives."[35] These flowers would stay in place until the floral arrangements donated by the Columbus Flower Growers and Dealers Association arrived.[36] One observer described "evenly placed caskets, their lids now closed, gray and pearl and black, a spray of roses and lilies on each one."[37]

Undertakers were kept busy throughout the day and by noon on Tuesday, April 22, had finished more than two hundred embalmings. They planned to finish the rest by nightfall. Arrangements had already been made to transfer eight bodies to the Whitaker mortuary for funeral services. Likewise, protocol was in place to make sure all of the Cincinnati victims were returned to their homes for burial. Embalmers from all over central Ohio also worked quickly. The bodies were checked by coroner Murphy.

In the days ahead, sobbing wives, relatives, and friends began the grueling task of identifying hundreds of cadavers. The protocol for claiming the bodies began with a visit to the warden's office at the Ohio Penitentiary, where next of kin were given passes that would get them into the temporary morgue in the Horticulture Building. Pass in hand, relatives were transported to the fairgrounds, where they waited outside the building until the body had been located, before being taken inside to view it. One reporter described the relatives of the dead men "assembled in droves at the temporary morgue . . . where victims were laid out in caskets of gray, white and pink."[38] Weeping relatives moved along the long line of caskets. Several women passed out when they spotted their loved ones. The army trucks that had brought the bodies to the fairgrounds would also take them to railroad stations for the final journey to their hometowns. If families could afford the expense, hearses were available as well.[39]

At 5:30 Tuesday evening an army officer from the Horticulture Building apprised waiting survivors there would be no more identifications that night. At this point 149 bodies, nearly half of the 317 dead, had been identified, and 37 had already been released for shipment. The army officer informed the milling crowd that transportation and lodging would be provided by the Salvation Army to anyone who wanted to wait until the next day. Several who waited moved in for a last look at the "evenly placed caskets, their lids now closed, gray and pearl and black, a spray of roses or lilies on each one." For the 168 families who decided to wait the night out there would be "another black night of suspense lighted only by the hope that a beloved face would be white, and whole and familiar."[40]

There was very little that could be done to make the Horticulture Building welcoming to bereaved family members, but building manager C. K. Rowland "did what he could to make the grim room less dreary" by moving plants that would have decorated the grounds at fair time into the makeshift mortuary. By one account, "they were the only 'bouquets' for those who had gone west, and somehow they made the grisly scene a bit more bearable."[41] The weather seemed to have reverted to winter, with light frost expected in exposed areas as the sky cleared. Indeed, it was so cold that the opening baseball series between the Columbus Senators and the Milwaukee Brewers had to be rescheduled to June. Tuesday night the mercury had plunged to thirty degrees, and the following morning was expected to be fifteen to twenty degrees below normal. It was imperative, therefore, to offer some type of seating inside the building. But the fifty chairs set up for mourners provided minimal comfort.

The fairgrounds housed many of the overnighters in its colosseum. Around "a roaring fire" one family sat with "immobile faces, benumbed by catastrophe. A daughter and granddaughter watched anxiously a tired old face which alternately dropped in slumber and raised in vague grief." Two Newberry boys,[42] of the four the old woman had raised, were listed among the dead. One had not been identified yet, but once he was, his mother could say "they played together, lived together and now they have died together." That's all she wanted at this point. She managed to smile as she took a tin cup of coffee that was handed to her.

Although the state capital, Columbus, was used to visitors, it is doubtful that anyone could remember so many cars from so many different Ohio cities in town at the same time. "Car after car bearing licenses issued from remote corners of the state and which gave the evidence of being driven at a terrific clip over the state's highways pulled into the fairgrounds disgorging drawn faced occupants."[43] It wasn't long before the fairgrounds were teeming with so many cars that it became necessary to close the gates to all but selected visitors, in an attempt to create a bulwark between the bereaved and morbidly curious rubberneckers. Anyone found lurking around just out of curiosity was "routed in short order." Among those volunteering to keep curious bystanders at bay were a number of "actives and pledges" of Pi Kappa Alpha Fraternity at Ohio State University, who helped guard the doors to the Horticulture Building.[44]

Orders were sent out Tuesday night by Colonel J. S. Shetler, from the 37th Division of the Ohio National Guard that relatives of the victims would not be allowed to enter the Horticulture Building until Wednesday morning, April 23. Shetler's 150 guardsmen would remain on duty until Wednesday night to keep the curious throngs from the building. Relatives who were able to provide burial and shipping permits were spared the ordeal of the initial protocol requiring first going to the prison to make arrangements for the bodies. Instead, they could now go directly to the fairgrounds, where state officials assisted in identification and bodies were neatly grouped in sections arranged in alphabetical order. By the end of Tuesday fingerprints had been taken of fifty-five yet to be identified men in hopes of establishing their identities.

Word came Wednesday that the 318th convict had died, thirty-year-old Edward Willis, doing five to seven for larceny. Cause of death was reported as pneumonia. Wednesday morning at 9 a.m. the "parade of sorrow started," as relatives from distant reaches of the state who had been notified by telegram that their loved ones had perished gathered at the Horticulture Building to identify husbands, fathers, sons, and brothers, "some seared beyond almost recognition." They found 318 "different colored coffins in rows the length of the building," some covered with flowers placed by friends or relatives. One reporter described long lines of women making their way down the rows of caskets, "seeking but fearing to find."

The *Ohio State Journal's* Mary V. Daughtery, one of the few women to report the tragedy, was perhaps better able to empathize with the bereaved women than her male counterparts. She noted, "Women used to screaming, screamed, and mothers with suddenly bitter faces [railed] against the state" for the deaths of their misdemeanant sons. "Then there were quiet little women with ancient black hats perched, dusty and bent, on their wisps of hair. They did not weep or rail, but now and then an epidemic of frenzy caught the long line in its grasp, and then they searched their purses for handkerchiefs, and reached for support."[45]

Daugherty interviewed one grandmother who had told her grandchildren that their father was dead rather than admit that he was in the big house. She said, "I'd hate to have anybody see me here. You see I tried to think of him as dead too, for the children's sake." But she admitted having saved money for his burial. During their conversation the grandmother "shivered at the sudden scream of another woman." The reporter described "a tall, lanky figure in a brown coat" reaching toward a casket and taking off the roses that had been placed there. She threw them to the ground and then "ground them into the floor with her heel." A "Junior League Woman" who had accompanied her tried to offer support, but the "woman turned on her violently, as if to strike." A man in uniform rushed over to intervene. "It was the end as she fell to the floor in a violent fit of weeping which continued until she was removed in a state of collapse."[46]

No matter where one looked, "serenity was rare on any face, whether of the waiting bereaved or of the hundred or more workers from the Red Cross and Salvation Army who went to and fro among the moving ranks, giving comfort and advice." On the edge of the crowd, correspondent Mary Daugherty espied "two well-dressed gentlewomen" who seemed to be in their late thirties. Daugherty apparently learned their stories from Salvation Army volunteers or "sympathetic bystanders." It turned out they were sisters who had found their younger brother among the dead "on the rough tables." The dead boy had made the mistake of joining a friend, the son of a bank cashier, in a bank heist. Their brother had agreed to drive the car and help take care of the stolen bonds. The cashier's son escaped with the cash, leaving his partner in crime to face the music as a co-conspirator. He was due to be paroled in June, in part because of his extreme youth.[47] Little did he expect that he would get out much sooner—but in a coffin.

Almost anywhere the reporter turned there was a human interest story. There was the case of a youthful mother of five. One of her children happened to be in a Cleveland hospital with a serious disorder at the same time she was re-claiming her husband's body and trying to find out if she had insurance to cover expenses. Daugherty saw her walking around the fairground for almost an hour "in a sort of apathy" before collapsing.

Once the dead had been removed from the prison and the fairgrounds, it was time to take stock of some of the Ohio Penitentiary personalities who had perished. Among them was Robert Stone, serving a life sentence for the murder of a railroad detective, the brother of celebrated magician Howard Thurston.[48] One of the more infamous victims was Oren Hill, a former Ohio Penitentiary guard who was imprisoned for helping an inmate escape on March 10, 1929. His fate was set once he harbored the fugitive John Leonard Whitfield. Though the jailbreak was well planned, Whitfield was traced to Hill's house the very next day. Rather than give himself up, Whitfield took his own life after being cornered by Columbus city detective Norwood E. Folk and Ohio Penitentiary record clerk Dan Bonzo. Both Hill and his wife were indicted for helping the fugitive. Hill was sentenced to one year, which turned into a death sentence on Easter Monday.[49]

In a great example of "Beware of what you wish for," John Bowman had been given a 128-month sentence for forging an eight-dollar check. He was originally sentenced to the Mansfield Reformatory, but asked the judge to relo-cate him to Columbus so he could be closer to his parents. Thirty-two-year-old

Albert Holland had only been behind bars for several hours, beginning a six-to-thirty beef for forgery and a robbery in Coshocton, Ohio, when he perished.[50] He was known for his connection to Irene Schroeder, Pennsylvania's "notorious gun woman,"[51] who was confined in the Lawrence County Jail in New Castle, awaiting execution for the murder of a Pennsylvania state trooper. Future best-selling popular historian Bruce Catton, who reported on the fire for a Texas newspaper, chronicled the irony of several of the deaths, including Holland's.[52] Ernest Brown and Mack Talley had just become eligible for parole after serving three years but died in the fire as well.

Carl Lyons, twenty-one, came to the fairgrounds to look for the bodies of his brother, Charles, twenty-five, and cousin Everett, twenty-nine, both in their fourth year of a twenty-five-year stretch for highway robbery. Scrupulously searching the Horticulture Building, he found his brother but no sign of his cousin. Garland Runyon from Lawrence County had only been admitted hours earlier to serve a stint for abandoning his children in Ironton. Joining these unlucky victims was Joe Pedro, who had just been admitted on Monday.[53] Jack Beers had just recovered from an illness and had been transferred back to his cell from the hospital in time for the fire. Tubercular Leslie Humphrey, a lifer and a patient in the prison hospital, was probably a roommate with Beers. But he left the hospital "and groped through smoke to help other prisoners until he dropped exhausted."[54]

John Anderson, a convict from the Columbus area, ran from his cell at the outbreak and raced over to his brother's cell, but too late. "Big" Ben Henderson, a highway robber out of Cincinnati, also failed to save his brother from a burning cell. He pointed out the cell on the sixth tier to a reporter, telling him, "This is where my brother died." The reporter described him as half sobbing, with "no rancor visible in his voice. Only Sorrow." Big Ben continued, making sure everyone would know his story, "Yep, Hank died in there like a rat. He never had a chance. . . . There is what is left of his radio. And there is the box where he kept his stuff." Ben turned away, perhaps to compose himself, still speaking. "I did my best to reach him when they released me from the white cell block [White City]. . . . But we couldn't get near the place." Hank had entered the Ohio Penitentiary in 1922 and was serving one to fifteen years for burglary; Ben followed in 1929.[55]

Even more memorable was the story of the four Anglian brothers, all housed together in the "doomed cell block." Two of the brothers, William and John, serving life for murder, were held in the lower tiers and were among the first to be released when the fire broke out. Both risked their lives trying to save others in the ruined cellblock as they searched in vain for their brothers Frank, twenty-one, and Theodore, twenty-three, both serving ten to twenty years for robbery with intent to kill.[56] Two other brothers, Walter and Harry Smith, died valiantly after carrying out close to ten men each. Both were overcome by fire and fatigue and took their last breaths in the prison hospital.[57]

All but a few, who were burned beyond recognition, were eventually claimed. A number of victims remained unidentified, leaving it to the state to establish identifications based on fingerprints. Any trouble identifying a corpse was usually remedied by checking fingerprints, as Bertillon officers went through the painstaking process of "pressing lifeless fingers on ink pads and paper."[58] As the week came to an end, most of the bodies had been sent home either by train or hearse, but that still left a number of unclaimed, and unidentified bodies. Plans were to bury the men at the East Lawn Cemetery on Friday afternoon, but last efforts to check fingerprints pushed the "wholesale burial" to 11 a.m. Saturday. Two trenches were dug in the east end of the cemetery, 150 feet long, 7 and a half feet wide, and 5 feet deep.

Just a mile away was Evergreen Cemetery, where African American victims, unclaimed or unidentified, were set to be interred in a separate ceremony.[59] A grave 75 feet long and 6 feet wide had been prepared for the fire victims. But according to the *Chicago Defender*, an African American newspaper, only "two bodies were buried in the Jim Crow cemetery" on Sunday: convicts Robert Thompson, twenty-six, from Lucas, Ohio, and Dempsey Brown, twenty-four, from Hamilton, under the direction of cemetery manager J. W. Williams. According to a *Defender* reporter, "No ceremonies and blowing of trumpets were accorded them. These demonstrations were held in lily-white cemeteries where ministers of many faiths and various organizations took part in burial services."[60]

Lloyd Vest, a Columbus police officer, was asked several days after having visited the fairgrounds whether he had seen anything unusual. He reported that his attention was called to "a knife, [a] dagger about two and a half inches long, that was cut to a knife edge and come to a point, very sharp, and had a wooden handle on it wrapped." He said it had been taken off one of the victims. He was alerted by workers to other items of interest, with one telling him, "We have a lot of other stuff over here we have taken." Vest was then shown a box, two feet long and eighteen inches wide, a .32 automatic Colt inside of it. He was informed that "it come off of the prisoners. . . . We taken that off of a man that we taken [*sic*] $140 in money off of." Other items that could have been put to deadly use included files and saws. One of the fire investigation inquisitors, Director of Public Welfare Hal H. Griswold, shrewdly observed, "They all have knives in there now, don't they?" Vest said, "I don't know anything about it," which was probably true since he worked outside the prison as a police officer. Griswold flippantly responded, "If they don't have them it is probably the only institution in Ohio where those things are not manufactured."[61]

On April 22, as the bodies were being prepared at the fairgrounds for burial, Governor Myles Cooper, who had arrived early the morning after the fire, was convening a Board of Inquiry (BOI) to look into the causes of the fire. The outset of the investigation was marked by conflict between the county and state authorities over whether to suspend Warden Thomas. The issue was settled quickly when Governor Cooper took the case out of the hands of the local prosecutor and assigned the attorney general to take over the official inquiry. The hearings began in the prison records office, which had been converted into a temporary courtroom.

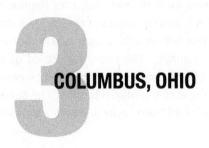

3 COLUMBUS, OHIO

Here were all ranks and ages, from the man of high life to the
meanest pickpocket, from the gray-haired man of 80 down to the
boy of 14.

—*James Finley, 1850*

The Ohio Penitentiary was "most unsuitably situated in the midst of the
city of Columbus, a few blocks from the main street."

—Handbook of American Prisons and Reformatories *(1933)*

Anyone approaching the Ohio Penitentiary (also known as the Ohio State Penitentiary) in Columbus from "a distance" and a "southern standpoint" at the end of the nineteenth century, particularly those who were "unacquainted with the character of the vast edifice that looms up against the sky, might envy the residents of a structure of such palatial dimensions." But as one approached closer to the prison structure, its details came more into focus—"the massive walls, armed sentries, battlemented gables, grated windows and towering turrets, resembling the feudal castles of romance and barbarism." Getting even closer to the looming structure, "the real character and purpose of the institution would be apparent to any intelligent mind; and perhaps would fill the place of [misplaced] envy for its unfortunate inmates."[1]

Columbus, like a handful of other American cities—Huntsville, Texas, Clinton and Ossining, New York, and others—became synonymous with its famous prison, contrary to the expectations of the local chamber of commerce. The Ohio Penitentiary maintained a commanding presence on West Spring Street from 1834 to 1998, and even before that building was constructed, being "sent to Columbus" meant hard time for Ohio convicts. The prison became "a local landmark as easily identifiable with Ohio's capital city as the statehouse."[2]

As it stood in 1930, the Ohio Penitentiary was just the most recent version of a series of carceral structures purpose-built to handle an expanding clientele as Columbus grew throughout the nineteenth century. Formerly part of the Northwest Territory, Ohio joined the union as the seventeenth state in 1803. As a state, it adopted a number of law codes from surrounding states. The following decade was one of progress and development, in no small part due to the rapid influx of settlers and the removal of the Indian threat after the War of 1812. But it took almost a decade for the government to consider providing a facility specifically dedicated to the incarceration and punishment of malefactors. The first stride toward providing a prison for the new state took place in December 1811, when the legislature accepted a donation of two ten-acre plots of land, agreeing to the donor's requirement that one plot would be used for a state house and the other for a state penitentiary. The offer also hinged on establishing the permanent seat of government on the donor's land, located on the east bank of the Scioto River. After these proposals were accepted, the following February, "in accordance with them, a town which was destined to become the city of Columbus was surveyed," with a patch of land set apart for the state prison.[3]

Construction on the first prison began in 1813. Two years later the brick structure was completed on a ten-acre lot at the southwest corner of town bordering Scioto Street. The three-floor structure measured sixty feet by thirty feet, comprising a basement used for cooking and a dining room, a second floor for the keepers' lodging, and accommodations for the prisoners, housed in thirteen cells on the third floor. Crimes that formerly merited a lashing or public humiliation in the stocks or pillory were now punished with terms behind bars. Paralleling the rapid growth of the community was an increase in lawbreakers and other miscreants, necessitating either the enlargement or replacement of the prison only a year after its inauguration.[4]

Like so many rudimentary prisons built in the era, as populations increased and cities expanded, these institutions would always be grappling with more prisoners than they were meant to confine. By 1818 it was necessary to build a new prison nearby and the old one was reconstructed for the keeper's residence. The new prison measured 150 feet by 36 feet and contained 54 cells (plus five solitary cells below the surface of the first floor. Beginning in 1822, the newest rendition of the Ohio state prison was formally designated the Ohio Penitentiary; within a few years, it was also overcrowded.[5]

Having experimented with various versions of prisoner incarceration, Ohio could take advantage of recent advances in prison construction coming out of New York State. In 1820, a state committee expressed interest in what became known as the "Auburn" plan of solitary confinement, modeled on Auburn Prison in New York. It would become the most popular corrections model in the United States well into the twentieth century, but implementing it in the existing prison structure proved to be impossible. A new facility would have to wait until the following decade.[6]

On February 8, 1832, legislation was passed that provided for the erection of a new Ohio penitentiary, and a site was selected on the east bank of the Scioto River, north of Columbus. By most accounts, the location had been presciently selected. According to one report, the building of the facility was "greatly facilitated by some advantages in the site of the Prison, not anticipated at the time of its selection," such as the fortunate availability of "excellent clay for brick making." What's more, "the value of the sand alone, in the construction of the buildings and walls of the institution, [was] more than twice as great as the whole cost to the state of the prison site of fifteen acres."[7]

Contracts were quickly bid out for stone and brick to build the prison. One of the directors decided to see for himself what was so distinct about this Auburn Prison that everyone was talking about. The new Ohio Penitentiary reflected the influence of the Auburn model not just in architecture but "in its overall program, rules and regulations and the punishments meted out to inmates." Most renditions of the Auburn design had previously featured "a tier-on-tier interior, dimly-lit cells, a program of daily work and Sunday religious services and Sabbath school." Garbed in "ugly and bizarre uniforms," inmates suffered from a "meager and monotonous diet," prison smells, and an "ever-changing cast of politically appointed personnel, petty rules and cruel punishments."

When the Auburn-based Ohio prison opened in 1834, it could hold up to seven hundred prisoners "in two inside cell ranges that flanked a central keeper's house and a guard room." Each cell was seven by three and a half feet in area and seven feet in height. The cells were built back to back on five ranges "connected by balconies and separated from the exterior wall by an eleven-foot space. Stoves located in the open areas between cells and the cellhouse exterior walls provided heat. Workshops and a separate female cellblock were arrayed on the remaining three sides of the walled enclosure."[8] The facility was built with convict labor and was surrounded by a perimeter wall four hundred feet long and twenty-four feet high, earning the sobriquet common for high-walled institutions of the era, "The Walls."[9]

In 1833 a hospital building was added, and in late October 1834, although not all the buildings had been completed, the new improved Ohio Penitentiary received its first complement of prisoners under the watchful eye of its first warden (known as the "keeper" until a change in nomenclature in 1834), Nathaniel Medbury. Within four years, a separate facility for female prisoners, offering eleven cells and capable of accommodating many more, was built just east of the main building. The "first large penitentiary in the West,"[10] when completed in 1837, it cost $93,370.50 and 113,462 days of convict labor. Prisoners did almost all of the work, including the grading, leveling, ditching, brickmaking, and stonecutting. Convict blacksmiths even forged the grates, doors, and locks.[11] Now it was up to prison administrators to put contemporary correctional practices of the day into the prison-management regime, which, like the penitentiary itself, was always a work in progress.

Following the Auburn regime, prisoners worked together in a congregate setting by day and slept in solitary cells at night. Auburn's prison industries exceeded the profits of the competing Pennsylvania system, exemplified by Philadelphia's Eastern State Penitentiary, where prisoners worked on piecemeal projects alone in their cells and had no contact with other prisoners, effectively spending their days in twenty-four-hour solitary confinement. Ultimately, the Auburn model won out over the Pennsylvania system because it was cheaper to operate and more financially productive. While the Pennsylvania model offered spacious accommodations, including better sanitation and heating, observers weighed heavily the physical and psychological impact of solitary confinement (as they still do today) on prisoners at Eastern State Penitentiary against the opportunities for profit in the Auburn model and its attendant routine.

There was another particularly American consideration for choosing the Auburn design. Prison architectural historian Norman Johnston suggested that America, with "its tradition of hard work and its chronic labor shortages[,] could not really tolerate the degree of relative idleness" permitted under the Pennsylvania system.[12] Between 1827 and 1834 prisons in Connecticut, Massachusetts,

Maryland, Vermont, Tennessee, New Hampshire, Georgia, the District of Columbia, and Ohio adopted the Auburn multitier-cell plan. Eventually most prisons in
nineteenth-century America would follow suit.[13]

By 1840 the prison featured an industrial building where prisoners were kept
busy making the prison profitable, manufacturing harnesses, shoes, barrels,
brooms, silk hats, bolts, and other items not otherwise manufactured in Ohio.
Early prison officials kept control through a combination of hard work, discipline, and hefty doses of religion. According to one early chaplain, "Here were
all ranks and ages, from the man of high life to the meanest pickpocket, from the
gray-haired man of 80 down to the boy of 14. They were all dressed in striped
clothing; all seemed depressed and broken down in spirits; all were silently at
work, without the hope of remuneration, under the inspection of well-appointed
watchers."[14]

By the mid-nineteenth century, the Ohio penal system consisted of the state
penitentiary at Columbus, county jails, and numerous city lockups. When the
pen was completed in 1837, it housed exclusively felons, convicts sentenced to two
or more years, irrespective of age, gender, and mental condition. It was not until
an act was passed in 1857 that any real strides were taken toward classification and
separation of convicts according to their "age, disposition and moral character."
The new legislation also specified that inmates assigned to work for contractors
were to be paid. What's more, it now required the warden to send illiterate and
poorly educated prisoners to classes each evening for two hours during work days
from October through April, and for an hour and a half on the rest of the working
days.[15]

By the 1830s, Columbus was little more than "a thriving village, with little
upon which to predict prosperity and greatness."[16] Conditions must have improved during the following decade, since British writer Charles Dickens, while
traveling through Ohio in 1842, proclaimed Columbus "a clean and pretty town"
and predicted that "of course it is going to be much larger as it is the seat of the
State Legislature of Ohio."[17] By the time Dickens visited, Columbus was indeed
in the midst of a growth spurt, tripling in population from 6,048 souls to 17,882
by 1850. Even so, Columbus at midcentury had little to recommend it by most
accounts, beyond the fact that it was home to the state's capital and "the site of a
rather fine new penitentiary opened in 1834."[18]

Columbus was spread over forty square miles in the rolling Scioto Valley at
almost the geographical center of the state, where "the Scioto River sweeps gen-
tly into town through miles of parkway owned by the municipality, to be joined

near the walls of the Ohio penitentiary."[19] Its strategic location at the confluence of the Scioto and Olentangy Rivers guaranteed the "ease of transportation" so vital for "moving inmates safely and cheaply from the rest of the state." Moreover, its central location minimized "the cost of moving raw materials and finished products offered by the projected prison industries."[20]

Ohio experienced new waves of immigration in the 1840s, including New Englanders and, from overseas, Irish, Germans, and others fleeing from the economic pressures and religious persecutions of the era. All would contribute to Ohio's "rapidly changing economy" in the 1860s as an era of industrialization saw the population of Columbus pass the twenty thousand mark. By the turn of the twentieth century, German immigrants made up much of the city's population and transformed the city in a number of ways. On the south side, for example, was a distinctive neighborhood "replicating the cobbled streets and narrow houses of neighborhoods in Munich and Dresden." Germans would open a number of successful breweries on the western edge of "German Village." But these would be pushed out of business by Prohibition.[21]

Crucial to the development of Columbus and the 1930 prison riot was the evolution of the capital city as "an important military center." Fort Hayes, in particular, originated as an arsenal during the Civil War, and by war's end Columbus had become the state's "principal mobilization point for military forces," a distinction it still maintained in 1930, when the National Guard and militia were called out to quell the prison mutiny following the fire.

Columbus "grew up along its two principal streets, Broad and High."[22] As the years ticked by, the city continued to develop around the Ohio State Penitentiary, and by 1930 only thirty-foot stone walls separated city residents from the thousands of prisoners inside. In the year following the fire, visitors from the Osborne Association noted that the Ohio Penitentiary was "most unsuitably situated in the midst of the city of Columbus, a few blocks from the main street."[23] Much had changed since the previous century, when towns competed to house state prisons, which city boosters "regarded as the enhancement of the community,"[24] much as they vied to acquire state capitol buildings.

According to one 1930 observer, the physical relationship between the prison and the Columbus community was such that "the penitentiary buildings [were] scattered about a limited acreage not a mile from the Ohio State capitol at Columbus, the whole surrounded on the most part by a wall more than thirty feet high, and the top of which is a walk along which armed guards patrol. At the corners are placed small guardhouses, with an outlook in all directions."[25] The massive prison walls separating the free community from the inmates "served as not only a final barrier to escape but as a symbol of society rejection . . . a fort to keep the enemy within rather than without." The perspective of the prison's neighbors would have been familiar to criminologist Gresham Sykes, who described the New Jersey State Prison in 1958: "From outside you can see guards in their towers on the wall, and each armed with revolver, gas grenades to quell a riot or strike down inmates desperate enough to attempt to escape."[26] Anyone who lived in Columbus or served a stint behind bars in prison there would have been well acquainted with these depictions of the Ohio Penitentiary in the first three decades of the twentieth century.

Columbus in the years leading up to the fire was on the ascendant as a commercial, academic, and tourist destination. Home to a growing university, a Greek Revival capitol building, and venues hosting sporting and cultural events, it seemed to have something for everyone. The city even featured an excellent zoo and Red Bird Stadium, "one of the finest minor league baseball parks in the country, the lighting equipment for night games being outstanding."[27] In the late 1920s, the American Insurance Union Citadel was completed, at its time "the tallest building west of Manhattan and the fifth-tallest building in the world."[28]

In the year of the stock market crash and just months before the fatal fire, Columbus was selected as a transfer point for the fastest coast-to-coast means of travel, "where plane meets train." By combining train and plane travel, a passenger could reach Los Angeles from New York City in just forty-eight hours, half the time it took by train alone. Train passengers from New York City would arrive and transfer to a Ford Trimotor aircraft at the recently dedicated Port Columbus airport.[29]

As far back as 1899, hungry and deprived children waited at the prison's southeastern gate for baskets of scraps left over from the convict mess hall.[30] Thirty years later, conditions were still tough on the less privileged, especially with the onset of the Great Depression in 1929. Although by most accounts it hit hardest in Ohio's northern industrial cities, such as Cleveland, Youngstown, Akron, and Toledo, Columbus and other cities "had their breadlines." Meanwhile, enrollment at Ohio State University plunged by a thousand students between 1929 and 1933. Delinquent tax rolls increased, and more and more families found themselves evicted into the streets. Few could dispute that by 1930 the Great Depression was upon them, and a job working in the prison was a much-sought-after position.

The convergence of hard times, unemployment, and labor strife in the 1920s and '30s was not new to Ohio. In the early 1820s, a protective organization among workers emerged from the widespread unemployment of the era. By 1828,

Cincinnati printers inaugurated the state's first labor organization. Columbus was also beset with unrest "over the contract-labor system at the Ohio Penitentiary," which local free-world workers saw as unfair business competition.[31]

At the time of the 1930 fire, Columbus was a segregated city. If shops, restaurants, movie theaters, and recreational facilities allowed African Americans inside, it was only "reluctantly."[32] The local university, Ohio State, denied its eight hundred black students space or use of its student union, forcing them to find lodgings in the segregated black section of town. Future author, inmate, and fire survivor Chester Himes ended up withdrawing from Ohio State in 1927.

The newspaper coverage of a mass murder in Columbus, just one month after the fire, offers some insight into not just race relations in Ohio, but its coverage by the African American and the white-run newspapers. According to the *Chicago Defender*, a white woman and mother of ten, Mrs. Ethel Yeldem, shot and killed seven of her children "because six of them would have to face American prejudice and color bars due to the fact that that their father was not white." She shot the seventh because he was "weak-minded, therefore also unable to cope with the world's problems." Curiously, she had posed the family for a picture at a Columbus art gallery just hours before the shooting on May 6. After the children she shot herself, succumbing ten days later.[33] The most poignant aspect of this story was a postscript, that the incarcerated husband had written her a letter just days earlier informing her that he had escaped injury in the Easter Monday prison inferno.[34]

4 OHIO PENITENTIARY

Ten thousand pages of history of the Ohio Penitentiary would not give one idea of the inward wretchedness of its 1,900 inmates. The unwritten history is known only by God himself.

—*Prison superintendent, 1893*

Most American prisons, including the Ohio Penitentiary, experienced population increases between 1870 and 1904. Prison architecture during this era continued to follow the Auburn pattern, with improvements that sometimes included the introduction of ventilating systems and steel cells that offered plumbing and running water. However, the bucket system of human-waste disposal persisted in many penitentiaries well into the 1930s, as underfunded prisons were forced by circumstances to modify existing structures and add new cellblocks to house the growing legions of new inmates.

The Ohio Penitentiary was expanded several times during its first forty-five years. In 1861, East Hall was finished, adding five hundred more cells to West Hall's original two hundred. Following the American Civil War, the prison, like most other prisons in the country, continued to experience tremendous growth. Preventing prison escapes was foremost in the minds of prison officials both before and after the 1930 fire. Despite thirty-foot-high walls sunk several feet into the ground, the Ohio Penitentiary was plagued by at least fifty successful escapes during its more than 150 years. Confederate general John H. Morgan, who chiseled through the floor of one of his men's cells and escaped via an air chamber beneath the block on the night of November 26, 1863, led the most famous breakout. Morgan and six others clambered over the wall with the help of an improvised rope and grappling hook and fled back to the South, where they received a hero's welcome.[1]

Several efforts at improving management led to the passage of an 1867 law that borrowed from New York's penal system, adding a board of directors and providing six-year appointments for its three members. The new board had the power to appoint major officers, create rules, and approve labor contracts. Concurrently, it was suggested that Ohio's seventy-seven counties, with their myriad derelict jails, would benefit from some type of central supervision. In 1867, Ohio followed the lead of Massachusetts and introduced a state board of charities.[2]

In 1877, Ohio's New Hall, which would be the site of the Easter Monday fire, was completed. Together, the three halls "formed an impressive 813 foot façade looming large along Columbus's Spring Street."[3] At this time the prison walls contained numerous shop buildings, many of which had to be rebuilt over the years "due to periodic fires set by disgruntled prisoners." Before the construction of New Hall, the prison had become overcrowded for the first time since the Civil War years, when two thousand military prisoners were held there. New Hall was built thanks to the work of two hundred convict laborers, who also improved the old cell building. Coterminous with the surge of prisoners, its completion was just in time "to profitably employ the large number of new inmates"; otherwise, the construction would have proved a "'white elephant' of no small dimensions."[4]

Foreshadowing the introduction of the electric chair in the years ahead, electricity was added to Ohio's punishment regime in 1878, with what would become known as the "hummingbird." As one newspaper put it, "the Penitentiary management, determined not to be outdone by Edison, have introduced electricity as a mode of punishment." A visiting journalist was shown the apparatus by the deputy warden, accompanied by the prison physician. The reporter described a macabre electric device containing an "electromagnet" and housed in a box measuring ten inches long, three inches high, and three inches wide. Protocol required the prisoner to be taken to the "ducking box, formerly in use in the insane department," where he was stripped and blindfolded prior to being introduced to the "water box," referred to as the "ducking-tub." The convict was then "led around a corner of the interior cell building and placed in the box, handcuffed but not shackled at the feet." The room remained quite warm, having a fire burning day and night. The prisoner was forced to sit down in water three inches deep as "one pole of the battery is placed in the water" and "a sponge attached to the end of the other pole." The deputy warden supervised this punishment, which entailed "touching the bare skin of the convict in various places rapidly with the sponge." Another prisoner assisted by "turning a small crank attached to the electric apparatus." Prison officials of the era minimized its fear-inducing qualities, noting, "The concern is so small that it looks like a toy, but it makes the subject of punishment yell sometimes, as though he was badly hurt or badly frightened." Fortunately, the reporter did not have to witness the procedure as the prison officials touted its benefits. The physician said the "mode of punishment does no harm," and "in some cases he says it is a physical benefit."

According to officials, the punishment was effective because the man was blindfolded and thus "has no idea where or when he is going to be touched, and is not nerved against it as one would be who takes hold of the poles of a battery with his eyes open and thoughts concentrated for the expected shock." This punishment had "reduced the visits to the room 45 per cent. The dungeons have been dispensed with except five. About one man per week is sent there. The water box, or ducking tub, is painted red and has a lid. When the lid is lifted up and turned back against the wall the visitor reads on the underside of it, 'Long Branch.'"[5]

In 1885, Ohio was directed to carry out all executions at the Columbus facility, replacing the public hanging spectacles that sometimes took place in the counties where the original crimes had been committed. To separate the condemned from the general population, five cells were constructed on the "south side of east end-screened off cells known as 'the cage.'"

The warden at the time was so impressed with the New York electric chair, first introduced in 1890, that he had one installed at the Ohio Penitentiary in 1896, just below the trapdoor of the second-floor gallows. Prior to its abolition in 1963, 315 inmates would die in it.[6] Put another way, during the sixty-seven years of electrocutions at Columbus, five fewer convicts died in the contraption than the 320 who perished in the Easter Monday fire in one hour.

In the last decades of the nineteenth century, states such as New York were opening new prisons and reformatories to replace aging and obsolete facilities. By contrast, "Ohio was unable to decide on a site for even a second prison, and continued to add new buildings" to the Columbus penitentiary until the cells numbered 1,800, "greatly exceeding any other prison in the world."[7] Ohio prison officials did not receive authorization to begin sending some younger inmates to the unfinished reformatory in Mansfield until the main population surpassed two thousand in 1896. But this did little to relieve the congestion in the Ohio Penitentiary.

By most accounts, the administration of Warden E. G. Coffin between 1886 and 1900 was a high point in nineteenth-century Ohio corrections. Several "flattering books were written" about the prison during this era, a time when visitors could buy picture souvenir books showing convicts in military formation marching across the "lushly landscaped prison yard." On Christmas Day 1888, Columbus newspapers lauded Coffin's decision to abolish primitive punishments such as the ducking tub. Coffin would later note, "A hard box to sleep on and bread and water to eat will cause them to behave themselves. It may not be so speedy but is more humane." That same year Coffin noted in one of his books how he charged visitors twenty-five cents for guided tours of the prison. Prison tours continued to be offered until the 1950s. These were especially popular during the week of the Ohio State Fair, when "many out-of-towners had it on the list of places to visit."[8]

Convict Charles L. Clark witnessed the Coffin regime firsthand. In his memoirs, he recalled entering the prison through the main gate on the way into the guardroom. From there he passed through another gate into the prison yard, where hundreds of bodies would lie in the repose of death just thirty years later. Clark, who was no stranger to America's penitentiary system, asserted that the Ohio Penitentiary "had probably one of the finest lawns of any prison in the U.S." He was more than impressed with the Ohio Penitentiary in general. He described a prison yard divided up like a self-contained small town. It "formed a square, surrounded by the Warden's house and cell houses, a dining hall, the Hospital, Chapel and Green Houses. Other parts of the yard contained shops and the streets that were numbered or named from 1st Street to 7th Street and running in the other direction 1st Avenue to 7th Avenue and these streets and buildings all run under the contract system."[9]

Though the following decade would see many improvements, the 1890s were still marked by the punitive correctional philosophy of the day. In 1894, an investigative reporter for the *Columbus Dispatch* was taken into the inner sanctum of the prison, where he found prisoners locked in sweatboxes for punishment, leading the newspaper "to denounce the state for 'a partial return to the dark ages.'" It was still a time of the ball and chain, bread-and-water diets, and political graft. Some of the less-connected inmates were still being blindfolded and tortured with water hoses, while well-connected inmates, who today would be considered "white-collar criminals," were ensconced in large, airy cells on the so-called Bankers' Row. Here they enjoyed special privileges and reveled in a standard of living that sometimes included a private cell. One observer described a typical cell featuring carpeted floors, curtain-covered doors for privacy, mirrors, and other luxuries. Rather than the bland prison uniforms, they were clothed in a manner that bespoke their former prominence, wearing white shirts and generally holding clerk positions in the prison and being permitted to buy their own food.[10]

When William Sydney Porter, later known by the sobriquet O. Henry, arrived at the Ohio pen on April 25, 1898, he was asked his occupation. He responded, "newspaper writer," which was indeed his last full-time job; he had worked for the *Houston Post* as a columnist and feature writer. He then added, "I am also a registered pharmacist." That was his ticket to better treatment, since a pharmacist was always needed in the prison hospital, situated about a hundred yards outside the prison walls. (He would also work later as a bookkeeper, another job he had held before prison.) His white-collar background allowed him unfettered freedom. He would never be assigned to a cell, but slept, ate, and worked at the hospital, where his working day ended at four each afternoon. Using his trustee status, he could walk into town and visit friends and even the local beer halls. Not bad for a convicted bank embezzler sentenced to five years in prison (he was out after three years and three months).[11]

In 1908, one Ohio historian suggested that the Ohio Penitentiary and its thirty-six-inch-thick walls "looked like a penitentiary should. Its weighty blocks of Ohio limestone rose three stories, creating a forbidding countenance in gray—dark and brooding. The largest penal institution in the world when it was built possessed a 'massive grandeur.'"[12] Five years later the state of Ohio adopted plans for "abolishing the old style of prison and erecting a farm industrial prison in its stead." According to Frederic C. Howe, director of the People's Institute, the Ohio Penitentiary complex was set to be replaced by a new prison "located on 1,600 acres of land in Madison County, to which the great body of prisoners will be taken." Governor James M. Cox asserted that the "underlying idea of the new prison" was "to save men." He stated, "Money is not our object, the State of Ohio does not want to coin gold out of the tears of unfortunates." He claimed the new prison could be maintained at little cost. The inmates from Columbus would be taken out of the walls and "a great construction camp like a big railroad camp will be organized, and the men will live in tents and other temporary structures, moving into the buildings as fast as they erect them. There is no thought of using any of the cell blocks of the old prison."[13] Like so many other plans before it, this vision never came to fruition.

It was common for wardens to complain that "their best efforts are hobbled by the architecture of their institutions."[14] On the eve of America's deadliest prison disaster, the Ohio Penitentiary had a well-earned reputation as a firetrap. While an aging penitentiary "is not of itself bad," it did not mean that every institution was worth renovating. One journalist suggested that rather than refurbishing the Ohio Penitentiary, it "ought to be razed." Federal prison director James V. Bennett, speaking about the older prisons in general, but in terms that were particularly evocative of the Ohio Penitentiary in April 1939, said, "these ancient bastilles reach a point where no more money should be spent upon them" and that any attempt to "modernize a century old institution by patching up long-outmoded cell blocks, or crowding modern kitchen facilities or a hospital amidst a jumble of cell blocks, shops, or storehouses is wasteful in the extreme."[15] Indeed, it was the renovation of two cellblocks at the Ohio Penitentiary that would indirectly lead to the country's worst prison disaster.

The construction on the G&H blocks, where the 320 men died, had been completed about seven to eight months prior to the fire. While it was going on, the inmates were housed in the neighboring I&K block, which was empty at the time of the fire and was being renovated as well. Both cellblocks dated back to 1876 and were covered by a wood roof with a slate covering on the outside. While the roof had been repaired sporadically over the years, it had not been replaced in fifty years. At the time of the fire, the timbers and sheeting on the inside were all wood and exposed to the interior of the building, further contributing to the spread of the deadly fire.[16]

Once renovated, the G&H blocks contained six ranges or tiers. Each cell was about eight feet high and square. The cells were outfitted with two folding bunks, located one above the other and attached to one wall. Each bed was supplied with a mattress and a blanket. Prisoners also had four folding chairs and a two-foot-square table, often used for playing cards and checkers or just writing letters home. Finally, the cell had several shelves attached to the rear walls. However, there is little doubt that the biggest upgrade was a commode and a washbasin.[17]

On October 8, 1925, investigators from the National Society of Penal Information visited the Ohio Penitentiary and later delivered a scathing report on its condition, published in the 1926 edition of the *Handbook of American Prisons*.[18] To secure their data at each prison they visited, the organization eschewed a questionnaire method and decided "the only way to make an adequate study was to visit each of the prisons and spend enough time for inspecting and gathering the data." Two investigators were sent to each prison. Their typical protocol was to inspect the prison and talk with its officials to draw as complete a picture of the institution as they could. Naturally, prison wardens were not always receptive to these studies, and some, such as Ohio Penitentiary warden Preston Thomas, did not cooperate thoroughly.

The representatives were required to send the finished reports back to each warden for any questions or clarification. Once the corrected reports were back in the hands of the society, the reports were published in the next volume of the *Handbook*. The reports usually suggested improvements and offered criticism. The society was confident in the assertions of its representatives, who were vetted for their knowledge of contemporary prisons and the prerequisites for making accurate comparisons.

Some of the findings from the 1925 investigation would continue to crop up in new editions of the *Handbook* in the years to come. The Ohio Penitentiary was among the prisons that continued to "show neglect in upkeep, repairs and general sanitation." The prison also came under fire for the large number of idle inmates, ranging from two hundred to eight hundred at any given time. With so many men serving long prison sentences that had been originally decreed at hard labor, many were "forced to serve long years in idleness and semi-idleness, the worst possible industrial training for men." Investigators mostly agreed that there was "no one feature of the prison situation today that is so appalling as the lack of work."[19]

At the time of the 1925 visit, the Ohio Penitentiary held 2,554 prisoners, which increased to 2,649 by the end of the year, all serving indeterminate sentences. In an era of primitive prisoner classification, according to the 1926 report the penitentiary's "trouble makers were put into one company and mental cases in another. . . . Men adjudged insane were transferred to the state hospital," but a number "of borderline cases are held at the prison." The Society inspectors were especially troubled by the punitive nature of punishment, branding it "more rigorous than most prisons today." They also remarked that the warden himself held court each Monday to weigh in on any disciplinary cases brought before him. Punishments included the loss of privileges, yard recreation, or tobacco for lesser offenses. More serious transgressions were penalized with solitary confinement on a bread-and-water diet in the "semi-circular steel cage," which was constructed in such a way that they were forced to stand for eight or more hours each day. Confinement lasted from several days to a few weeks.[20]

The prison mess halls were described as well-lit and clean but "not entirely free of odor." When inmates marched in for mealtime, they all sat facing one way, toward the backs of prisoners in the row in front of them. During the 1920s, the Ohio prison system did not have any prison farms that could supply the men a varied and healthful diet, and they were forced to survive on a rather limited food regimen.

In 1928, the National Society of Penal Information reported that the penitentiary had the worst crowding in the country. Little progress was reported the following year, when the 1929 *Handbook of American Prisons and Reformatories* labeled it one of the worst in the nation, citing overcrowding, low-paid guards, and blanket treatment for all felons. One observer described the ill-fated cellblock house, containing the G&H and I&K cellblocks, as "among the most ancient" buildings of the institution. Making matters even worse were a regime of idleness, lack of classification, loss of hope, and overcrowding. It was still a time of bread and water, straitjackets and the strap, and solitary confinement, and recent legislation prohibited prison industries from competing with free-world markets, leading to diminished jobs and idleness.

Ohio was no stranger to deadly building fires. But none of the previous fires foreshadowed the 1930 Easter Monday fire as closely as the October 8, 1928, dormitory blaze at the State Brick Plant at Junction City, Ohio, where fifteen inmates died and twenty-seven were severely injured. Indeed, the day after the Columbus disaster, one journalist noted that the Brick Plant fire had called attention to the perilous conditions that reigned in prison farms and road camps and other related facilities, describing them as "firetraps" lacking adequate provision for the immediate release of inmates in the event of a fire.[21]

Unlike the dangerously overcrowded Ohio Penitentiary, holding close to 4,500 inmates, the dormitory at the Brick Plant was a "barn-like structure of wooden frame and corrugated iron covering, erected upon a ten foot brick foundation," with accommodations for 275 prisoners "sleeping in two-tiered bunks arranged in pairs with narrow aisles between." Including 13 trusties, who did not sleep in the dorm, there were a total of 288 men at the Plant.[22]

Several inmates discovered the Brick Plant fire at midnight, but by the time the alarm resounded through the dimly lit dormitory room it was too late. The fire spread quickly along the building's floor and framework, leaping "from bunk to bunk across narrow aisles, while convicts cursed and screamed as they struggled to open doors and windows."[23] Making matters even worse, the fire hydrant did not work. As in the Columbus blaze in 1930, the convicts were awakened in time to escape, but upon reaching the nearest exits found them locked and barred. According to guards and convicts, it was probable that "many of the dead were trampled to death in a 'mad rush for the exits.'"[24]

Convicts who had made it out into the fresh air remembered looking back through windows "into the flaming interior," where they witnessed sights that they would never forget, seeing fellow prisoners "wreathed in flames, rushing to and fro" before disappearing in the smoke and flames that enveloped them as they fell to the floor. The roof and walls soon collapsed, showering the onlookers and writhing victims with burning embers.[25]

As in the Columbus fire, stories of convict heroism abounded. Among the heroes was a convict overcome by smoke and burned to death as he tried to rescue his friend. Another prisoner, who had been responsible for the prison commissary, ran inside to fight the flames but perished "on his job."[26] One inmate, Andy Kiebert, who made it out safely, ran back into the burning building to rescue the convict mascot, a terrier named Tiny King. The animal lover suffered burns but fought his way back out, emerging with the relatively unscathed dog under his coat.[27]

News reports would describe the fifteen fire victims as "charred bodies, part of them only small piles of bones," with "few or none . . . possible of identification."[28] A dozen of the more seriously burned were taken to the hospital at the Ohio Pen for treatment. A cursory identification of the dead was attempted, but remained tentative, their identifications being based for the most part on the location of the body when found. Prisoners aided in the task "to some extent," but not with any degree of certainty. In the early going, the only ones identified were two African American inmates.[29] A prison dentist examined the victims' teeth to aid in the identifications. The remains were buried in the New Lexington Cemetery, where markers were set up for those whose identities had been established. Twenty men were missing, three of whom, officials believed, had seized the opportunity to escape during the confusion that followed the fire's discovery. Others, including many cons, insisted none had escaped. Despite the opportunity for a learning moment, few lessons had been learned at the Junction City fire.

The penitentiary in Columbus was frequently plagued by incendiary fires in the years leading up to Easter Monday 1930, bolstering its reputation as a firetrap and serving as harbingers of the tragedy to come. A number of shop buildings had to be rebuilt after being periodically torched by disgruntled inmates. In 1857, someone started a fire in the north range of the workshops. Although no one died, the Ohio Tool Company shop, Hayden's blacksmith shop, Hall, Brown & Co.'s cooper shop, the state shoe and tailor shops, and Day's wood-type manufacturing were all destroyed. Losses to contractors totaled almost $50,000. One observer asserted, "It is hardly possible this conflagration could have been so complete without having been the work of some scoundrel."[30]

Although arson was never substantiated, there is a high probability that prison arsonists were responsible for several factory fires in the late 1880s.[31] The Columbus fire company, with better equipment, had to be called on in 1886 when the prison fire department proved "unable to accomplish anything" due to a lack of "requisite [water] pressure."[32] Losses were tallied at $20,000, with perhaps half covered by insurance. Fire struck again in April 1900, when a large three-story building within the walls of the penitentiary, occupied by a bolt-manufacturing shop, was destroyed by fire, at a declared loss of $100,000.[33]

It is doubtful that any of the members of the 1930 Board of Inquiry investigating the Ohio Penitentiary fire were aware that there had been well-established strategies and protocols for responding to smoke and fire in the Columbus big house dating back to the previous century. In his history of the prison published in 1891, Warden B. F. Dyer, who ran the prison from 1879 into the 1890s, devoted extensive coverage to the prison's firefighting capabilities during his administration. He described an Ohio prison fire department "situated in the angle formed by west wing and rear extension of the Chapel," replete with a fire alarm created by prisoner Charles F. Kline. Society's loss was the prison's gain as he invented

> an indicator, having 16 figures on its face. Numbers 2–15 [were] for fire purposes only, so arranged that an alarm bell will ring from 14 different places, the alarm boxes being located in different parts of the prison. All that is needed is to pull the handle attached to each box. If the number of any box is pulled it rings a gong in the engine house, new hall and guard room and general alarm on the large bell in the Chapel belfry, locating the fire. Beyond cost of battery, which was small, cost state nothing.[34]

The prison fire department had access to two hose reels and two chemical fire extinguishers. Moreover, two inmates were "constantly present," and at the first bang on the fire alarm gong they could expect to be joined by other trained prisoners as they took their places with the fire equipment. There was a hierarchy, with a fire chief commanding the inmate firemen. According to one late nineteenth-century observer, "It is an exciting scene to see the firemen rushing from their cells upon a night alarm being sounded." It appears that these trusted firemen were never locked into their cells; as soon as the gong was sounded an officer in charge of the prison fire department building would pass along to consecutive cells word that a fire was in progress, and in "less than ten seconds" the firemen were "up and away."[35]

Supplementing the fire company were fire "watchmen" who were employed by shop contractors to be on duty from 6 p.m. until the convicts were unlocked in the morning. In addition, there were six guards who stood fire watch from "the sound of the bugle" at 6 p.m. until 10 p.m. each night.[36]

By 1905, the Ohio Penitentiary fire department was held in high enough esteem to be chronicled in one of Ohio's leading newspapers.[37] According to the reporter, in the stillness of night, when prisoners in the penitentiary were supposed to be asleep, a "Clang! Clang! Clang! Clang!" would occasionally break the silence, a sound he compared to that that "a bevy of boys would make hammering old dish pans." There was a fire department outside the cellblock "regularly organized" for impending action.[38] When the prison fire alarm was sounded, "there is the same hurry and rush among the men who comprise the company, as would characterize an up-to-date fire department." Once the fire was located, a hose cart was staffed and a mad dash through the prison yard to the fire took place.[39]

One feature that captured the fancy of the reporter was the "primitive way" the alarm was sounded. "There is an old saw, such as woodsmen use in sawing logs, hanging outside the building where the fire apparatus is housed. When a guard discovers a fire he runs to this saw, draws it from the building and hammers at it with a club." Once the strange alarm alerted the inmate firefighters, who (except for the chief) slept about thirty yards away from it, there was a "response which would surprise a city chief."

It is unclear when and why the prison firefighting system was dismantled, but one of the greatest criticisms leveled at the administration of Warden Preston Thomas in 1930 was that none of the prisoners or staff could remember anything resembling a fire drill, let alone a cellblock fire company. The response by the Ohio Penitentiary guards in 1930 paled in comparison to this "primitive" yet apparently effective system in use twenty-five years earlier. The fire inquiry would reveal that by 1930 there was no firefighting apparatus in the cell buildings.

In the early 1920s, the future head of the Federal Bureau of Prisons, James V. Bennett, visited the Ohio Penitentiary on a fact-finding tour. His escort led him around to various shops that were "poorly lit, filled with obsolete and worn out equipment." In most of the shops, many of the prisoners were just "squatting against walls of rooms or loitering by the drinking fountains." The laggard inmates did not seem bothered by the proximity to their keepers in charge of the workshops, who sat in chairs on platforms just three feet above the floor, "with heavy clubs in their hands. Every now and then, a guard would pound his club on the platform and point at a prisoner, or shout an order, and the prisoners would understand. I thought the prisoners looked dispirited and hopeless, but the guards could not be blamed."[40]

Almost half a century later, Bennett would recount in his autobiography that "the enormous cellblocks depressed me beyond despair." One of the cellblocks housed "more than 900 men, with two prisoners in every ten-by-five-foot stone walled cubicle." His inmate guide noted, "He lived on the top floor and it got 'damned hot in summer.'" As they continued down a corridor, Bennett hesitated when he came upon "several men in their cells pacing up and down with unusual intensity, jabbering to themselves, rattling their bars, or shouting obscenities." His escort told him not to pay any mind: "they were psychos," kept among the general population "because there was no other place for them."[41]

The 1929 *Handbook* contained one of the best descriptions of the Ohio pen at the time of the fire. It was based on a visit by members of the National Society of Penal Information on August 1, 1928, when the prison population stood at 4,345, with most serving sentences under five years. Prison labor was guided under the state-use system.[42] On the day of the visit, more than 1,200 of the inmates were idle, 597 were on maintenance details, 1,505 were working within the walls, and 663 trustees, or "honor men," were outside the prison. Investigators found the prison dormitories "among the worst" that they had seen. Most noticeable was that there was simply not enough work for such a large number of inmates. Due to "a condition of overcrowding worse than in any large prison," the Ohio Penitentiary could not continue to properly care for the growing population and was "too large a prison to be operated on any other lines than those of blanket treatment."[43]

"Labor," according to one prison historian, "was one of the few features of prison life that changed considerably from the nineteenth to the twentieth century."[44] Historian Blake McKelvey echoes this observation. The "biggest change in the internal life of American prisons" in the 1920s, he writes, "was the rapid decline in the number of inmates employed."[45] As far back as the 1820s, during the relative infancy of the penitentiary system in America, reform groups such as the Boston Prison Discipline Society lobbied for the use of convict labor because it was "productive, it is healthful. It teaches convicts how to support themselves when they leave prison."[46] For a short period, prison factories did indeed flourish, with some institutions even earning profits. But the 1840s were also a time when only five prisons, in New York, Massachusetts, Maryland, Pennsylvania, and of course, Ohio, had more than two hundred prisoners.

Prison industries had flourished in America since the early nineteenth century. But between 1895 and 1923, antilabor legislation led to a 10 percent drop in prison industrial employment (from 72 percent to 62 percent). Leading the charge against prison labor was organized labor, citing the unfair business competition free labor posed to free-world workers. In times of unemployment or economic

stagnation, organized labor found a responsive audience among American workers who felt they should be the ones getting the work opportunities that prisoners
had.[47] Legislation in some states between 1923 and 1929 began to drive industry
out of prisons in many states, eliminating the sale of prison-made products on the
open market.

In 1929, Congress passed the Hawes-Cooper Act, which allowed *all* states to
prohibit the sale of any state prison-made goods within their borders. Although
the federal legislation did not become effective until 1934, most states by then had
already passed their own legislation placing limits on the sale and shipping of
prison products.[48] As a result, prisons returned to their earlier concentration on
punishment and custody.

As of 1929,[49] only four states had yet succumbed to the pressure of free industry and confined prison industries to the state use system: Ohio, Pennsylvania,
New York, and New Jersey. The prison systems of these states became notorious
for idleness, living up to the biblical adage that "idle hands are the devil's work-
shop." Big houses such as the Ohio Penitentiary found no viable alternative to
productive labor. During the heyday of a typical prison's "idle house," it was easy
to understand the origins of the term. The "idle house" housed the "idle men
who do nothing all day long but sit on benches crowded together, all day, every
day of the week, every week of the year, and every year of the prison term."
One penal critic described a typical idle house as a "large bare loft," where he
found "400 men dressed in their prison suits, sitting, all facing one way. Around
the room were keepers, seated on high stools responsible solely for watching
these idle men. In the morning after breakfast the men were marched to the idle
house,"[50] with the same routine repeated after their succeeding meals.

Some critics as early as the late 1920s questioned the veracity of the free-
worker stand against prison labor. Penal historian Harry Elmer Barnes went as far
as claiming, "Convict labor has never been a serious competitor with free labor
in American industry," pointing out that in 1905 "convict labor produced less than
one-quarter of one per cent of the goods manufactured." Barnes was among
those who asserted that the "scandalous degree of idleness which prevails among
the inmates of American prisons . . . is a chief cause of the demoralization of
convicts and of prison riots."[51]

Inmate idleness continued to rise in the decade before the fire as another
dozen states were added to the list of those that restricted inmate labor to the
state-use system, where goods produced by inmates were sold not on the open
market, but to government agencies in the state where the prison was located.
The most common products manufactured for state use included license plates,
printed material, shoes, brushes, clothing, towels, bricks, and office furniture.[52]

By the end of the 1920s the years and months of enforced inactivity of inmates threatened prison stability and gave convicts plenty of time to sit around and hatch escape schemes or plan illicit activities. Combine the idleness with the boredom and frustration and all the ingredients were in place for future prison mayhem, especially as the prisons continued to become dangerously overcrowded.

When it came to the biggest of the big houses, idleness at the Ohio Penitentiary "was much more conspicuous [here] than in many prisons." The Columbus penitentiary was home to an "idle room," on the third floor of a manufacturing building, where "hundreds of men spend their days sitting on benches in absolute idleness, under the eyes of guards."[53] One contemporary account described the building as "almost ready to collapse." Few of the convicts were constantly employed. Between fifteen hundred and two thousand inmates were idle at any given time, confined to the large raftered, barn-like room furnished with benches and tables. Here, convicts languished from morning until nighttime lockup. It was not uncommon for cocaine and morphine addicts to be housed in the idle house as well. One inmate noted, "You can spot them in the Idle House, sitting silent, staring into space with lack-luster eyes, their entire bodies twitching from time to time in that peculiar agony that comes upon the dope fiend when he hasn't any drugs."[54]

According to one survey, idleness was "much more conspicuous here than in many prisons by the use of the 'Idle room,' in which hundreds of men spend their days sitting on benches in absolute idleness under the eyes of the guards."[55] Some would argue that the Idle House was still a more humane alternative than sitting locked up all day in cells or in dark, crowded dorms.

With little work in prison factories, prison officials could only legally have the convicts make commodities used in prisons, including uniforms, chairs, cots, and other goods. Besides this work there were few assignments left to keep inmates occupied except for tasks needed to keep prisons functioning, ranging from janitorial work, painting, and general maintenance to groundskeeping and preparing food. Add all these jobs up and there was still not enough work to go around at big houses. One historian noted that one Ohio prison warden "was so desperate for work assignments to occupy inmates that he ordered one inmate to spend his entire day keeping salt and pepper shakers on mess hall tables neatly lined up."[56]

State prison populations increased almost 140 percent between 1905 and 1935 to house the legions of new convicts, and old prisons such as the Ohio Penitentiary were stretched to the breaking point, leading to remodeling efforts and new construction at old institutions. The Ohio Penitentiary was well over capacity as early as 1927. Indeed, according to the Wickersham Commission, it was "worse than it has ever been, taking the country as a whole." Moreover, unemployment had declined to such an extent that just over one-third of the prison population was "kept in idleness."[57]

A number of contemporary observers blamed the increase in prison commitments across the nation on a raft of new crimes created by federal legislation such as the Harrison Narcotic Act (1914), the Dyer Act (1919, concerning interstate theft), the Mann Act (1910), new immigration laws, and laws covering interstate commerce violations. For example, one 1929 survey by the Justice Department reported that fraudulent bankruptcy violations increased in number from 2 to 295 and Mann Act and other sex offenses from 53 to 220. Liquor law violations increased from 248 to 557 (there were liquor law violations prior to 1920 as well), drug convictions from 0 to 1,540, Dyer Act violations from 0 to 572, immigration law violations from 9 to 70, and interstate commerce law violations from 0 to 98. Although more prisoners than ever were being convicted of federal crimes, about half of the nation's federal prisoners in 1928 were confined to state, city, and local lockups, since the federal prison system was still a work in progress.[58]

Critics charged that "the Federal government cannot continue in its present course of manufacturing new crimes without at the same time making still more jails." Regarding the $15 million that President Hoover wanted to spend, critics responded that one could not spend one's way out of overcrowding. Indeed, "the idiocy of the present situation is apparent to all intelligent observers. The Federal government has been creating Federal crimes at an appalling rate. In the days still remembered by middle-aged men, the only federal crimes were those involving violation of postal laws, involve fraudulent bankruptcy, counterfeiting, interfering with Federal officers, treason and a few others of equal rarity."[59]

One editorial went even further in its criticism of the federal predilection for creating new crimes. "Under the whip of political parsons and the immature moralists, the Federal Government has invaded the police powers of the States and taken responsibility for an even greater regulation of individual and business affairs," causing prisons to become overcrowded and "making the US, in the eyes of the world and some of its own citizens, a nation of criminals." One newspaper editor decried the "abominable" prison policy that neglects to provide prisoners with useful work. "Spineless politicians, yielding to complaints of organized labor and organized capital, are responsible" and have "condemned the inmates of Federal penitentiaries to useless loafing" with disastrous results as in the case of the 1929 Leavenworth riot.[60]

One of the greatest barriers to saving prisoners on Easter Monday was the primitive cell-locking mechanisms still used at the Ohio Penitentiary. One survivor recalled fifty years later, "They didn't have automatic locks in that prison, where you would pull the bar and it would spring all the cells at one time."[61] What proved particularly devastating was the penitentiary's reliance on nineteenth-century cell-door technology, featuring cell doors "hung on hinges" and constructed of "flat straps of iron that were interlaced in a latticework pattern." Contemporary prisons, such as the new federal penitentiaries at Atlanta (1902) and Leavenworth (1906), had adopted a more secure type of cell door years earlier, doors that "slid on tracks, were operated mechanically from a single point on the tier, and were constructed of cylindrical, case hardened, tool resistant cell bars. These would become standard in twentieth century prisons. New York's Sing Sing Prison had a mixture of cell lock technology that included individually padlocked cell doors, sliding grille doors, manually operated grille doors, and a centralized locking apparatus," which was deemed less vulnerable to tampering.[62]

The situation at Columbus demonstrated that just because new technologies were available did not mean there was anything near universal adoption of the latest advances in prison technologies. In 1930, many prisons still endured night buckets, poor lighting, and "other undesirable remnants" of the previous century's prison regime. Nevertheless, cell-lock technology had come a long way since the 1830s, when iron doors consisted of "grillwork in the upper portion and [were] fastened with gang locks.[63]

To his credit, warden Preston Thomas had been complaining about the vulnerabilities of the Ohio Penitentiary lockup for years, even going in front of twelve successive state legislatures to urge action. Each time he was met with indifference. Unfortunately, it took the Easter Monday fire to make the state legislature more receptive to the warden's urgings. The victims of the fire perished in the G&H cellblocks. As in its neighboring I&K blocks, both sets of tiers were positioned back to back inside a building constructed in 1877, dubbed New Hall. Ohio historian Richard Barrett compared the building's architecture to "a large barn." His description of it would be familiar to anyone conversant with Auburn-style prisons. The cellblocks "were free standing structures" built within the greater "stone-trimmed brick" building. A twelve-to-fifteen-foot clearance was left between the cellblocks and the building's outer wall. This arrangement was intended to prevent convicts from reaching the walls from their cells except at ground level, diminishing most avenues of escape.[64]

The two pairs of cellblocks were positioned in the cell building so that the temporarily empty I&K cells under construction faced back to back in the northern section of the building, that is, the back of the I tiers faced the back of the K tiers. The occupied G&H blocks were similarly positioned in the southern half of the building. One chronicler of the Ohio Penitentiary fire aptly described the positioning of the blocks: "G was parallel with H section and was its mirror image," that is G on the east side and H on the west.[65] Except for a temporary ten-to-fifteen-foot-tall wooden partition, meant to keep dust particles and other detritus from coming over to G&H from the construction, there was normally "no structural barrier" between the two halves.[66] Each cell measured 8 feet by 8 feet and was topped with an 8-foot-high ceiling.[67] Four convicts were held in each cell in G&H. Both sides contained six tiers, with 37 cells to a range, 17 cells on the G and H sides, adding up to 204 total cells.

The New Hall building, containing the affected cellblocks, measured 410 feet long, 53 feet wide, and extended almost 60 feet up to the roof. The 30-foot walls surrounding the building were close to 2 feet thick and featured windows "high up and barred." These bars would prove a barrier for the firemen trying to get a full stream of water from ground levels into the windows, forcing them to change tactics at the start.

The southern half of the building, containing G&H, measured 176 feet long, 32 feet wide, and reached 49 feet in elevation. So clearly it did not reach to the wooden trusses supporting the roof, less than 1 foot above. At the time, the roof was supported by "heavy wooden trusses and its construction above it was sheeting of wood on the inside, then the wooden purlines, then a sheeting of wood on the outside and then a slate finish."[68]

Together with the wooden building materials necessary for the I&K project, there were plenty of combustible materials on site at any given time. Fire inspectors would later report seeing "wooden forms and timbers of different shapes for construction . . . strewn over the top of the cell block." By necessity there were also plenty of other oil and gasoline products on hand. In order to build the concrete walls it was essential to regularly use wood for scaffolding as well as concrete wood forms coated with petroleum. The forms were treated over and over with oil to make it easier to extract the cement from the wooden forms. There were also drums of combustible oil present. So, if the fire was of incendiary origin, as many suspected but could not prove, all the elements were there.

Convicts had access not only to the oil, but also to a substance known as Vondelene, a cheap grade of gasoline used in the automobile tag shop. It was an inexpensive way to wash off paint from the forms on which the auto tags were painted and "could easily be carried away in small containers by those working in the factory."[69] Moreover, the easy access to cigarette lighters that needed gasoline to operate meant that there were plenty of ways to touch off an incendiary. In addition, candles could be found in a number of buildings, including the chapel. The fire investigators were well aware that candles had been used in previous incendiaries.

The I&K reconstruction effort underway involved removing the old structures and erecting new cellblocks in their place. In 1930, G&H contained the prison's oldest cellblocks, which still had their original brick walls from 1877. Most, if not all, of the convicts were apparently aware that they were building new solitary confinement cells in I&K, and this did not sit well with any of them. G&H had already been updated and modernized seven months earlier, bringing them into the twentieth century with running water and toilets.[70] The I&K construction had just reached the fifth tier level (out of six). During the week leading up to the fire, the wooden forms had been treated with oil and placed in position on range five and were ready for the pouring of cement on April 22.

When the hue and cry of "Fire!" was raised on Easter Monday, officials and prison staff responded on the assumption that a brick-and-stone edifice was fireproof. They were apparently unaware that a kindling-dry wooden roof that was scheduled to be replaced once the construction process was finished in an estimated two months still covered the building. The old timber roof had been permitted to stand during construction to protect workers from inclement weather. More importantly, until the structural work was completed on the sixth tier of the new cellblock, the weight of a new fireproof concrete roof could not have been sustained.

Ultimately, the fire, which took 320 lives but caused only $11,000 worth of property damage, would have never happened if the concrete roof had been completed beforehand, which would have sealed off the ancient wooden roof above and would probably have just burned off without allowing the heat and toxic smoke to enter any of the cellblocks. However, by April 21 the cement ceiling under construction ended above the G&H blocks, and the wood sheeting was still exposed in I&K.[71]

A wooden purpose-built scaffold was located on the north end of G&H construction. It was used for welding wickets onto the screens surrounding parts of the cellblocks, and it could be rolled around to paint the block. The scaffold would play an important role in fire rescue efforts and bringing down the dead from the upper tiers. Convict George "Cleveland" Johnson later stated, "It was lucky it was still up in the block."[72]

The main entrance into the Ohio Penitentiary was on Spring Street, on the southern side of the prison complex. The entrance took visitors first to the executive offices and "just beyond" to the guard room. Moving farther north from the guardroom led one into the so-called bull pen, a "small enclosure surrounded by bars." Continuing north led into the prison yard, the scene of so much death and suffering on Easter Monday. From the walkways above the prison walls armed guards could keep track of activities below.

Stepping into the Ohio Penitentiary's main entrance on Spring Street, to the left was the hall that led into the 182-foot-long E&F dormitories. Inmates assigned to these lodgings would describe them charitably as something akin to a barracks rather than the traditional cell setup. The dormitory ran east and west, coming together with the G&H blocks along Dennison Street to complete an L shape. One 1930 Ohio Penitentiary report described the building containing G&H and I&K as a "great hollow rectangle running north and south parallel to Dennison Street and separated therefrom by the great prison wall."[73] To get into the G&H blocks one would have to walk through the F dormitory to the south end of the cellblocks, passing through a partition and a door between the two structures, then turning right and entering the south end of G&H.

The G&H block held some of the most industrious inmates, including most who worked on the adjacent I&K renovation. But until the cellblock was ready, G&H was overflowing with more inmates than it was designed for. Once construction had ended on Easter Monday sometime between 3:40 and 4:00 (rather than the usual 4:30–5:00),[74] the workers followed routine, leaving "the current on in the lighting equipment." The fact that it was left on at the time of the fire led many to initially presume that the fire was started by an electrical short. Making matters worse from a security perspective was the fact that once the convict workers quit for the day, there was no patrol or guard on I&K, effectively eliminating any early warning system in case of an emergency. After the workers finished dinner they returned to their cells for the evening.

One of the most contentious issues surrounding the disaster was the failure of the prison guards to respond to the emergency in a timely fashion. Since there had never been any fire or emergency drills, much of the debate centered on who was responsible for the tragedy and whether the inmates could have been saved if the guards opened the cells in G&H at the first hint of smoke. In the aftermath of the fire, most of the survivors, as well as many officials, agreed that if the cells had been opened beginning at the first hints of fire sometime between 5:20 and 5:30, all, or at least more, of the prisoners could have made it out alive.

The ensuing mix-up over the keys exemplified not just the lack of readiness and preparedness on the part of the staff, but also the tenor of the times, when prison riots seemed to occur on a regular basis and no guard wanted to take responsibility for letting inmates out of their cells without direct orders from supervisors. Moreover, guards were more afraid of losing secure jobs, which could be threatened if they allowed inmates to escape. But perhaps the most glaring weakness demonstrated was the lack of training and the utter ineptitude of officers given decision-making power.

Each cellblock was manned by two guards. The first tier of cells in G&H, according to Roy "Whitey" Steele in 1H, was the sick range: "that is the reason it is on the bottom."[75] The tier was open and accessible on the same level as the route one would take from the guardroom through the E&F dormitory. As one guard put it, "You walk right in from outside into the brick floors of cells."[76] But if someone needed to get into the five tiers above he would have to first have the key that unlocked the cage gate leading to the stairs. On the night of April 21, guard Thomas Watkinson controlled the cage door key that effectively sealed the entire block above the first level.

The confusion that transpired in the minutes leading up to getting the cells opened was to a great extent tied to the transition of staff from the day to the night watch. Since the fire began between the day and the 6 p.m. night shift, the timing of the fire, between two overlapping shifts, could not have been worse. Ordinarily, the two night guards took their first count of the convict population as they began their twelve-hour shift at 6 p.m. Another count was conducted at midnight and the final one right before the day shift took over at 6 a.m. the next morning. On the night shift two guards were detailed to replace the previous watch, taking turns patrolling the upper and lower ranges, switching places each hour or so. Night guard William Baldwin later recounted that "our job is to walk the ranges every hour, and sometimes even every half hour." Asked if both night guards went inside together, he explained, "When one man goes on range we lock him in; if anything happens—someone makes a break—he can't get out. We don't go up in cell block at same time unless [the] man refuses to come out of cell, or there is a fight that requires the intercession of more than one guard."[77]

Day guards controlled the cellblock during working hours until locking the prisoners in for the night after the evening meal. Protocol required them to drop off the keys in the guardroom for the night guards. There were two keys, including a reserve key that would unlock all cells on a specific range but would not work on any other ranges. One key unlocked two ranges. For example, the key to the second range would unlock the G and H sides but no others. Except for the tier four key, which had inexplicably disappeared, there was a reserve key for each range.

There was also some confusion as to how long it would take to release the convicts from the tiers in the event of an emergency. Guard Thomas Little later asserted that the "best a man could do with no excitement would be three to four minutes per side." He explained that it was probable that most men, if excited, "would hit that [key] hole three or four times, like a man who had a drink or two and keeps missing."[78] Although there had never been a formal experiment to figure out how long it would take to open all of the cells in an emergency, most estimates were around five minutes per range, or thirty to thirty-five minutes to unlock all the cells. However, this would be in the best of conditions. When Warden Thomas was questioned several days after the fire, he admitted that not only had there never been any fire drills, but there had never been a test to determine how quickly the men could be unlocked in an emergency, and certainly he had never tried.[79]

Inmate Leo Lyon, on 3H, claimed after the fact that he could have unlocked every man after the first hint of fire. Like most convicts, he was attuned to every motion around him, which meant he knew the rhythm of the guards when they unlocked cells. "He will hit the first cell, he will unlock it, one, two, three steps, one two, three steps, one, two, three steps. . . . You can carry in your memory a sort of rhythm" of the way each guard walks, usually about three paces between cells (about three seconds each).[80] Another inmate on the same tier, the Canadian Percy J. Sullivan, asserted that each cell could have been opened in three seconds. A couple of days after the fire he pantomimed his "quick move" in front of the Board of Inquiry.[81]

When Warden Thomas was queried as to why he had not insisted on more up-to-date locking mechanisms in the Ohio Penitentiary, he responded that he was indeed familiar with other locks, but didn't like the so-called snap lock or double lock, which could be unlocked at one time in a given block, because there had been instances in other prisons where they were unintentionally opened.

Once free-world contract labor was forced from prisons, big houses such as the Ohio Penitentiary found no viable alternative to productive labor. As state prison populations increased almost 140 percent between 1905 and 1935 to meet the needs of legions of new convicts, old prisons were stretched to the breaking point, leading to remodeling efforts and new construction at old institutions (such as Ohio's). In fact, it was a renovation project in the aging cellblocks G&H

and I&K that contributed to the tragic Easter Monday conflagration. There was plenty of blame to go around for the conditions at the Columbus big house leading up to the deadly fire. An almost perfect storm of more punitive sentencing policies, overcrowding, and thousands of idle inmates was a recipe for disaster by any standards. One federal commission summed up these fears best, noting that without work "convicts waste physically and suffer in morals and mentality. Discipline becomes difficult and the guard system more expensive. It is a facile descent from idleness to mischief and worse."[82]

5 THE BIG HOUSE

It is not solitude that plagues the prisoner but life en masse.

—*Gresham Sykes, 1958*

A nation's correctional institutions offer "a kind of barometer of society's attitude toward its malefactors."[1] Perhaps the Russian novelist and former prisoner Fyodor Dostoevsky put it best when he wrote in 1862, "The degree of civilization in a society can be judged by entering its prisons."[2] His observation would have been applicable to the American prison system during the first decades of the twentieth century, when prison conditions were unashamedly punitive. Few Americans cared about the quality of inmate chow or how large and airy their cells were, especially during economic hard times when Ohioans were more concerned with keeping a roof over their head and bread on their table. Furthermore, it was a common conceit that whatever retribution was doled out behind bars was "probably well deserved."[3]

The big house emerged in the early twentieth century and lasted until at least the 1940s and 1950s (and in some cases even into the 1980s). Criminologist and former inmate John Irwin calls it "the dominant type of prison in the 20th century." He argues that it "emerged, spread, and prevailed, then generated images and illusions, and with considerable help from Hollywood, displayed these to the general society."[4] The era of the big house would cast a shadow in most industrialized states outside the South, constituting an important phase in the evolution of the American prison, following on the heels of the silent and solitary systems pioneered at Auburn Prison and Eastern State Prison respectively.

Irwin describes the typical big house as a "walled prison with large cell blocks that contained stacks of three or more tiers of one- or two-man cells. On the average, it held 2,500 men. Sometimes a single cell block housed over 1,000 inmates in six tiers of cells. Most of these prisons were built over many decades and had a mixture of old and new cell blocks."[5] In the weeks prior to the Ohio Penitentiary fire, journalists noted, the "prison population" had appeared to peak. One sage wrote, "New York has the greatest number of prisoners in its history, so does New Jersey, so does the Federal government."[6] The same held true for Ohio. A number of explanations for the rise were offered, ranging from the simplistic, that there "more coming in than going out," to the more practical, that the increase was perhaps due to the "number of revolvers and pistols manufactured and sold in the United States." Those in favor of nascent gun control suggested that unless the brakes were put on the sale of arms and ammunition to young men and women, the "prison population, murders, stick-ups will continue to increase."

By the 1930s, the big house was a subject of much derision. John L. Gillin, in his *Taming the Criminal*, wrote, "What monuments to stupidity are these institutions we have built—stupidity not so much of the inmates as of free citizens! What a mockery of science are our prison discipline, our massing of social inequity in prisons, the good and the bad together in one stupendous *potpourri*."[7] Inmate-turned-penologist Frank Tannenbaum averred likewise: "There is something unkindly about the American prison. There is something corroding about it. It tends to harden all that come within the folds of its shadow."[8]

Following the 1930 Columbus inferno, newspapers jumped on the prison reform bandwagon. The New York correspondent for the *London Daily Telegraph* went as far as to suggest that "the sacrifice" of more than three hundred convicts should have "clinched the case for American reformers, who maintained for years that many of the jails are 'Black Holes of Calcutta,'" adding that the U.S. prison system was "an unendurable disgrace to this civilized country."[9]

The end of the Civil War and Reconstruction coincided with a sudden increase in America's state prison populations. Between 1870 and 1904, the population of state prisons increased by more than 60 percent. Shortly before the outbreak of

the conflict the prison population stood at almost nineteen thousand, rising to
thirty-three thousand in 1870, forty-five thousand in 1890, and fifty-seven thousand in 1900. With many model prisons deteriorating badly, states responded
by modifying existing structures and building new ones to house the rising state
prison populations.

It is somewhat ironic that Columbus, Ohio, was the site of America's worst
prison disaster, given that Cincinnati, Ohio, only one hundred miles away, had
hosted the first National Prison Congress sixty years earlier. International prison
congresses had been held in Europe in the 1840s and 1850s, but only one American
representative attended. American prison reformers reasoned that if the United
States became more involved, the organization of an international prison reform
movement could be jump-started. Ohio governor and future president Rutherford B. Hayes welcomed more than 130 delegates representing twenty-four states,
Canada, South America, and Europe.[10] Among the attendees at the 1870 meeting
in Cincinnati were judges, wardens, prison chaplains, and governors.

Included among the forty papers and addresses delivered were several from
Ohio prison officials, including Samuel D. Desselem, who weighed forth on convict apparel.[11] One of the more troubling papers was given by Rev. A. G. Byers,
secretary of the Ohio Board of State Charities, who noted that between 1864
and 1869, of the 1,120 convicts received at the Ohio Penitentiary, more than
one-quarter of them were under the age of twenty-one, with 97 percent locked
up on their first convictions. Of these, more than one-quarter had been sentenced
to one year, and almost four-fifths of the youthful convicts were serving sentences
not exceeding three years.[12]

Zebulon Brockway (1827–1920) was one of the most influential attendees and
prison reformers of the era. The scion of a venerable New England family, he
had begun his career in corrections as head of a New York almshouse and then
of a penitentiary in Rochester. He captured the imagination of the assembled
reformers at the 1870 congress with his presentation, "The Ideal of a True Prison
System for a State." His suggestions would resonate for decades. Brockway may
have been a zealous proponent of indeterminate sentencing and the classification
of inmates according to age, gender, and offense, but he never shied away from
his support for life sentences for career criminals. The "Declaration of Principles"
adopted at the National Prison Congress represented an extraordinary step forward for progressive prison reform. The congress ultimately threw its support
behind the principles that defined it, including the upgrading of sanitary conditions, abolition of political appointments, progressive classification of prisoners,
adoption of the indeterminate sentence (this innovation would not gain wider
currency until the late 1850s and 1860s, when twenty-three states adopted it),[13]

rewards for good conduct and work, and increased emphasis on education, vocational training, and religion.[14]

~~~

During the 1890s, prison reform became part of the general reform movement known as Progressivism, inspired by a number of new trends, including the rise of a new professional class, the use of scientific methodology in the social sciences, industrialism, urbanism, and a growing tendency to depend on government intervention to solve social problems. However, when it came to prisons it was slow going. By the turn of the century, large-scale industrialization had changed the character of the cities and the countryside, and as the urban population grew, so too did poverty and crime.

The notion that Progressivism created the big house, a new type of institution run by professionals rather than short-term political appointees, has gained increasing currency in recent decades. The big house might have been designed to eliminate the more abusive forms of corporal punishment and prison labor, but, according to one critic, it "exemplified the superficiality of Progressive-era reforms. . . . Indeed, in the world of granite, steel and cement, the dominant features were stultifying routines, monotonous schedules, and isolation."[15]

The first reliable figure for America's total prison population listed 30,000 in the 1880 federal census.[16] By 1910, when the expression "big house" became part of the underworld lexicon, the country's prison population more than doubled, before quadrupling to 120,000 by 1930 (the year of the fire), when, according to one noted penologist, there were as many Americans behind bars as in the military,[17] the majority housed in big houses. More than one-third of the nation's convicts resided in just twelve state facilities scattered across the country, most located in midwestern states. Columbus was home to the biggest of the big houses, with more than 4,300 inmates, but others earned notoriety as well, including San Quentin, California (4,300); Jackson, Michigan (3,800); Jefferson City, Missouri (3,800); Joliet-Stateville, Illinois (3,100); Mansfield, Ohio (2,900); McAlester, Oklahoma (2,500); Folsom, California (2,200); Pendleton, Indiana (2,000); Michigan City, Indiana (2,000); and Chester, Illinois (2,000). By comparison, in 1890, just forty years earlier, there was only one prison holding more than 1,000 inmates (which represented more than one-third of the country's convicts at the time).[18]

Prohibition and the early days of the Great Depression coincided with rising prison populations across America. In the thirty years leading up to the Easter Monday fire, American prisons were custodial, punitive, and industrial. Except for several modest changes, imprisonment between 1900 and 1930 was substantially similar to the previous century. Many of changes that took place in the 1920s might have been superficial, but had a "profound cumulative effect" on prisons and prisoners. Striped uniforms and lockstep marching and the compulsion to produce profits had mostly been left behind, but the "drab ill-fitting garments and often aimless shuffling from one prison yard to another seemed an uncertain gain."[19]

In 1908, burglar Walter Edward White made it over the wall using a pole and rope assembled out of bedsheets, making it the last successful attempt that entailed going *over* the wall. In 1929, Arthur Brooker, twenty-three, died from gunshot wounds while trying to escape his life sentence for first-degree murder. His accomplices, Guy R. Tennant, thirty-two, and William Miller, twenty-one, armed with a shotgun and pistol, were both serving ten to fifteen years for robberies. The escape made the national news, especially after it came out that the three convicts had "chiseled through a steel reinforced concrete ceiling of their cell in the new escape-proof block into the attic of the prison." They were able to work their way through the building before cutting through a brick wall facing the prison walls. Using ropes knotted from torn bedsheets (as did General Morgan), the three men dropped to the catwalk leading to the tower in the southeast corner and there disarmed a guard (he was subsequently suspended). They dropped another rope over the wall and slid to the ground, but not before other guards noticed them and opened fire. They returned fire, several bullets striking the wall of the execution chamber where several guards had positioned themselves. The first guard, taken by surprise, was taken to the prison hospital unconscious, but recovered a short time later after having his scalp stitched up and his broken nose reset. Hunted by a posse of thirty peace officers, the mortally wounded Brooker was captured about four hours later and died later that night, November 4, 1929. Tennant and Miller were captured.[20]

In one survey of thirty-seven wardens, the nineteen who replied either declined to comment or were at a loss to explain the rising prison populations. Some cited "the mounting desire to obtain funds without work, and the liquor situation placing money in possession of wrong people, plus a lower respect for law and rights of others by general public."[21] Others looked to the heavier sentences meted out under minimum-maximum sentencing policies such as the Norwood Act in Ohio and the Baumes laws in New York.

Prison overcrowding was at the root of virtually all of the prison disorders of this era, including at the Ohio Penitentiary. The evolution of the big house coincided with the rise of minimum sentencing in a number of states, which contributed to increased prison overcrowding. Ohio, for example, was one of six-teen states that declared parole could be granted at the expiration of the minimum term of the sentence, *at the option of the paroling authorities.* Seldom mentioned as a source of overcrowding in Ohio and other states was the issue of judicial control over minimum sentences.

During the 1920s and 1930s, crime emerged as one of the nation's leading political and social issues as popular attention was lavished on the exploits of bootleggers, gangsters, public enemies. and crime waves, both real and imagi-nary. In fact, while America's homicide rate doubled between 1900 and 1919, in the 1920s there was actually little or no increase.[22] Lurid crime reporting led the public to demand action, essentially supporting the awarding of more power to judges and juries."[23] Ohio was just one of a number of states that created stricter legislation to counter the "crime wave." The state's Norwood Act, which only applied to the Ohio Penitentiary, was passed in 1921. Its advocates pitched it as a response to the perceived surge in crime since World War I. The law gave judges the right to set the minimum sentences for commitments of persons to the Ohio Penitentiary, "provided that he set it no lower than the minimum nor as high as the maximum, fixed by the law of each crime." Consequently, sentencing guide-lines could be manipulated by judges, who were able set the minimum sentence at just one day less than the maximum, in effect creating a fixed sentence. Making matters worse was the fact that pardons and paroles were becoming much harder to come by. Ohio Penitentiary warden Preston Thomas cited the Norwood Law as "one of the greatest causes of the greatly overcrowded conditions of prisons, unparalleled in its history."[24] The law would be repealed in 1931.

It was no coincidence that some of the worst big house riots took place in New York prisons, where, due to the so-called Baumes laws, more inmates were doing life as four-time losers than ever before. These stringent sentencing pro-visions had been introduced by the New York State Crime Commission, better known as the Baumes Commission, after its chairman, State Senator Caleb H. Baumes. Established in 1926, the commission passed a slate of retaliatory laws that critics blamed for the widespread overcrowding in the late 1920s. Particularly punitive was the "fourth offender act," which provided that when an individual was convicted for the fourth time it automatically resulted in a life sentence, thus taking all sentencing discretion out of the hands of judges.

Another punitive Baumes law was the "second offender act," which kicked in when an individual was convicted for a second felony. Then "he must be sen-tenced for a term not less than the longest, nor more than twice the longest, term prescribed in the penal code for the first conviction."[25] Making matters worse, the Baumes Commission reduced a number of rules that greatly reduced good-conduct time. One source of particular hostility came from the fact that individuals sentenced under Baumes laws were often working next to individuals who had committed the same crimes but had the good fortune to have been sentenced prior to 1926, when the new policies were put into force, and were thus serving much shorter sentences.[26]

New York governor Franklin D. Roosevelt was highly critical of the Baumes laws. In May 1929, President Herbert Hoover, who had proposed in his inaugural address to create a federal commission to study crime, criminal justice, and the racketeering linked to Prohibition, appointed a panel of eleven men to serve under former U.S. attorney general George W. Wickersham on what became known as the Wickersham Committee. The committee was just getting organized when prison riots broke out in New York at several institutions in the summer of 1929. Although the Wickersham Commission was derided in some corners as "a monument to equivocation" for its failure to reach any conclusions about the ties between crime and Prohibition,[27] it is considered the first national commission to consider issues of crime and law enforcement in a serious manner as well as to make recommendations. Between 1929 and 1931, the commission released its finding in a fourteen-volume report, one volume of which was devoted to the penal problem.

Investigations of New York prison conditions in 1919 and 1926, led by George W. Alger, apparently had gone nowhere. Alger cited the 1929 New York prison riots as "the inevitable culminating result of the conditions which I found and on which I reported to the Governor." Alger cited the "disgraceful living quarters" of Clinton and Auburn Prisons, where decaying cellblocks built in the previous century were still being utilized.[28] Both institutions had been overcrowded for years, due to the current predilection for longer sentences and more punitive parole policies that "induce many prisoners to join in a general plan for escape."[29] All of these conditions existed at the Ohio State Penitentiary in 1930 as well. In both the New York and Ohio prison systems many prisoners were serving much longer sentences than they would have served prior to the Baumes laws and the Norwood Act, respectively.

The year leading up to the 1930 Ohio Penitentiary fire witnessed a cycle of prison riots and fires that "startled and shocked not only the United States in which they occurred, but the entire civilized world." The indecisions and blundering responses on the part of the guards and officials to the Easter Monday fire and the prisoner mutiny that followed can best be understood in the context of a series of prison disorders that had shaken the country in the ten months leading up to April 21. Violent prison riots took place at New York's Auburn and Clinton (Dannemora) Prisons; Leavenworth, Kansas; Cañon City, Colorado; and elsewhere. When the Ohio Penitentiary fire broke out, "there was a menacing undercurrent inside the Ohio prison" in the wake of the especially bloody riots in Auburn and Cañon City. By some accounts, Warden Thomas mentioned he sensed tension inside his big house, detecting some restlessness among the convicts. But there was little vacillation from the warden when all hell broke loose on Easter Monday and he decided to make a stand outside the prison walls, where he established what was generously called a "third line of defense" as he prepared with other officials for a mass jailbreak.[30]

The first major big house riot broke out on July 22, 1929, in the sweltering Clinton Prison at Dannemora (a "bleak Siberia" in winter as well), an upstate New York institution for hardened offenders. Some thirteen hundred inmates mutinied, smashing and burning the hated factory shops and storming the walls to break out. In the five-hour frenzy, three Clinton inmates were shot dead by guards and a score wounded (two buildings burned and $200,000 worth of property was destroyed) before guards drove them back into their cells with machine guns, shotguns, tear gas, and hand grenades.[31] Unlike New York's Sing Sing Prison, Clinton was not yet modernized, and inmates confined to narrow cells and overflowing into every nook and cranny, including the corridors and the tuberculosis hospital.

Five days after the Clinton disturbance, on July 27, 1929, at historic Auburn Prison, seventeen hundred prisoners fought guards for five hours before the four ringleaders escaped over the walls. The violence left three dead from gunshots and eleven others wounded. Close to $500,000 in property was destroyed as inmates seized arms and ammo from the arsenal and burned six buildings.[32]

On August 1, 1929, a riot erupted at Leavenworth Penitentiary, the federal prison in Kansas. An investigation afterwards found that it was "spontaneous, triggered by an unpalatable meal, but more importantly, it reflected the tensions of severe overcrowding and lack of work, exacerbated by a severe heat wave."[33] One official labeled this variety as the "old 'Oliver Twist'" type (as in "Please, sir, I want some more"). It broke out over meager food rations as the prison system was forced to feed more with less. At Leavenworth, no one tried to escape or planned to. After the dining hall had been cleared and the men segregated in the prison yards, it turned out that it was just a few "ignorant troublemakers" who had provoked the short-lived rebellion.

In every riot, the majority of prisoners suffer for the actions of just a handful. In the overcrowded big houses there was no chance for segregation, giving "this little handful a tremendous opportunity for stirring up the dull witted and ignorant."[34] Most penologists observed that these riots would never have occurred in institutions where prisoners were held in single cells, something unthinkable in the current prison environment.

On the heels of the New York's July prison "mutinies," in September 1929 one observer, Winthrop D. Lane, cautioned that the nation's prisons "were at the breaking point."[35] One 1929 article even suggested that "It Pays to Revolt," if that was what it was going to take to end prison overcrowding, citing the "succession of prison mutinies within a few days of each other" in prisons ranging from New York to Kansas, California, and Colorado.[36]

On October 3, 1929, an attempted breakout at the Colorado State Penitentiary at Cañon City that left thirteen guards and inmates dead riveted the nation. Until the 1971 Attica riot in New York,[37] it was the deadliest prison riot in twentieth-century American prison history.[38] It would serve as a template in the minds of prison managers, who were constantly on guard for such worst-case scenarios in the event of a thwarted breakout attempt at their prisons. It was probably on the minds of Ohio Penitentiary warden Preston Thomas and his subordinates that Easter Monday in 1930 when he made the decision to position himself outside the prison walls.

The Cañon City mutiny began on a "warm Indian summer day" in October. Inmates at the Colorado State Penitentiary seized virtual control of the facility for six hours, then barricaded themselves and withstood a two-day siege that ended in the deaths of seven prison guards and six inmates. Three of the guards were killed outright as the prisoners negotiated with authorities over the lives of another four guards held hostage. The convicts bargained for automobiles and a free road to make their escape. After seventeen hours of negotiation, their demands were rejected. In response, convict leader Albert A. "Danny" Daniels murdered the remaining guards one after another and ordered their bodies thrown from windows to the ground below. A convict eyewitness testified that when Daniels "told his pals the jig was all up, at their request he shot all four of them and then himself."

All the deceased convicts involved in the killings at Cañon City had previously escaped from prison. They were armed with weapons including two revolvers and some sharpened butcher knives supposedly smuggled in, as well as a rifle taken from the first guard shot down at the start of the riot. Although other prisoners set several buildings on fire, it was "clear that the mutiny was far from general among the prisoners."[39] This was probably true. A year later, in October 1930, Ohio warden Thomas, speaking at the annual meeting of the American Prison Association, commented, "prison riots are seldom participated in by more than one tenth of the population, leaving 90 per cent who have not been a burden of adverse public opinion."[40]

On December 11, 1929, New York's Auburn Prison suffered its second major riot in five months. During six hours of mayhem, state troopers and militiamen tracked the rampaging convicts through "dim corridors and cells" as "spotlights flooded the courtyards and machine guns barked from the walls." By the time the spree had been resolved, the chief keeper and eight inmates had been killed and numbers of other staff and convicts "wounded and gassed." The riot leaders were reportedly inmates who had been in solitary since the previous summer "for their part in the July riot."[41] One journalist suggested that the recent bloodshed at Auburn not only "horrified the whole country," but "made these 'houses of forgotten men' one of the paramount issues of the day."[42] Observers blamed much of the carnage on a lack of prisoner classification and rampant overcrowding. One Roman Catholic priest who administered last rites "among gas fumes and flying bullets" asserted that "there ought to be segregation of the desperate and hardened characters," particularly third- and fourth-time offenders.

"Idleness, lack of recreation facilities, and brutal repressive policies" were important contributors to the spate of riots in New York and elsewhere. Perhaps New York's *Buffalo Courier-Express* addressed the prison conundrum best: "The average criminal would not live if the hope of escape was not continually with him in prison. Plotting of escapes would go on whether or not there was segregation of hardened criminals, as at Dannemora, or insufficient housing, as asserted at Auburn, or poor food as asserted of Leavenworth . . . adequate housing and decent food will not solve the prison problem. . . . Prison management should be a profession. It is, except in too infrequent cases, a political job."[43]

The highly influential Wickersham Report compared the era's prison cells to small, escape-proof fortresses. Cells varied in size "from those in which the occupant can touch the opposite wall with his elbows to those six or seven feet wide and eight or nine feet long, perhaps eight feet high, in which the inmate has some room to move." The cells usually stood in long rows, "so that an observer in front sees a series of cages which might contain wild animals." To complete the big house portrait, the report noted, "One row of cells tops another, so that what we have is a series of tiers of cells, and he will see an exactly similar piece of construction on the other side. This is a conventional cell block."[44] Wickersham's description would have sounded familiar to the more than forty-three hundred denizens of the Ohio State Penitentiary.

At the sixtieth meeting of the American Correctional Association in October 1930, speakers castigated the big houses and the systems that created them. It was not difficult to enumerate the underlying causes for the riots in 1929 and 1930,

which included inadequate and inedible food, overcrowding, lack of work, abolition of good time and the merit system, constant denial of parole, and long and
hopeless sentences with no chance for liberty in sight. Many attendees agreed.
Moreover, it was a marvel there were not more riots.[45]

Supporters of the Ohio Penitentiary warden pointed out that the Easter
Monday fire was different from the outbreaks of prison violence in other prisons.
While the Ohio Penitentiary was like the other big houses in being dilapidated
and overcrowded, the riot there did not occur until after the fire deaths of 320
inmates, after which inmates panicked as a "natural result of physical fear born
of ghastly disaster. No one could control the terror stricken men, and free men
would have reacted the same."[46] Warden Thomas even acknowledged that the
majority of the men were "orderly, heroic and helpful." However, he also seemed
to take umbrage that the "world pictured it as a vast mass of prisoners rising
bodily against authority."[47]

Most states' prison populations had increased between the early 1920s and
1930. New York prisons, the scene of several recent riots, rose from 4,598 to 6,618
in just seven years, a 44 percent increase. During the same period, Illinois's number of inmates nearly doubled and Ohio's rose 120 percent, from 3,837 to 8,613
prisoners. At the Ohio Penitentiary alone, 4,345 inmates carved living arrangements out of cells designed for 2,184 men. Even more troubling was that its "idle
squad" of nonworking prisoners ranged between 1,200 and 2,000 at any given
time.[48] According to one penologist, among the factors that most contributed to
prison riots were overcrowding and the lack of work. "Poor food and archaic cells
contributed their share" as well.[49] There was no consensus on solving the growing
American prison problems, but the Columbus tragedy would focus the nation's
attention on this issue like never before.

THE WARDEN

The appointment is primarily a reward for political service
rendered.
    —Wickersham Commission, 1931

As for the prisoners, they were getting what they deserved.
    —Ohio Penitentiary warden Preston Thomas, ca. 1930

For most of the nineteenth century, the job of prison warden was
one of many coveted rewards offered by political spoils system. The duties of
Ohio wardens, originally identified as "head keepers," included purchasing tools
and clothing for prisoners, keeping inmate accounts, arranging for the sale of
manufactured goods, and making sure there were adequate materials and stock
on hand. In addition, they were expected to provide "coarse and wholesome food
for the prisoners, to punish convicts by confinement in solitary cells if necessary
and pay all prison debts."[1]
    One of the unintended consequences of the spoils system was that it re-
sulted in frequent turnovers in personnel, making it almost impossible to create

a stable professional staff, while undermining the enforcement of rehabilitation.[2] Between 1850 and 1860, the Ohio prison system was controlled by five different prison boards of directors and eight wardens. The 1931 Wickersham Report found that in some western states the warden's term began and ended the same date as that of the governor and that the "the appointment is primarily a reward for political service rendered."[3] This constant change at the top, not surprisingly, led to shifting, often conflicting policies due to a lack of continuity in standards of professionalism. During this era officials were "hired on the basis of political partisanship or business accomplishments, as well as social standing, gentlemanly behavior and Christian character." One early warden, Lewin Dewey (1846–50), seeking to improve the Ohio Penitentiary's "moral environment," insisted that his guards be models of Christian deportment, which meant no whistling, shuffling, laughing loudly, or any other undignified behavior.[4]

As the Ohio prison system moved into the twentieth century, it was still common for wardens to be appointed by whichever political party won the last election and to be removed after it lost the next one. Some had worked in law enforcement or as sheriffs, but many, such as Ohio's Preston Thomas, brought no relevant experience to the job. Thomas would serve under both Democratic and Republican governors, which suggests that the spoils system was perhaps in decline, at least when it came to selecting prison wardens. Born in West Cairo, Ohio, on November 30, 1871, Thomas spent his childhood on the family farm and was educated at local rural schools. He later studied at Ohio Northern University, earning a bachelor of science degree in 1892. His marriage two years later to Mary Elizabeth Blume produced two children, Amanda and Don, both of whom would figure in the fire story. Following college, Thomas entered the teaching profession, spending thirteen years inculcating students with the same "habits of industry and self-reliance" that he was brought up under, and that he later tried to impart to his prison charges. His teaching acumen brought him attention and prominence, and he was soon in "great demand, for he was regarded as a man of progressive ideas and methods and he did much to place the schools in his locality on a higher level, inaugurating more advanced systems, and . . . always kept well to the fore in all that pertained to educational affairs." The last five years he taught at Wapakoneta, Ohio.[5]

Thomas had his first brush with penology and correctional administration when he taught at the Ohio State Reformatory at Mansfield between 1904 and 1908. He left teaching to become a parole officer and five years later resigned this position when he was appointed warden of the Ohio Penitentiary on May 1, 1913. Ohio governor James M. Cox made no bones about what he expected from the new warden, telling him during a phone call that he wanted Thomas to make "the best prison in the world." Thomas would later report that he told the governor that this goal could not be accomplished with the "material at hand," explaining the conditions of the buildings and so forth, but told him he would do the best with what he had to work with.[6]

In the years leading up to the Easter Monday fire, Thomas was lauded for some of his "commendable reforms." He reportedly did what he could to eliminate politics from the management of the institutions and introduced the indeterminate sentence law and the trustee system at his institution. He implemented these reforms to such an extent that the Ohio pen had a "greater number of that class of convicts [trustees] than any other prison in the United States." Moreover, "the ratio of 'walkaways' men who abuse the privilege of trust is less than one in fifty." Thomas is also credited with suppressing "the use of 'dope.'"[7]

By the late 1920s, Thomas was approaching sixty years old. In his fictionalized account of the fire disaster, the inmate scribe Chester Himes described the warden of his story, obviously based on Warden Thomas, coming over to talk to new convicts in order to let them know "he was tough." He was "the remnants of a large man gone to seed, dressed in an expensive suit. . . . His head was practically bald and his face seamed and sagging, looked as if it had melted through the years and had run down his jowls which in turn, had dripped like flaccid tallow onto his belly."[8] Surely the years weighed heavily on the teacher turned warden.

One inmate recalled one of the "warden's pet expressions": "Look out for the guy that talks on the side of his mouth," he would say. "I never talk on the side of mine. I try to talk straight."[9] Another inmate at the time of the fire, Robert Farr, recalled that it was seared into his memory how Warden Thomas would hold court. He would come out in the morning and if he knew you would say, "Well you're here again, out of the corner of his mouth, hard boiled as if he imagined convicts talked or tried to create the impression among the prisoners." To further rub it in, he would then ask "what you had for breakfast." The warden followed his question up by bragging, "I had my ham and eggs" then "pat his stomach" for extra effect. Farr noted that you did not dare respond, all you could do was "sneer at him," especially after the warden added, "Well I will have my dinner too, my chicken too probably." Still "you don't say anything," or risk going into the hole on a bread-and-water diet.[10]

If Preston Thomas seemed ill suited for his job, it is worth noting another exemplar perhaps even less qualified to run a prison. At the time of the bloody Cañon City, Colorado, debacle in October 1929, the prison was in the hands of Warden F. E. Crawford, described as "strong willed but mild mannered," who was perhaps "too nice a man" to be a warden.[11] He had served under previous wardens as the chief clerk and business manager of the prison. Appointed warden only three months after the death of his predecessor, Crawford was essentially just an accountant from Kansas City. It was only through the nepotism of his cousin, a previous prison warden, that he was first hired at the prison. Even the governor opposed Crawford's appointment to warden. However, the civil service system had been instituted in Colorado in 1918, under which, by law, the holder of the highest score on a general exam received the appointment. That was Crawford.

As much as Warden Thomas was denigrated, there were numerous testaments to his softer side. In late 1929, just months before the fatal fire, for example, he welcomed Dr. James Snook to Ohio Penitentiary's death row. An Ohio State University veterinary professor and former Olympic champion (in target shooting), Snook was convicted of murdering his lover, a young coed named Theora Hix. The murder, like so many other lurid and sensational cases, was covered as if it was a "once in a century" case. When Snook joined the forty-three hundred prisoners in the overcrowded nineteenth-century penitentiary, the warden was then in his twenty-fifth year of service to the state of Ohio, seventeen as warden. Initially, Thomas considered releasing daily bulletins to the press, covering Snook's daily menus, activities, and so forth, explaining "this is not a matter of pandering to a murderer's public. It is a case of self-defense against a flood of inquiry we expect to receive from a sensation loving world."[12] He must have thought better of it, however, and the bulletins were never issued. Instead, the warden made it known that he planned to publish a "psychological treatise" after the execution (he never wrote it). He was apparently fascinated by the professor, whom he described as having "the coldest nerve of any man I know whoever sat on Death Row." The warden and his secretary would often stop by Snook's cell to chat and try to gain some insight into the professor for his purported future monograph.

The warden demonstrated his benevolent side in the case of Snook, probably best exemplified during the 1929 Christmas holiday. Aware that this would be Snook's last holiday meal, the warden withheld the fact that Snook's stay of execution had been denied, hoping to give the condemned killer some peace of mind as he enjoyed the holiday feast cooked up for the rest of the convict population in the prison kitchens. The meal included four thousand pounds of pork, oyster dressing, applesauce, candied sweet potatoes, blackberry pie, celery, bread, and coffee, followed by a nightcap of cigarettes and cigars. Snook would be executed on February 28, 1930, less than two months before the prison came under the national spotlight.[13]

It is probably understandable that virtually every description of Warden Preston Thomas offered by inmates before and after the fire portrayed him in an adversarial light. The warden does not come across any better in the autobiography of James V. Bennett, who rose to become the director of the Federal Bureau of Prisons between 1937 and 1964. As a lawyer considering his career options in the 1920s, he decided to gain "additional seasoning and insight" by setting out on a tour of some typical state prisons, starting with Columbus. It was here that Bennett had what he described as "probably the decisive experience of my early career." His "first view of the antiquated institution was frightening and foreboding" as he looked at "the stone prison, with its high walls and bristling towers patrolled by guards." For a brief moment, he considered walking back out, having lost some of his "desire to present my letter of introduction to the warden [Thomas]."[14]

Bennett was kept waiting through what he considered "an unnecessary delay" before being led into the office of Warden Thomas. The warden "sat at a bulky, square oak desk that had large round, carved legs. The desk seemed as solid as the stones of the prison wall. Thomas checked my credentials, asked to be remembered to a congressman we both knew, and sent for a guide, who, I thought, was to take me around to the workshops. Later I learned he [the guide] was a former treasurer of the state who had put his hand in the till." Thomas then ordered the guide to "show Mr. Bennett around and bring him right back here."[15]

Upon Bennett's return from his tour, he was welcomed back to the warden's office to what he thought would be a productive dialogue about penology. The warden explained that he had "an extremely tough job, and he was not too impressed by 'softies' and 'do-gooders,'" his shorthand for prison reformers. While the warden was a supporter, he said, of prison industrial work, he saw it as a fool's errand at a time when "there was not enough of a market for prison product in the state agencies." He reserved some of his rancor for the unions, commenting that "the laborskates" had too much influence. And "as for the prisoners, they were getting what they deserved."[16]

When Bennett's time to speak came, he began by asking Thomas how prison officials were able to "maintain discipline and how they punished offenders." Deciding it was easier to show than tell, the warden told Bennett, "Come with me. . . . I'll show you." The two men proceeded back across the prison square toward a small brick structure. The warden banged on the wooden door. It opened almost immediately and they strode into a "small, dark room with a huge bench at the far end." He explained that this was his "'courtroom,' where he and his deputies sat in judgment upon prisoners who violated the rules." Punishments could range from losing visiting and correspondence privileges to losing good behavior credits and receiving a stint in "the hole." It was then time to visit the hole, which was conveniently located in the same building.[17]

The warden ordered a guard to open up the room to show the young "do-gooder" some old-fashioned justice. They entered the room through "a barred, steel door" that had to be unlocked before they proceeded through a "steel boiler-plate door." They then entered "a narrow corridor lined with more steel doors, and Thomas motioned to a guard to open one. There stood a pathetic creature, his eyes staring vacantly, his hands handcuffed to a bar halfway up the wall." Asked how long he had been there, the prisoner said five days. Apparently, the warden was not expecting this answer. Thomas told him, "I don't believe you" and rushed Bennett back out through the corridor. One might have thought that Thomas had already revealed too much about his punitive regime, but he insisted on showing Bennett the cells reserved for laggards who refused to work. These men were forced to stand "for hours or for days in tiny scrap-iron cages, in which there was no room to sit down, until they agreed that washing pots and pans or shoveling coal was not such a bad fate."[18]

Bennett decided it would be foolhardy to ask any more questions or to argue with the warden about what he had just witnessed. He wrote that he "had seen enough, and I never wanted to get out of a place so badly in my life." He thanked the warden "half-heartedly" for "taking the trouble to show me around and headed for the gate." He then canceled the rest of his prison inspection itinerary.

Between 1900 and 1948, the Columbus penitentiary had seven wardens, with an average tenure of 6.9 years. Such turnover was typical at the time; Thomas's twenty-two years at the helm were an exception. Between 1906 and 1955, the lead-ing cause of turnover was a change of administration (35 percent), followed by poor health or entering business (22.7 percent), death (12.5 percent), and dismissal or removal from office (12.5 percent). The rest left through promotions, moving to new positions at another institution, or being killed in the line of duty.[19]

By the 1920s, the warden's position was not particularly remunerative, with top annual salaries ranging around $4,700, equivalent to about $63,000 in 2017 dollars. However, there were a number of benefits that supplemented his income, including room and board and "practically unlimited opportunity to use inmate labor for per-sonal assignments," as was the case with Warden Thomas.[20] This was not enough for some wardens, who turned to corruption to further enrich themselves.

The warden's job was a juggling act between keeping the inmates under control while exercising a modicum of diplomacy, an attribute that Warden Thomas was clearly deficient in. According to contemporary sociologists Edwin

Sutherland and Thorsten Sellin, "Prison wardens from all parts of the country were almost without exception qualified to do nothing other than superintend a custodial program."[21] According to one study of nineteen prison wardens in the 1930s, eight had begun their careers with a significant amount of police work under their belt, three had had an army career, and four started as prison guards, including the iconic Warden Lewis Lawes of Sing Sing fame, who first worked as a guard at Clinton Prison.[22]

In 1926, one criminologist noted that the warden is "in immediate charge of the prison."[23] According to the influential Wickersham Report, issued the year after the fire, the prison warden was "the all mighty. From him all pleasures and benefits and all ills and sorrows are derived." It is no wonder that due to "the intensity of the situation, the men are inclined to credit the warden even with things for which he is not responsible."[24]

The demands on a warden in 1930 were wide-ranging, and expectations were high. According to the Wickersham Commission, the warden was "expected to be a good businessman and run his institution at a profit," though that was all but impossible in the era of idleness that Warden Thomas worked in. He was also expected to be a "humanitarian, great educator and at some time a disciplinarian and custodian for the hardened and the embittered, the desperate and the weak."[25] This became an even taller order when the job of state executioner was added to his tasks.

Warden Thomas's admission that he had no plans to deal with fires, combined with the clear breakdown of command structure during the fire, left his image in tatters. To be fair, the warden had been warning of the dangers of the big house for years. He had urged twelve successive Ohio state legislatures to take action, and was only met with indifference. Nevertheless, much of the blame on Thomas was well placed, especially when it was determined that after the fire broke out he had essentially left seventy-one-year old Captain John Hall in charge of the institution until the deputy warden returned, while positioning himself outside the walls to see no one escaped—considered a dereliction of duty by observers of all stripes.

The warden had his reasons for staying away from the prison yard, according to Earl Hofstetter, sergeant of the guards the past three years, and prior to that, a guard for eighteen years. He would tell investigators that during a prison break three years earlier inmates planned to waylay the warden on his walk to the prison court, catch him in the yard, put a knife to his throat, and bring him to the gate, forcing him to either open the gate or have his throat slit. Hofstetter recovered this information from several conversations and letters and notified the warden of the danger that awaited him if he entered the prison yard during any unrest. (He had given a similar warning to a previous warden.) Hofstetter claimed that prisoners had almost followed through with their plan one time already, but apparently thought better of it when the convicts came to the conclusion that threatening to kill the warden would still not be enough to get the guards to open the gate After the sergeant's warning, Warden Thomas gave the order that in the event that convicts tried to use him to force the gate open, the guards should "let them cut my throat . . . but never open the gate."[26] Nonetheless, Thomas still went in from time to time, "usually when the inmates were locked up," and it was not uncommon to see him walking the yard alone or with another officials. In any case, if prisoners were in the yard the guards "got close enough to be in good shooting distance if anything started."[27]

Following the tragic conflagration, Warden Thomas had even more good reasons not to enter the prison yard, since he was blamed by most inmates for the unnecessary deaths. It was two days after the fire before he entered the yard, and from then on he would only risk it under some form of military guard. During the inquiry following the fire, inmates became more incensed when they heard that when Thomas was asked why he had installed an ancient style of single-lock cells in a new building, the warden responded, "to have provided the lever system of locks would have been too costly."[28]

While Sergeant Hofstetter portrayed the warden as a marked man, other prison administrators gave a different image. During the October 1930 meeting of the American Prison Association, one Thomas booster reported, "Shortly before the Ohio trouble, I heard the great prison population at Columbus prison cheer Warden Thomas to the echo. We all know how very quickly in a prison crowd hissing and murmurs are forthcoming if the men have a grudge or grievance against the individual. The men in Ohio for years have known their Warden was doing the best he could for them under terribly adverse circumstances."[29]

This would seem to be hyperbole of the highest order, because in fact the prisoners had little positive to say about him. Inmate Robert Farr, serving twenty to twenty-five years, said that contrary to his perception as being "square and fair" and giving prisoners a "square break," in reality the inmates used monikers for him such as the "pig," "the ground hog," "the red neck," and "hog."[30] The consensus among the inmate population was that he "should have been ousted years ago." Testifying to the investigation committee in the days following the fire, Farr was among the prisoners who gave a litany of transgressions by the warden.

7 THE KEEPERS

The pay is so low that it is impossible to secure any but the least competent.

—*Wickersham Commission, 1931*

I am the old turnkey, you see,
I know my duty well;
For many years, 'mid sobs and tears,
I've locked them in their cell.
I've seen the strongest hearts break down,
But what is that to me?
'Tis the law, 'tis the law
'Tis the duty of the old turnkey.

—St. Michael's Almanac, *1899*

In her best-selling *Kind and Usual Punishment,* Jessica Mitford ponders how one should respond to a young boy who, when asked, "What do you want to be when you grow up?," responds, "To be a prison guard." Would it be a dramatic overreaction to brand this "a trifle worrying" or "cause perhaps to take him off to a guidance clinic for observation and therapy"?[1] In 2015 and in many other years, the profession of corrections officer was listed among the ten worst jobs in America.[2] Indeed, along with their counterparts on police forces, modern prison guards have "the highest rates of divorce, heart disease, and drug and alcohol addiction and shortest life spans of any state civil servants due to stress."[3]

From the moment a new prison keeper enters the closed confines of the prison, he or she (only men guarded men in the early twentieth century) is well aware of entering "into an alien environment, and is enveloped in the situation 24 hours a day without relief." Modern studies demonstrate that, at least in the beginning, the new guard "is stunned, dazed and frightened." This would probably hold true for the Ohio prison keepers at the time of the penitentiary fire. A 1967 study concluded that new recruits experienced shock equivalent to the "17-hydroxycortico-steroid levels comparable to those in schizophrenic patients in incipient psychosis, which exceed levels in other stressful situations." This was exacerbated, no doubt, by the fact that the "recruit received little, or erroneous information about what to expect, which tends to maintain his anxiety."[4]

For guards starting work at most state prisons in the 1920s and 1930s, particularly at the Ohio Penitentiary, training typically consisted of being given a brief tour of the prison before being handed the keys to the kingdom. Perhaps noted prison historian David J. Rothman puts it best: "The staff was qualified to fulfill one task only: holding the inmates."[5] One penologist in the 1920s noted that the function of the guard, or warder, is "primarily a jailer. This is his business. . . . He is a jailer first; a reformer, a guardian, a disciplinarian, or anything else, second."[6]

The origins of the modern-day corrections officer can be traced back to medieval gaolers (jailers) and keepers, who ran their jails like small businesses. Keepers typically purchased their appointments or were selected on the condition that they gave the jail owner a percentage of the profits. Although, like their modern-day counterparts, they earned uniformly poor wages, there were always applicants waiting for positions. In fact, the job could be made even more lucrative by enterprising keepers. Since medieval prisoners were expected to pay for all provisions, including food, drink, and clothing, a keeper of that era could make a tidy profit selling commodities to his charges.

In the eighteenth century, prison reformer John Howard led a campaign to abolish these and other profit-making ventures enjoyed by keepers and institute a fixed salary subject to public oversight.[7] In 1823, Sir Robert Peel's Prison Act put Howard's theories into practice in Great Britain by requiring jailers to become paid employees of the local government, forbidden to charge fees of any kind to prisoners. However, it was almost impossible to enforce this law outside London, and what was good in theory was perhaps not ready for practice.[8]

The English brought many criminal justice practices to the New World in the pre-Revolutionary era, including the position of jailer, which proved just as lucrative an endeavor as it was in Britain. Like their medieval forebears, American jailers in some colonies earned most of their income from charging inmates for services, ranging from the removal of chains upon release from jail to furnishing food and bedding or in some cases providing a private cell.

By the 1840s, in response to a growing criminal class and the rise of modern penitentiaries in New York and Pennsylvania, American prison reformers introduced discipline to augment the already elaborate regimentation. In New York's prisons, where the Auburn system gravitated toward a "paramilitary model," new daily routines were introduced, including lockstep marching, which required inmates to move in close order and single file, in unison, each head inclined to the right, with each man looking over the shoulder of the man in front.[9] Prison guards hoped to prevent conversations between inmates and keep convicts from dallying from place to place. Other innovations borrowed from the military model included the introduction of striped uniforms for inmates (and guards), keeping watch, and assembling at specific hours. New regulations were adopted that expected guards to comport themselves in a "gentlemanly manner," which meant acting like an officer while on duty, "without laughter, ribaldry, or unnecessary conversation while on duty."[10] Around the same time that prison guards began to adopt a more professional mien, some states were promoting a message of security and isolation by designing prisons to look more and more like medieval fortresses.

As mentioned previously, in 1870, at the First National Prison Congress, held about a hundred miles from Columbus in Cincinnati, leading prison reformers gathered and adopted a "Declaration of Principles." A number of reforms were addressed, including "job training for prison officials." Prison guards throughout the American correctional system at that time commonly received little to no training. Prison officers' training schools were "an entirely new feature of prison work," and the few that existed in the world by the early 1930s were considered to be of "very recent origin." The Ohio Department of Rehabilitation and Correction did not have a training academy until director Richard Seiter created one in Orient, Ohio, just south of Columbus, in the 1980s.

Prison training did have a long tradition in Europe, dating back to at least 1791, when Heinrich Balthasar Wagnitz suggested establishing seminars wherever a state prison was located so that "prison administrators and guards might be given training and in which 'not only their moral character and mental powers be tested—which would, no doubt, be most important—but where they would also be instructed for their future service."[11] The United States, however, did not begin experimenting with training schools for prison officers until the early twentieth century. In 1921, the Massachusetts Department of Correction began offering a lecture course to guards "already in service."

As early as 1908, Japan, after fifteen years of experimentation, began a training program.[12] But in many countries the training of prison staff took place in fits and starts, and programs often proved ephemeral. The best-known schools were conducted by the U.S. Bureau of Prisons, the New Jersey Department of Institutions and Agencies, and the New York Department of Correction. In 1932, there were three training schools in Great Britain, one in Belgium, one in Holland, two in Germany, and six in the United States. By some accounts, the first Prison Officers' Training School opened in Wakefield, England, in 1925, and all of the others opened after the 1930 Ohio fire.[13] According to one pioneering criminologist, although the programs were intended to teach recruits, once "these were absorbed into the prison system, nothing short of an enormous turn-over in the staff could keep the school in constant operation, unless the prison system was exceedingly large."[14] It would be years before recruits were trained prior to entering the prison service, and, just as importantly, before definite programs for training in-service were established and common.

More than a decade before the Easter Monday catastrophe, a report by the State of New York Civil Service Commission admitted, "The prison officer received no special training before entering his duties. He is appointed after a civil service examination in which emphasis is placed on his height, age and physical condition generally and upon 'great personal courage, a kindly but firm disposition, sound judgment and discretion, inclination to carry out order of a superior faithfully, and a personality and temperament calculated to command respect and obedience of persons in their custody.'"[15]

When the future iconic Sing Sing warden Lewis Lawes began his prison career as a guard at Clinton Prison in March 1905, his first lesson in penology was to "tread softly and carry a big stick." He found that he needed to take this lesson literally. On his first night, as he recounted in his autobiography, he "was handed a pair of sneakers and a club. The sneakers, to enable the guard to make his rounds noiselessly, so as not to disturb sleeping forms within the cells, and the club to be used in emergencies should any of those forms become unduly active."[16]

During his initial weeks on the job, Lawes received plenty of free advice. Some urged him to "Treat em rough," others to go easy on the cons. One wizened old guard, retiring after thirty years, offered the rookie Lawes a learning moment. He recounted that during his early days as a guard he caught inmates in adjoining cells communicating through ventilators and ordered them to desist. One of the cons got down off his bunk and called the novice over. Having seen his share of incidents during his long years behind bars, he told the new guard, "Don't see too much," implying that sometimes it's better to give inmates some slack.[17]

"Rookie" guards were given little slack by "old timers," one of whom warned the twenty-one-year-old Lawes, "You never know what they're up to. So you've got to watch your step. They haven't any respect for new guards. . . . You've got to have eyes in the back of your head. . . . Don't trust any of them [prisoners]." Lawes admits to having had preconceived notions when he joined the prison staff. "I thought that the prisoners were a desperate lot and had to be treated accordingly. I was determined to be hard-boiled, to show no quarter and ask for none."[18]

Little changed in the following decades in other big houses. At Auburn, Frederic A. Dorner reported, "The prison officer enters upon his duties ignorant of how to meet the problems which hourly present themselves; too often he covers his ignorance by roughness, which in addition to the deadly monotony of his daily duties leaves him, at the end of a few years, a 'bully' or at best a machine with little human sympathy or understanding." Moreover, "If an officer had any friendly feeling and made any display of it, he was criticized by the officers and called soft and unfit to do his duty by the institution."[19]

Few argued with the contention that the Easter Monday catastrophe could have been averted or at least better handled if the guards had been trained properly. In his syllabus on "Training Schools for Prison Officers," Dr. H. H. Hart explained, "many of the past failures of American prisons can be traced to the mismanagement of officers who were selected without regard to their ability or training for the important work they are called upon to perform. A task requiring character, education, experience, and the scientific attitude often has been entrusted to novices and politicians merely in quest of a job, men who were incapable of social vision and constructive work."[20] A quarter century after the fire, one journalist recognized that the Ohio Penitentiary guards on the night of the fire had been trained only to keep inmates locked up, and several reacted "automatically," unable to bring themselves to unlock the cell doors.[21]

During the first decades of the twentieth century, there was a thin line between the keeper and the kept. The guards, or "screws" in prison parlance,[22] received much of the blame for the outcome of the Easter fire. They were a poorly paid and untrained lot, with little chance for advancement. Nevertheless, it was a job, something precious during the years of the Great Depression. They spent twelve-hour days watching after their charges and probably felt as locked up and isolated as the convicts. One investigatory body suggested that the guard's "labor is very long. . . . He is himself virtually a prisoner."[23] Criminologists describe prison guards as suffering from "lock psychosis" because of their stultifying routine of constant "numbering, counting, checking and locking." As a result, "their personalities [are] 'warped by the unnatural life they lead.'"[24]

One early criminologist suggested that the disregard for inmate conditions on the part of the guards was fostered by the big houses themselves. "There is something unkindly about the American prison. There is something corroding about it. It tends to harden all that come within the fold of its shadows. It takes kindly, well-intentioned people and makes them callous. . . . In some inexplicable manner the prison 'gets' not only the prisoners but the prison guards as well."[25] An early penologist suggested that "the keynote to understanding the psychology of the prison keeper" was "the exercise of authority and resulting enjoyment of brutality."[26]

One of the most severe challenges faced by 1930s' prison personnel was the psychological transition they were forced to make from rookie to keeper. Most of the officers' duties revolved around keeping inmates from fraternizing. In fact, this was considered the source of most conflict between the keepers and the kept. Most guards came from the same backgrounds as the inmates. Based on their low salaries and dreadful working conditions, one could conclude that prison work was (and often remains) an option for the unskilled and uneducated. The Wickersham Commission found that "the pay is so low that it is impossible to secure any but the least competent."[27]

Victor F. Nelson, who chronicled his years behind bars in the era of the big house, concluded, "Prison guards are not for the most part educated and intelligent men. They sense the antagonism of the prisoners and in most cases react in the natural way. That is, they too become hostile to their inmate charges. They resent the hostility of the roughneck type prisoner and resent the intellectual superiority of the more intelligent prisoner; and thus a wall of active hatred springs up between guards and inmates."[28] Historically, the keepers and the kept have had a rancorous relationship. Prisoners complained of harassment and daily graft, claiming guards often took half their food and coffee rations. The "constant hostility" and "hostile attitudes of inmates toward guards" is reflected in the prisoner slang for guards: "bulls," "hacks," and "screws,"[29] as well as in the nicknames applied to particular guards and wardens. These often referred to physical characteristics such as weight and height, or where they came from. According to one prison guard turned scholar, "These negative attitudes and names indicated that inmates are keenly aware [that] their relationship to guards is an adversary one, and guards represent the state's intent to curtail or squelch the wide range of illicit goods and services inmates deem necessary for their survival."[30] In the late nineteenth century, one Ohio prison guard suggested, "A convict is like a rubber ball. He will stay as long as you press him down, but flies up when the pressure is removed. He must feel the pressure all the time."[31]

One British visitor touring American prisons in the 1930s was surprised that so many guards were over forty years of age, commenting that "many old men [were] in charge of American institutions."[32] Any chronicle of the prison staff at the Ohio Penitentiary in 1930 offers examples of aged and/or debilitated personnel. For example, day guard Thomas Watkinson, known as "the Englishman," was fifty-five years old. Captain John Hall was seventy-one, an advanced age in that era for any profession. His physical condition was brought into question when he couldn't keep up with the younger guards responding to the fire. When Warden Preston Thomas, in his sixties, testified before the Board of Inquiry after the fire, he noted that another guard captain named Cottingham "wasn't very well, they sometimes pity him, say 'Go ahead Cottingham, I am here anyway' and go on the gate for him."[33]

No one exemplified the age disparity between the keepers and the kept more than night captain John Hall, who began working in the prison on May 28, 1909. Hall earned a reputation for cruelty, and if one inmate is to be believed, he had "lost all pity if he had any." By one report, when a convict garbed only in underclothing and overalls complained about the freezing temperatures, Hall purposely turned off the heat and opened windows. In another case, he was accused of refusing appeals from sick inmates to go to the hospital.[34] These stories might be apocryphal, but there are enough of them to suggest that Hall was indeed a petty tyrant.

Captain Hall had just come on for the night and was outside the locked cage with one of the guards when the cry of "Fire" rent the air. Rather than let prisoners out of their cells, his first inclination was to order guards and trustees to "smash the windows!" and "don't let one of the [convicts] out!" After giving his orders Hall left the cellblock and by most accounts was not seen again during the fire. Prisoner Jim Morton later stated, "I doubt anyone would have been lost" if he had given the order to release the prisoners. "If the night guard, who had just come on, had turned over the cage keys to two of the day men who rushed in, hundreds of lives would have been saved."[35] Convict Roy Williams testified to the Board of Inquiry, "Hall had no business with his job. It should be a younger man on the job."[36] However, given his age, Hall must have been full of vim and vigor; one inmate described him as "one of the most hated and despised human beings in the institution," treating inmates "like dogs and cattle, kicks them around."[37]

Guard Thomas Watkinson, the "Englishman," who played a controversial role in the subsequent fire investigation, had resided in the United States for a quarter century. He had been a miner in England and then in Ohio. He moved to Columbus three years earlier after losing his mining job during the 1927–28 coal strike in southeastern Ohio.[38] He later recounted that "when the strike came on, I came up to Columbus knowing there was no use to stay down at the mining camps; there was nothing doing there. . . . I came up to Columbus, picking up what work whenever I could, and I got work at the bakery." After five months, unable to support his family on such meager pay, he decided to look for work at the local state prison. Asked if he had an applicable trade, he responded, "I don't have any trade; I've been mining all my life."[39] This must have seemed good enough, because he was hired and almost immediately started on the night watch, which he described as being "on the inside of walls, going over in the yard, see, on the inside, going all around, that was my arrangement."

At the Columbus penitentiary, guards worked twelve-hour shifts, beginning at either 6 a.m. or 6 p.m. Typically, there were on average 137 guards on each shift, responsible for controlling the more than forty-three hundred inmates. The April 21 fire broke out around 5:30, just before the second shift came on. With the blaze beginning so close to the transition between shifts, there was an overlap in day- and night-shift personnel, and it was unclear who was in charge. This played a role in the confusion over who could open the cells to save the men in the G&H blocks.

Ohio prison guards were paid according to their "class," or "ability." Asked whether they were paid according to length of service, Warden Thomas responded that captains were all "ranked as first class" (Grade A) and received the highest salary, $150 per month (equivalent to $2,255 in 2018). Grade B received $140 ($2,105) and Grade C $130 ($1,955).[40]

For some guards, the job offered them a second chance at redemption. Guard William G. Baldwin, who performed heroically the night of the fire, had started working nights at the Ohio Penitentiary the previous year. He had served a previous seven-month stint as a guard before being fired. As Baldwin would later tell the board, Warden Thomas had asked him to resign for beating up another guard. There was bad blood between the warden and Baldwin. The warden had congratulated him for his efforts the morning after the fire, and investigators asked him what they talked about. He responded, "I don't say much to the warden, the warden let me go once."[41]

Baldwin's cellblock partner Thomas F. Little, who would acquit himself honorably on the night of April 21 as well, had been on the job for four months. He had served on the Columbus Police Department for eight years, only to be fired when the "State men" arrested him for selling liquor in violation of the Prohibition laws.[42] Another guard, Charles M. Donaldson, had joined the prison service in 1913, quit in 1925, and come back in 1928.

It is rare to find any official applications, but the author was able to find in the archives an application from 1935 for Arthur John Miller, who was applying to take the Ohio State Civil Service examination. He listed his age at forty-three, on the older side of middle-aged for the era, and married. At six foot-one and 235 pounds he must have been quite a physical specimen, in keeping with the stereotype of the brutal hulking prison guard of the big house era. He admitted having made it through the sixth grade before ending his education in 1908 and spending a stint in the military from 1911 to 1914. He had served as a prison guard for only one month in 1928; his duties included supervision and disciplining of inmates. He was applying for the job again, seeking $130 per month. He offered some impressive references that included James C. Woodard, a former railroad police captain and public works manager who had been the deputy warden at the penitentiary since 1913 and would succeed Preston Thomas as warden.[43]

It was not uncommon for guards to pummel inmates. Sometimes it went unreported and sometimes it did not. Early chroniclers of the Ohio fire contribute to the negative portrait of the prison keepers. Inmates and others relished passing on stories of men being thrown into the "black hole" for minor infractions of prison rules, or being forced "to fight like beasts to satisfy the whims of moron guards, many of whom are of lower mentality than those they rule by gun and club."[44] Another dark portrait had guards waking up prisoners in the middle of the night and dragging them to the hole for no reason other than disliking particular inmates. Following protocol, in the morning the victim would be hauled in front of the so-called warden's court, "which is a second cousin to the 'kangaroo court,' and there he is given a hearing, with the grouchy and vengeful guard a 'prosecuting witness.'" The guard could trump any charge that was thrown at him by the prisoner, "for he knows the prisoner dare not contradict him, for to brand the guard as a liar or even cast mild aspersions upon his integrity would only be courting further and probably more drastic torture."[45]

If anyone knew something about prison discipline, it was James C. Woodard. He began work at Ohio Penitentiary as a storekeeper in 1909, and as deputy warden was in charge of discipline. Asked by the Board of Inquiry if he knew of any brutality, he admitted, "Prisoners have been hit—I hear of it or if it's reported it comes to my notice," but he added, "There might have been cause for them to be hit. There was some cause for the guard hitting them." He offered several scenarios where this might occur, such as when a prisoner attacked a guard. According to protocol, whenever this happened, a guard was supposed to file a report stating the prisoner's name and the cause of the assault and hand the report directly to Woodard. Woodard explained that he also tried to get the other side, generally speaking from the inmate, when he was brought to prison court. He then would write a report detailing the guard's justification. He proudly told the committee that he had once suspended two guards for ten days for an unnecessary beating.[46]

More historical information is available on wardens and others in a supervisory capacity than on guards. Prison guards tended to have rather peripatetic careers, sometimes serving multiple nonconsecutive terms as guards at the same prisons. Compared to prison administrators and literary inmates, "We know less about the career lines and personal characteristics of the rank and file guards, but on the basis of their low wages and abysmal working conditions it seems fair to conclude that prison work had to be a last resort for the unskilled and uneducated."[47]

Most of what we know about prison guards, particularly at the Ohio Penitentiary, was through the jaundiced eyes of the inmates, who unsurprisingly had little good to say about them. One prison historian suggested that besides the reporters and officials, information about the lives of prison guards can be gleaned mostly from "institutional reports, committees charged with investigating prison riots, brutality, scandals, and from biographies and memoirs of prison administrators and inmates."[48]

Between 1929 and 1930 the average income of an American family was around $2,335 ($35,109.85 in 2018 USD), but would drop by almost 40 percent over the next several years. A letter carrier, for example, could expect a salary of a little over $2,000 per year in 1929–30 ($30,072 in 2018 USD), which was considered "a mediocre salary." However, this was an enviable job nonetheless during the Depression.[49] In 1930 the average salary for a lawyer had dropped from $5,534 to $5,194 since 1929. However, during the years of the Great Depression a lawyer's yearly salary only fell under $5,000 in 1933.[50] According to the 1931 Wickersham Commission findings, at the seventy-five prisons that reported wage scales to the Attorney General's Survey of Release Procedures, 44 percent of the guards earned between $535 and $1,000 per year ($8,004 and 15,036 in 2018), and the rest between $1,100 and $2,000. The low wages reflected the economic exigencies of the Great Depression, when pay scales precipitously declined compared to previous years. But it should also be remembered that prison guard salaries have historically been low. For example, in the late 1920s, prior to the stock market crash, the maximum yearly salary for guards in 19 percent of America's prisons was less than $1,000, while 46 percent reported wage scales between $1,000 and $1500, with only 11 percent over $2,000.[51]

A prison guard's salary was not much in this era, but for the uneducated and unskilled there were few comparable job opportunities at the time. Moreover, one should consider that although the average cost of a new house, $7,145 ($107,434), might not be in the cards, monthly rent was $15 ($225), and a Pontiac Big Six Car could be had for $745 ($11,202).[52]

The travesty of the low salaries was only exceeded by the long hours expected of the officers. The Wickersham Commission calculated that 70 percent of guards worked ten or more hours per day.[53] Conditions began to improve only in the mid-1930s, when most prisons instituted a forty-eight-hour work week, although 30 percent still required between seventy and eighty-four hours per week."[54] Depending on the market for unskilled employees, there was often a high staff turnover. Almost one-third disliked the occupation and resigned after just a year or two; those with fewer options were likely to stick it out for the long run. By the 1930s most states included guards on civil service lists, so that political party turnover no longer forced wardens to hire or fire staff members (although this arrangement persisted in fewer than twelve states) during the periodic housecleaning that accompanied every turnover in political administration. In the majority of the states, including Ohio, two-thirds of guards served five years or more, with some 15 percent making it past fourteen years.[55]

Three years after the big house fire, the subject of the recruitment and requirements of guards was discussed at the annual meeting of the American Prison Association. As usual, the prison administrators viewed penology from a rather utopian perspective. One attendee thought that the more desirable candidates should have an education "equivalent" to the eighth grade, with a "knowledge of and interest in social problems." Moreover, "mention [was] no longer made of the desirability of former police and military service," a clear break from the 1920s, when officers were employed more for their "brawn" than for any affinity for social problems.[56] However, the transition from belligerent keeper to social worker was mostly a pipe dream. As late as the 1950s, one journalist suggested that those inclined to take the job were drawn to it because it "gives them license to use a club," while others regarded it as a steady job offering the security of "government work."[57]

According to one modern prison historian, it was only in the 1970s "that judicial, administrative, and worker union pressure have come together in an attempt to elevate the status of the correctional officer."[58] As late as 1947, the hiring of prospective prison guards was accomplished under "methods of selection" that were "generally loose and [had] little experimental study of validity," and of the "13,000 guards in this country, it is safe to say that over three-fourths have been selected by unscientific methods."[59]

THE CONVICTS

Hundreds of men in every prison do not belong there at all.

— *Warden Lewis Lawes, Sing Sing Prison*

I grew to manhood in the Ohio State Penitentiary.

— *Convict author Chester Himes*

In the late 1920s and 1930s, the specter of prison riots, bloodshed, and overcrowding spurred a number of social scientists and journalists to look for solutions to America's big house crisis. The lives of guards and convicts came under the spotlight, examined in numerous publications and government reports. In 1930, the same year as the fire, for example, a Washington, DC–based report noted that a caged convict lived by necessity "an abnormal" life. "He is denied his liberty, held against his will. He is separated from his family, his relatives, and his friends. His companions are all of his own sex and nearly of his own age. He has no contact with women and children. Often he must endure great physical discomfort. He may be housed in a narrow, cold, dark cell, with primitive toilet facilities . . . oppressed by the monotony of the prison routine," spending most of each day in unrelenting idleness.[1] The 1931 Wickersham Report was even more scathing, noting how heavily circumscribed a prisoner's life was, constantly following a regime in which "he moves to innumerable rules which leave him no chance for initiative or judgment." This "mechanical existence did little to prepare for resumption of law abiding life. The treatment is en masse, not individual."[2]

When future federal prison administrator James V. Bennett visited the Ohio Penitentiary in the mid-1920s, as he crossed the prison's interior courtyard he came across "a line of men moving across the square in a long, skating stride, each man with one arm on the shoulder of the man in front of him." He was witnessing the iconic "lockstep" movement, in which inmates "moved rapidly without a sound other than the shuffle of their shoes on the walk, and their eyes [were] focused on the ground." Bennett had occasion to observe "several groups of gray-clad men marching about silently" on his visit. The images stuck with him; he wrote in his autobiography decades later about "the large numbers inked on the backs of their rough, wrinkled shirts," concluding, "It was a depressing introduction."[3] These large inked numbers would play a crucial role in identifying some of the victims of the penitentiary fire.

Although Columbus prisoners consistently griped about a diet heavy on corn, molasses, and bread, they still often ate better than the city's impoverished residents. This is made especially clear in an 1899 photograph of poor residents forming a line outside the prison gates, hoping inmates would finish their meals quickly so they could take away any table leftovers. They had even brought their own containers to take the food away.[4]

As the last decade of the nineteenth century ended, not much had changed in the prison regimen experienced by new inmates entering the Ohio Penitentiary. In his autobiography, convict Charles L. Clark recounted getting his first bath and his prison grays before being taken to a large room called the "Idle House." Here he found a guard on duty immersed in a periodical as fifty men lounged around. "The cripples and sick men were kept in this room and those excused from work also went there, all new men were sent there for a day or two."[5]

At the time of the big house fire, tuberculosis had taken "a dreadful toll" at the Ohio Penitentiary. A contemporary account suggested that few outsiders heard about deaths from the disease inside the prison, explaining, "The tubercular are not permitted to expire within the walls if there is time to have them paroled and sent home."[6] The strategy of sending home terminal patients to die (when possible), so as not to reflect badly on the Ohio prison service, proved to be a savvy public relations ploy.

For convicts in the late 1920s, each day's well-rehearsed routine began at 6:30 a.m., when all prisoners had to present themselves at their cell doors after "the gong rings for count." Each inmate was expected to display two fingers through the cell door bars "to show he's still alive." Once the guards completed the count, they unlocked the doors and guided their charges to the "wash trough," where they had seven seconds to wash with cold water, not really enough time "to make a good job of it." The guards yelled at anyone lagging behind, in order to let those waiting have their turn.[7]

After the quick wash, inmates were marched back to their tiers until breakfast time. They knew it was time to come out and eat when the screws "whack[ed] clubs against the wall." After eating breakfast (or "slop" in prison argot) and returning to their cells, they had a brief respite before the 7:30 call to leave the cells once more and either go to work or lounge around in the idle house. At 10 a.m., the habitués of the idle house were ordered out and marched around the prison yard until 11 a.m., when they were returned to their cells or dormitories. It was not long before the working prisoners returned to their cells as well. Then it was time for all to march to the dining hall. By 2:30 inmates returned to either their work stations or the idle house, and at 6 p.m. they would have another count. At 8:30 the lights were dimmed, a bell was rung, and anyone caught out of their bunks could be thrown in the hole.[8]

On admission every prisoner was given a physical exam and vaccinated for smallpox and typhoid fever. During this process Wassermann tests, an antibody test for syphilis first introduced in 1906, were conducted and dental and eye condition determined. A local optometrist took care of fitting new eyeglasses. Separate wards for tubercular inmates fed them a special diet of eggs, milk, lemons, and sugar, while those suffering from venereal disease were placed under specialized treatment. However, it was still an era in which no psychiatric exams were given until symptoms occurred. While some groups were segregated to a degree, the Ohio Penitentiary was simply too overcrowded and understaffed to offer any scientific system of classification.[9]

On December 18, 1928, future author Chester Bomar Himes entered the Ohio State Penitentiary, just ten days after his trial, to begin a sentence of twenty to twenty-five years at hard labor for a home-invasion robbery.[10] He would be one of the few inmates to write of his experiences in the Ohio Penitentiary in the years surrounding the Easter 1930 fire. Although he would be paroled early, he later admitted, "I grew to manhood in the Ohio State Penitentiary."[11]

Himes's prison regime mirrored that of his fellow inmates.[12] In his autobiographical novel *Yesterday Will Make You Cry*, we follow his alter ego, new inmate

Jimmy Monroe, as he goes through the Bertillon routine, then is led to the chaplain to determine religious affiliation. Monroe next undergoes medical inspection, before being handed his gray uniform and hickory-striped shirt. In the commissary he spots "stacks of coats, vests and pants of different sizes, some new and some used." The clerks were instructed to give out the used items first, leftovers from convicts who had been released. All of Monroe's clothing is used except for his "Sunday shirt," which is matched with a constricted coat "patched at the elbows." Topping off his new sartorial look are pants that are "too short" and a vest that is "too big." After putting on his used thin-soled shoes, he derives some solace from the realization that he is "dressed as well as anybody, better than most."[13]

Monroe/Himes chalks up the dependence on used clothing to a state unwilling to toss funding at the prison system. As a result, money had to be saved wherever possible. He is given, like others, a pair of used gloves "made out of old uniforms." He imagines that they were cut out of cloth using the "imprint of a mammoth hand."[14]

Throughout the entry process, first-time inmates are typically petrified but do their best not to show it. There is little time to prepare for the prison environment. As they enter this foreign land, other convicts view them as outsiders until they can assimilate into the convict demimonde. This process has been referred to as "prisonization" by social scientists, penologists and others. Becoming part of the prison culture can be accelerated with assistance from other prisoners. Once he is accepted into this "band of brothers," he has become a moving piece inside the social system of the prison community. This association is imperative in helping the outsider make the transition to prisoner as he learns how to adapt to and tolerate the rigidity of the prison environment. Nonetheless, the transition of every new prisoner is dependent on his personality and psychological makeup.

Himes/Monroe describes his first impressions inside the cell house, "seeing the other convicts for the first time. . . . Sitting on their bunks, reading, talking, some walking around, others playing musical instruments, making rings and cigarette holders and inlaid jewel boxes, coming in and out from between the bunks with the sliding, sidewise motion of crabs. . . . And then he began to hear the noises peculiar to convicts—clumping of hard heels on concrete, yells, curses, off-key ballads, arguing, eternal arguing—all blended into a convict medley." Himes's alter ego notices, soon after being locked up in his cell, that it is common for other cons to possess "wooden boxes" fashioned like trunks "with wooden trays and fancy locks." These were stowed under the bunks after lights out and during the day were typically on top of the bunks "when the floors were being swept and mopped." Those fortunate enough to have this extra storage kept all of their personal items in it. Jimmy Monroe had to make do with "what the state had given him."[15]

Himes/Monroe admits he is scared, but does his best to hide it.[16] One of Himes's biographers, however, asserts that Himes not only "always carried a knife," but "was well prepared for prison life," having gambling skills that allowed him "to move easily within the prison walls, where much of the power and much of the prestige among inmates depended on gambling operations."[17]

Himes/Monroe takes the upper bunk next to the outer wall under "one of the high barred windows." At the top of his bunk is a label with his name and number. Looking down toward his toes, he would notice an "aluminum coffee pail, which served in the place of a cup." Himes/Monroe decides instead to use it to store his toiletries. He also gets in the habit of putting his "Sunday shirt of blue denim, and his white string tie underneath the mattress."[18]

The future author, a keen observer, quickly adapts to the prison regime. Watching his cellies, he gets into the practice of taking off all of his outer garments and sleeping in his "long cotton underwear with his prison number stenciled in the neckband." These numbers would come in handy for the identification of charred victims in the aftermath of the Easter Monday fire. Some cons were lucky enough to have their own pajamas, while most others just slept in their underwear or shirts and shorts. Underwear got the most abuse, with prisoners only allowed to change it once a week, meaning they wore it "continually for 168 hours."[19]

The day after Himes/Monroe enters the Ohio Penitentiary he is assigned to a group of convicts known as the "coal company," consisting of mostly black convicts. He is tasked with bringing shavings back from the planing mill. The shavings would be used as kindling to heat the convict coal company quarters "housed in the basement of a low building near the west stockade." He experiences his first "near-death experience" on a frigid winter day after refusing to dig out more shavings for kindling from under the snow, claiming to be totally disabled. The guards do not buy it for a moment and lock him out in the cold. They later transfer him to the hole, where they slap him around a little. Forced "to huddle all night under a skimpy blanket with two other convicts in the freezing, stinking cell," he vows never to resist openly again.[20] Little does he realize that he will face the worst near-death experience of his life just two years later, which he will survive only because he had been moved from the part of the prison housing the so-called punishment company, many of whom perished.

Penologist Donald Clemmer, in his mid-twentieth-century study *The Prison Community*, found that only 20 percent of the inmates in his survey fell into the category of "master criminals." Rather, "the great bulk of the prison population is comprised of awkward, amateurish and occasional offenders."[21] The ratio was likely much the same at the time of the Ohio Penitentiary fire, as it had been in the nineteenth century, when common laborers outnumbered all other occupations behind Ohio prison walls.[22] In 1840, the leading occupation among inmates of most northern state prisons, as it would have been in Ohio, was farming, with one in five inmates coming from this background, followed in descending order by shoemakers, boatmen, laborers, carpenters, blacksmiths, and sailors.[23] Twenty years later, as the Civil War approached, laborers took the top spot, followed by farmers, boatmen, carpenters, and shoemakers. Ohio prison records in 1880 listed "common laborers" and mechanics as the top two groups, accounting for more than half the prison population.[24] As one historian noted, "The same transition from agriculture to urban industrial background occurred earlier in most eastern states, later in prisons west of Ohio."[25]

In the second half of the nineteenth century, the ethnicity of the prisoners in the Ohio Penitentiary would have reflected the growing ethnic diversity of an industrializing America. A survey of the country's prisons demonstrated a higher proportion of the foreign-born behind bars than in free society. The largest groups included Irish and Germans, followed by English, Canadians, and Italians.[26]

The greatest number of prisoners in the Ohio Penitentiary came from Ohio (1,800) and neighboring Pennsylvania (214) and Kentucky (303). As testament to the growing diversity of industrializing America, there were 388 foreign-born inmates representing 37 countries. Most were from European nations, with a smattering from such disparate lands as Transylvania, Syria, Mexico, Arabia, Africa, and China. These numbers were broken down even further, supplementing the nativity figures with the prisoners' descent. There were forty-five categories of descent, most referring to national origins, including Albanian, American, Arabian, Hollander, Jugo Slavian [sic], Phillipino [sic], Scotch, and Syrian, reflecting the geopolitics of the era.

Also significant, but emblematic of the era, Jewish inmates (26) were listed under descent, the sole religion noted under that category.[27] According to one revealing study toward the end of the 1930s, "Jews seem to have fewer lifelong criminals," were more likely to be convicted for property crime than violent crime, were better educated, and were more likely to be married and foreign born than their "white counterparts."[28]

The Ohio prisoners were categorized by "color" as well, which broken down would include 2,916 whites, 1,410 blacks, and 3 Asians (recorded as yellows). The majority of the black prisoners at this time (1,160) were from outside Ohio.[29]

Inmates at that time lived under the vicissitudes of regimes that teetered between extremes of Christian despotism and deterrence through a capricious policy "of deprivation and terror." For inmates, Christian decorum meant a heady mixture of silence and repentance. Inmates were prohibited from communicating with each other, either verbally or through nods and winks. They were expected to kowtow to guards and visitors at all times under threat of solitary confinement, the shower bath, or up to ten strokes from the lash. Despite the punitive regime, when A. G. Dimmock took over the institution in 1852, he found the Ohio Penitentiary to be a "bedlam" in his first report and that discipline and order had broken down to such an extent that it seemed the convicts ran the prison. The new warden discontinued some of the former administration's policies, but inmates found he was no pushover either, stressing "rigid discipline, shorter sentences and fewer pardons." For him, deterring crime meant making prison a "terror to evildoers."[30]

Of the 4,329 convicts in the Ohio Penitentiary at the end of April 1930, more than half were serving up to ten years (2,240).[31] Another 571 were serving life sentences,[32] 7 were on death row, 18 were serving sentences ranging from thirty to forty-five years, and the rest were serving anywhere between eleven and twenty-nine years.[33] An examination of the crimes committed by the Ohio prison denizens indicates few master criminals inside. There were seventy-four different crime categories: 925 inmates were behind bars for one of the seven degrees of burglary), 799 for robbery, almost 700 for first- or second-degree murder or manslaughter, and over 200 each for larceny, forgery, or auto stealing. The numbers were in single digits for bigamy, blackmail, abortion, bank robbery, sodomy, horse stealing, interfering with a telegraph message, pandering, destroying and stealing ginseng, perjury, and other crimes. Outside of the financial crimes of embezzlement, false financial statements, defrauding an insurance company, false payroll, and similar crimes, there was little evidence of sophisticated crime. What is probably most surprising is the small number convicted for violating liquor laws (75) and narcotics laws (2).[34]

The convicts came from 132 different occupations. The largest category by far was 1,397 laborers, followed by 198 truck drivers, 148 auto mechanics, 120 cooks, and 102 barbers. In the double digits were other familiar professions—carpenters (74), butchers (26), musicians (48), teamsters (36), bakers (57), railroaders (35), chauffeurs (89), engineers (30), machinists (91), and electricians (51). Outlier occupations included a dash of singers, prizefighters, bartenders, newspapermen, policemen, and ballplayers, with a gambler, an oil prospector, a cigar maker, and an art model thrown in for good measure.[35]

Inmates ranged in age from seventeen to seventy-five years of age, including 92 over the age of sixty and 185 between the ages of seventeen and twenty. The bulk of the inmates were between those extremes: 1,117 between twenty-one and twenty-five, 1,051 between twenty-six and thirty, and 1,239 between the ages of thirty-one and forty. Ultimately, most of the inmates were between the ages of 21 and 39, with a decline in numbers at age 40.[36]

There were about the same number of married (1,651) and single (1,696) prisoners, with the remaining 982 made up of inmates who were separated (441), divorced (269), or widowed (272).[37] A large number had dependents, ranging from a wife or father only (691) to anywhere from one to thirteen children.[38]

Religiously, the inmate population proved surprisingly diverse, with thirty-four denominations and faiths listed, including 1,189 Baptists, 1,005 Methodists, 958 Catholics, 324 Protestants, 172 Presbyterians, 132 Lutherans, 87 United Brethren, 73 Christian Scientists, and 41 Jews. The other 24 categories listed a variety of other faiths, including Muslim (listed as "Mohamaden") (1), Spiritualists (2), Salvation Army (5), Holy Rollers (7), Dunkards (7), and 21 who listed no religion.[39]

Education statistics indicated that about one-tenth were illiterate, 3,084 had attended common school (first–eighth grades), 701 had attended high school, and 136 had some college training.

Finally, 3,270 inmates had no military training. Those who did have military training included veterans of the 1898 Spanish American War (20) and World War I (567). The rest had served in a variety of other related services.[40] Given the number of veterans of the Great War, which had ended less than a dozen years earlier, it should not be surprising that so many accounts of the fire and its morbid aftermath were peppered with wartime allusions. One World War I veteran, for example, compared the dense smoke to the gas attacks he had endured on the Western Front. Captain Tom W. Jones, who aided in the rescue, commented that what he saw that day was "worse than anything he witnessed in the Argonne or St. Mihiel."

Trustees were featured actors in the American prison world during the late nineteenth century and for much of the following one. The term "trustee," sometimes spelled "trusty," refers to inmates who are given authority to manage other inmates, unpaid guards if you will. The system was especially prominent in southern prisons that maintained large agricultural plantations. In the more modern era, the use of trustees was considered more of a cost-cutting strategy. During the 1930s, in prisons such as New Jersey's Trenton State Prison, trustees ran errands for guards, passed messages to inmates, and occasionally performed unpaid guard duty.[41] At the Ohio Pen, trustees often wore regular clothes and filled soft jobs ranging from clerks, bookkeepers, and stenographers to attendants and others. Like William Sydney Porter (O. Henry), mentioned in chapter 4, who was given unsupervised freedom thanks to his trustee status, numerous other prisoners enjoyed an amount of freedom behind the walls, and others even managed to accrue enough cachet to go outside in front of the pen on Spring Street, go uptown, take messages to the state house on High Street and drop into a picture show or a gin mill, or even go to ballgames and drive a car owned by the prison administration.

Former baseball player Clifford Wesley "Tacks" Latimer was probably the most prominent trustee at the time of the fire. His moniker, according to his biographer Jon Daly, may have referred to his edgy disposition. Coincidentally, he had been a childhood friend of the coed killer Dr. James Snook (see chapter 6), who was executed the February prior to the fire. According to Snook's biographer, Latimer, who worked at the time in the death row property room, helped him pick out the clothes he wore to his electrocution. After the execution Latimer recounted that they had never discussed the murder and mostly "talked about sports, and things we used to do back home (in South Lebanon, Ohio)."[42]

During his twenty-seven-game career as a major league catcher, Latimer had only eighty-six at bats over five seasons, which baseball statistics guru Bill James suggested "might be some sort of record."[43] He worked as a railroad detective for the Pennsylvania Railroad after hanging up his cleats. In 1924 he killed his supervisor in the culmination of a long-standing feud. While some witnesses labeled the killing self-defense, the fact that the fatal bullets came from behind was enough to convince a jury to convict him of second-degree murder. On January 6, 1926, he was sentenced to life in prison by Judge R. L. Gowdy.[44]

Latimer, who promised to toe the line in prison, was soon elevated to trustee. On the night of the fire, when mayhem broke loose as prisoners were released from their cells, he was trusted enough to be handed a shotgun by either the warden or the warden's daughter, Amanda.[45] According to one report, he was told to stand guard at the outer door, a position he knew well, having "stood vigil" there on a many an evening for several years.[46] A reporter who noted his actions during the night of the fire reminded readers that he had been "a hero of one prison break and one of the foremost trusties of the penitentiary." This was in reference to the events four years earlier, in November 1926, when he tried to stop a prison break at his outer gate post. By most accounts he protected Amanda Thomas from the thirteen inmate escapees, and he supposedly took a revolver from one of the inmates and fired at them. He also participated in the manhunt.

Like many trustees, Latimer was not well received by the rest of the prison population. Some convicts went as far as labeling him "the warden's pet." Few inside the walls regarded him a hero on Easter Monday.[47] One former inmate, who must have had a long-standing beef with the trustee, related how the ex–baseball player was "always whining about his aged mother waiting down at Xenia for her boy, despite the fact that he did a cowardly murder, shooting a railroad detective four times in the back." The inmate also took exception to how Latimer had been portrayed during the night of the fire. He regarded Latimer as a poseur, and was not impressed by how Latimer "covered himself with glory" by dashing upstairs in the warden's house to "protect the women." He noted that "Latimer and every-body else knows that those women didn't require protection—that there wasn't a ghost among us that would have harmed one of them."[48] Nonetheless, Ohio governor Cooper "personally" handed Latimer a pardon the next Christmas. In 1931 he married, and in 1933 he had a daughter. He would die of a heart attack at home in April 1936, almost exactly six years after the catastrophic fire.[49]

One of the more prominent convicts in the Ohio big house at the time of the fire, "Big" Jim Morton, was serving an eleven-to-fifteen-year stretch in Columbus after his conviction for a West Cleveland bank robbery. Variously known as "George Lawrence Moore," "Magnus Olson," "James Franklin," "Joseph Murray," and "Harry Fuller," he was part of the five-man bank-robbery team that took the West Cleveland Banking Company for $65,000 on June 16, 1919. He was already forty-six years of age when he entered the prison on January 9, 1920, and reportedly performed heroically on Easter Monday. He represented the professional but well respected criminal element in the prison. Having been arrested eleven times, he had served half his life in prisons from California, Utah, and Nevada to Minnesota and Illinois. Already a popular inmate, he was regarded by most of his fellows as easygoing and charismatic.

Never lacking initiative, the veteran con assumed a leadership role in the rescue attempts in G&H. Breaking into a storage locker holding sledgehammers, he passed them out to other inmates. Handling a sledge himself, Morton began breaking off cell-door locks, entering the dense smoke, and dragging out "unconscious forms of others." Prisoners would later "hail him as the foremost hero of the terrible conflagration."[50] Like a number of other lucky survivors who took part in the rescue attempt, he was overwhelmed by smoke inhalation but was "revived and suffered little ill effect."

Morton was paroled for his heroic actions shortly after the fire. But, like most other veteran criminals, he had a hard time adjusting to life outside the big house. He reappeared in the headlines in 1933, when police sought him in connection with a shooting in Morton's suburban Chicago bungalow, after a good friend of his was found inside mortally wounded. The initial gunplay was reported to the police after a physician, Dr. John Smith, was called to an "armament loaded house in Cicero, long the playground of gangsters," where "he found [Charles] Conroy doubled up from a bullet in his abdomen." Police found a "huge cache of guns, shells, [and] stolen dynamite," and assumed this was the "headquarters for a gang of bombers and bank robbers." The doctor told police another man showed him where the mortally wounded man was located and quickly left the premises. The doctor informed Conroy that the wound was mortal and he would probably die from his bullet wound, but Conroy, ever the hard case, refused to talk.[51]

Former inmate Victor Nelson admitted that "the prisoner is a breaker of laws. The idea that a rule should be obeyed, not because it is sensible or pleasant, but because it is the rule, is utterly beyond his understanding."[52] Some inmates went by their own personal codes of conduct that contravened the organizational structure adopted by the prison administrators. Nelson suggested that an inmate broke rules because he resented any attempt "to prevent him from doing things he wants to do."[53] Moreover, "The average prisoner dislikes the work of the prison; but he actually hates any work of a menial kind—such as emptying slop buckets. Many inmates prefer to go to cooler for 10 days on bread and water than do something they consider beneath their dignity!"[54] However, a prisoner constantly striving for autonomy will eventually come up against the punitive regime established by prisons such as the Ohio Penitentiary that have a disciplinary regime designed for such recalcitrant inmates.

It was not uncommon for prisons to offer incoming convicts a list of rules and regulations. At the Ohio Penitentiary, new prisoners in the late 1920s were given a rulebook, referred to as "a printed statement of advice." It provided a list of twenty rules, which one reporter branded as ones "that always deeply impress visitors."[55] The rules at least brought recidivist convicts up to date if there had been any rule changes since their last sentence and alerted new ones that the silent system was no longer in use. For example, if an inmate had been doing time at the Ohio Penitentiary a decade or two earlier, it would be news to them that they were now permitted to write two letters each month and to receive books and magazines directly from the publisher. Other changes could be immediately recognized, such as the elimination of prison stripes, which had also been consigned to the past more than a decade before the fire.[56]

Visiting regulations at the Ohio Penitentiary were typical for the era. Monthly visits were allowed, lasting up to three hours, and visitors were permitted to carry in a lunch and eat it at tables placed in the visiting room. Prisoners were also allowed to purchase tobacco, candy, and toiletries at the prison store, but could not exceed $1 in purchases each week (about $14 in 2017).[57]

When members of the Osborne Society reported on discipline in the Ohio Penitentiary shortly before the fire, they found that as "far as we have been able to determine, there have been no improvements in the disciplinary methods of the institution. For lesser violations, prisoners might expect to lose recreation yard privileges. More serious transgressions earned a stint in punishment cells located near the deputy warden's office. These cells were characterized by their small size, lack of plumbing, and "narrow shelves for beds." On the positive side, the cells offered some light. However, one of the most feared aspects of this punitive regime was the prospect of being locked in a standing position between the barred doorway and another door inside it, "which form a semi-circular steel cage"; prisoners were commonly left there for at least eight hours each day. Confinement in the punishment cells could last anywhere from a few days to several weeks.[58]

With more than 4,000 convicts and only 137 guards on each shift to guard them, it was a challenge to closely monitor their activities. In order to keep control over so many inmates, guards sometimes were forced to push the boundaries of the law when it came to discipline. Conversely, the vastly outnumbered guards could do little to stop inmates from gambling and indulging in illicit substances. One inmate trustee at the time of the fire, identified as "Robins" by several journalists, claimed that "whiskey, cocain [sic] and morphine were constantly being smuggled in the prison." Robins estimated that close to 23 percent of the inmates were addicts.[59] Moreover, not only was alcohol consumption "an open secret . . . if you had money in here you could get anything," but the trustee admitted that during his years behind bars he had seen "guys drinking in the Idle House and in the boiler room. . . . There are hop-heads here who haven't been off dope in all the years they've been in stir."[60]

A testament to the continuity of prison vice between the early twentieth century and the twenty-first century was the smuggling of illicit drugs into prison. It was a dirty little secret then, as it is today, that much of the contraband was brought in by guards who were either coerced or paid well enough. This type of informal business was especially seductive for poorly paid guards supporting families during the opening years of the Great Depression. And despite a prohibition against having cash on hand, it was common, by some accounts, for inmates to have plenty of greenbacks stashed in their cells or elsewhere. Paying cash to guards was known as "oiling the screw."

Despite the seemingly yawning chasm between the keeper and the kept, they actually shared a number of demographics, including education, economic class, religion, and a propensity for brutality and deviance. Perhaps one should not be so surprised then, that they were able to find common ground and work faithfully together rescuing inmates from the deadly inferno on Easter Monday 1930.

Ohio inmates in earlier years when prison stripes and lockstep marching were common. Courtesy of the Ohio History Connection, SC *763*, Ohio Penitentiary Collection.

Guards and staff, ca. *1890s*. Courtesy of the Ohio History Connection, AL *08391*.

The size of the Ohio Penitentiary dining hall offers a perspective on the sheer number of inmates in the overcrowded prison. Courtesy of the Ohio History Connection, AL 07551.

Aerial view of the Ohio Penitentiary after repairs, with the restored roof in the center of photo. Courtesy of the Ohio History Connection, AL 07605.

The most panoramic view of the prison inferno. Courtesy of the Ohio History Connection, AL 05870.

Firefighters and hoses at the southeast wagon stockade gate. Courtesy of the Ohio History Connection, AL 07600.

The Columbus Fire Department attempting to control the fire. Courtesy of the Ohio History Connection, AL *07601*.

Inmates and firefighters, able to do little at this point but watch the smoking inferno. Courtesy of the Ohio History Connection, *Columbus Dispatch* Photograph Collection, AL *05567*.

Looking for signs of life on the quad the night of the fire. Courtesy of the Ohio History Connection, AL 05869.

Tending to the injured and checking for life on the quad lawn. Courtesy of the Ohio History Connection, AL 05868.

Inmates conveying the injured and the dead on blankets away from the quad area. Courtesy of the Ohio History Connection, *Columbus Dispatch* Photograph Collection, AL 05668.

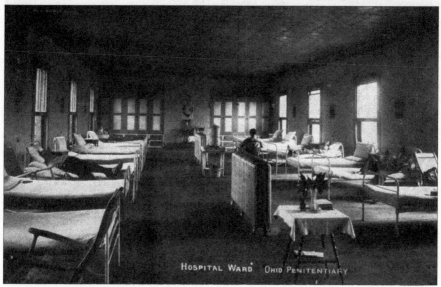

Ohio Penitentiary hospital ward in better times. Courtesy of the Ohio History Connection, AL 07753.

Women at the prison gates seeking passes to claim bodies of loved ones. *Columbus Citizen*, April 25, 1930. Courtesy of the Ohio History Connection, 9055.

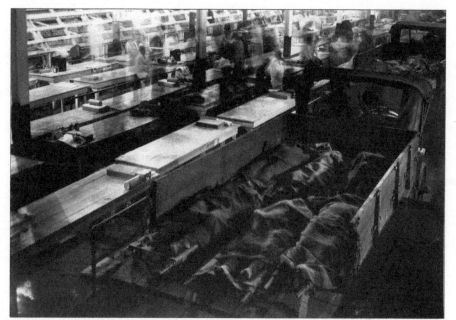

Bodies of victims delivered in trucks to the fairgrounds for casket preparation. Courtesy of the Ohio History Connection, SC 762, Ohio Penitentiary Fire Collection.

Bodies of victims being prepared for caskets at the makeshift morgue in the Horticultural Building at the state fairgrounds. Courtesy of the Ohio History Connection, SC 762, Ohio Penitentiary Fire Collection.

Caskets at the fairgrounds, ready for burial. The Columbus Flower Growers and Dealers Association donated a floral arrangement to place atop each casket. Courtesy of the Ohio History Connection, AL *03813*.

Burial of unclaimed coffin by Naval Reservists. *Columbus Citizen*, April 26, 1930. Courtesy of the Ohio History Connection, *9055*.

Twisted rebar amidst the collapsed cellblock roof. Courtesy of the Ohio History Connection, AL 07599.

Devastation in G&H cellblocks. Courtesy of the Ohio History Connection, AL 07603.

A scorched cell in the aftermath of the fire. Location is unclear. Courtesy of the Ohio History Connection, SC 762, Ohio Penitentiary Fire Collection.

GET PRAISE OF CONVICTS

WM. C. BALDWIN   CAPT. TOM F. LITTLE

GUARDS THOMAS F. LITTLE, 1323 E. Fulton-st, and W. C. Baldwin, 777 W. Broad-st, won the praise of the entire prison population by their acts of heroism in carrying out dead and injured convicts. They finally collapsed from their efforts.

The hero guards William Baldwin and Thomas Little in the aftermath of the fire. *Columbus Citizen*, April 22, 1930. Courtesy of the Ohio History Connection, 9055.

Postfire activity in the quad area adjacent to the destroyed cellblocks. Courtesy of the Ohio History Connection, AL 07604.

Postfire prisoner activity, probably lining up for breakfast. Courtesy of the Ohio History Connection, SC762, Ohio Penitentiary Fire Collection.

The stockade containing the tent city created in the aftermath of the fire. *Columbus Citizen*, May 1, 1930. Courtesy of the Ohio History Connection, *9056*.

Warden Preston Elmer Thomas being sworn in to testify before the Board of Inquiry. Courtesy of the Ohio History Connection, *Columbus Dispatch* Photograph Collection, AL 05670.

PICTURE STORY OF THE SOLVING OF PENITENTIARY'S FIRE MYSTERY

THEY STOLE FIVE GALLONS OF OIL

THEY WERE IN THE CELLS WHEN THE FIRE BROKE OUT

THREE TIMES THEIR ARSON ATTEMPTS WERE FAILURES

THERE WERE 322 LIVES LOST IN THE FIRE

A CONFESSION WAS FINALLY OBTAINED

JAMES RAYMOND

HUGH GIBSON

CANDLES WERE SMUGGLED OUT OF THE CHAPEL

JAMES MALONEY

THE FIRE WAS STARTED IN A PAN OF OIL

CLINTON GRATE

. Principal convicts named in the grand jury investigation of the Ohio Penitentiary fire and scenes sketched from descriptions in the confessions of two of them are shown above.

Hugh Gibbons, alias Gibson, and Clinton Grate have confessed to Prosecutor Hoskins that they used a candle in a pan of oil to start the conflagration which claimed 322 lives.

James Raymond, also said to have been in on the plot, hanged himself in a cell in solitary last August.

James Maloney says Grate threatened to kill him for his knowledge of the plot. He is believed to have had criminal knowledge of the conspiracy but will not be indicted by the present grand jury.

Maloney contends that he furnished the candles but was ignorant of their intended use. He claims he was told they were wanted to heat solder and since the request was not unusual in view of the work then in progress in the prison, he provided the candles.

The penitentiary arsonists and escape plotters. *Columbus Citizen*, April 2, *1931*. Courtesy of the Ohio History Connection, *9061*.

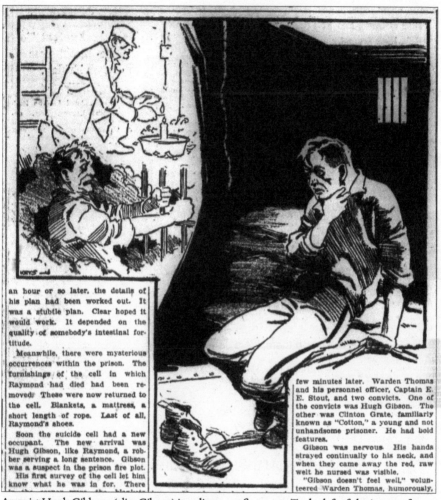

an hour or so later, the details of his plan had been worked out. It was a subtle plan. Clear hoped it would work. It depended on the quality of somebody's intestinal fortitude.

Meanwhile, there were mysterious occurrences within the prison. The furnishings of the cell in which Raymond had died had been removed. These were now returned to the cell. Blankets, a mattress, a short length of rope. Last of all, Raymond's shoes.

Soon the suicide cell had a new occupant. The new arrival was Hugh Gibson, like Raymond, a robber serving a long sentence. Gibson was a suspect in the prison fire plot. His first survey of the cell let him know what he was in for. There

few minutes later. Warden Thomas and his personnel officer, Captain E. E. Stout, and two convicts. One of the convicts was Hugh Gibson. The other was Clinton Grate, familiarly known as "Cotton," a young and not unhandsome prisoner. He had bold features.

Gibson was nervous. His hands strayed continually to his neck, and when they came away the red, raw welt he nursed was visible.

"Gibson doesn't feel well," volunteered Warden Thomas, humorously,

Arsonist Hugh Gibbons (alias Gibson) in solitary confinement. To the left of the image of Gibbons, one of the arsonists is depicted igniting the incendiary device. *Columbus Citizen*, April 5, 1933. Courtesy of the Ohio History Connection, 9073.

9 BOARD OF INQUIRY

I have no orders to let men out of here.

— *Guard Thomas Watkinson*

He just stood there like a damned fool.

— *Inmate Roy Williams*

The inquiry could not have been convened at a more tumultuous time than in the days immediately following the fire. As preparations were made for the final disposition of the dead at the state fairgrounds, a prisoner mutiny seemed to be on the verge of breaking out within the prison walls. Direction was urgently needed from the powers that be at the state capitol. Ohio governor Myers Y. Cooper was in West Virginia on vacation when his secretary, Charles A. Jones, first tried to contact him on Easter Monday. The governor managed to take the first train back home, arriving at the Columbus train station sometime between 3:15 and 4 a.m. the following morning.[1]

Cooper (1873–1958) was the fifty-first governor of Ohio. A highly successful businessman, he got involved in Republican Party politics in the 1910s and '20s. He ran for office for the first time in 1926, losing the governor's race to the incumbent Alvin Victor Donahey, but gave it another try in 1928 after Donahey decided not to run again, and this time he won. Cooper took office the year before the fire, and, except for the Easter Monday fire, served a relatively uneventful two years in office. Curiously, there is no mention of the fire and its aftermath in most of his online biographical references.[2]

Upon Governor Cooper's arrival back in Columbus, he ordered the director of the Ohio Department of Public Welfare, Hal H. Griswold, to launch a thorough investigation. With the eyes of the world on Columbus, it was incumbent on the governor to convene a reputable Board of Inquiry to satisfactorily explain how 320 prisoners perished so quickly and needlessly in the inferno. Unbeknownst to the governor, the Franklin County prosecutor, John J. Chester, had already beaten him to the punch. Shortly before dawn, while the governor was still on his way back from West Virginia, the prosecutor launched an investigation on behalf of his office. He first targeted Warden Preston Thomas and began interviewing him early Tuesday morning in the prison's administrative offices.

Chester's inquiry did not begin or end well. His first questions led to what could be best described as a "bitter exchange of views" with the warden.[3] Chester rebuked the warden for sending only three men (guards Baldwin, Little, and Hall) to unlock eight hundred convicts, as well as for his failure to direct additional help toward the liberation of the inmates. The warden first attempted to parry the criticism, pointing out that he had directed National Guardsmen and reinforcements to surround the walls and help firemen enter through the railroad stockade when they couldn't get in through the wagon stockade. This did little to appease his inquisitor. Chester, in an accusatory voice, asked the embattled warden, "Did you go down yourself, in any way, shape or form, to let those men out of the tier?"[4] He obviously knew the answer before the warden replied in the negative. The interview deteriorated rapidly after the county prosecutor had the temerity to accuse the warden of being responsible for the fire deaths and boldly asserted that he should step down until the investigation was over. Thomas vehemently refused. Chester was adamant that the warden be suspended straight away or at least until the inquiry had been concluded, but this proved wishful thinking.

With the return of the governor, there was a brief clash between county and state authorities over Chester's proposal to suspend Warden Thomas until all the facts were known.[5] The county prosecutor argued that since he had started an earlier investigation, by law he had the authority to investigate any crime committed in his county. The governor demurred, placing the inquiry in the hands of

Director of Public Welfare Griswold, who then selected Attorney General Gilbert Bettman to lead the inquiry. Born in Cincinnati in 1881, Bettman graduated from Harvard Law School in 1907. In 1929 he resigned his position as the dean of the YMCA Law School of Cincinnati (now Salmon P. Chase College of Law at Northern Kentucky University) after successfully winning the Ohio attorney general race.[6] Bettman was a justice of the Supreme Court of Ohio from 1941 to 1942.

With the inquiry now under the direction of the attorney general, county prosecutor Chester was no doubt piqued by this turn of events, but may have been mollified when Governor Cooper tossed an accolade his way, telling the assembled investigators that "I have asked the director of welfare to invite the County Prosecutor of Franklin County to participate so that the state may have benefit of his counsel and advice."[7]

An interesting inmate perspective on this transition from Chester to Attorney General Bettman can be found in a 1933 fictionalized account of the fire written by the pseudonymous inmate James Winning. Recounting how the county prosecutor strode into the makeshift courtroom, perhaps a little too aggressively, Winning insinuates that there may have been a more sinister reason for the state taking the investigation out of Chester's hands: "perhaps he may uncover something that would be better hidden, so the investigation is taken out of his hands and the attorney general of the state takes charge. Politics, so soon, begins to crush the fact that 293 men perished behind bars."[8] However, Winning's account is not substantiated by any other source.

The inquiry into the disaster took place in the prison records office, a long room in the main offices of the Ohio Penitentiary that had been converted into a temporary courtroom. Here the blame game began, as each witness gave his account of the night of the fire. The organization of the Board of Inquiry (BOI) was settled by 7:30 Tuesday morning, shortly after the return of the governor. Attorney General Bettman was tasked with leading it. From the start, Bettman felt that ascertaining the circumstances of the disaster would require the findings of "more than one mind." He designated an informal BOI comprising First Assistant Attorney General Earl C. Shively (Athens) and special counsels Joseph A. Godown (Columbus) and Harry G. Levy (Toledo).[9] There were also a number of observers. Cooper asserted that he invited "newspaper men in for the reason that this is an open investigation calculated to produce all the facts to which the public is entitled."

Governor Cooper, who sat at the head of the table, was only on hand to hear the first morning session. The inquiry heard and took testimony for five days between the morning of Tuesday, April 22, and the afternoon of Saturday, April 26. Ultimately forty-four witnesses would testify, including the warden and deputy warden, twelve guards, seventeen prisoners, and the chief of the Columbus Fire Department. The unredacted transcript of the trial goes on for 727 pages and offers the best chronicle of the hearings.

The board determined that it would take testimony from any witnesses under oath who "offered themselves as having any knowledge of the circumstances and also examine all the officials and guards of the penitentiary who claimed to have or whom the Board learned had any helpful information." To add to the details of the fire, "several prisoners, who by reason of their work in the Penitentiary or the location of their cells at the time of the fire," were also examined.[10]

Assistant Attorney General Snively took charge of the opening round of the inquisition, ordering the stenographer to read the testimony the warden gave to county prosecutor Chester earlier that morning. The highlights of the transcript at that point reveal that the warden received the first alarm at 5:35 from a houseman and proceeded to the guardroom to order whoever was in there to "get the men out." From the start he was convinced that all evidence pointed to an incendiary device.

Board members, led by Director Griswold and Attorney General Bettman and including their assistants Earl C. Snively, Joseph A. Godown, and Harry G. Levy, as well as E. J. Jenkins, the superintendent of prison construction, state architect T. Ralph Ridley, and a "corps of newsmen," then visited the ruined cellblocks. There they observed firsthand floors littered with half-eaten candy, unopened letters, water-soaked books, and overturned checkerboards. It didn't take much imagination for them to summon up images of the doomed men relaxing after their dinner, catching up on mail, and playing games when the blaze intruded. The tour group climbed up through water and debris to the sixth tier of G&H, where most of the victims had perished the night before. They were heckled at times by the survivors, who were dispersed by the guards. The magnitude of the destruction became clearer as the investigators mounted the stairs to the top two tiers. One reporter described a cellblock in which "concrete cells had been turned literally into bake ovens, fired and heated by the adjoining cell block construction." The walls of the top tiers, particularly at their north ends, were "burned white" under the "terrific heat." As the smoke and heat moved to the south end, it "charred everything flammable."

While a number of peripheral issues were discussed during the interviews conducted by the BOI, the principal focus of the hearings was on the actions of the warden and a handful of guards who controlled the keys for G&H. Throughout the inquiry witnesses concurred that no lives should have been lost. Columbus fire chief A. E. Nice, for instance, testified that not only were the prison officials lax in their consideration of the value of human life, but all prisoners could have been saved if released when the fire was first discovered.[11]

Before the first day was out, the warden, captain John Hall, and guards Thomas Watkinson, Thomas Little, and William Baldwin took the witness stand. Their testimony and actions that night were central to understanding why the inmates were kept locked in their cells until it was too late. Those same witnesses would testify at least once more over the five days of the inquiry. As could be expected, most of their testimony was repetitive, with here and there a potential bombshell, but mostly confirming what each other said. The one outlier was Watkinson, whose testimony conflicted with the others in the retelling of the so-called altercation over the keys at the cage gate.

As chronicled in chapter 1 and chapter 7, captain Hall and guards Little and Baldwin arrived at least fifteen minutes early for their 6 p.m. shift and were in the guardroom when alerted to the fire. All agreed that the warden briefly stopped by and told them to "get the men out." Little and Baldwin already had the keys to tiers two to six but would first have to get through the cage door at the bottom level. There is little doubt that Little and Baldwin, younger and in better shape than the seventy-two-year-old Hall, who suffered from a heart ailment, reached the cage gate before Hall did. The sequence of actions over the next five to nine minutes was key to getting to the bottom of what happened.

All witnesses agreed that Watkinson zealously protected the cage-door key when they arrived at the gate. The Englishman never wavered from his claim that Captain Hall personally ordered him not to open the cage door. Hall emphatically denied giving any order to Watkinson. In Hall's final testimony he said he did see Watkinson on the first tier but only stopped for a minute before vanishing from the scene because the smoke was affecting him: "You see I got organic heart trouble." Watkinson was the only one who claimed the septuagenarian Captain Hall ever personally made it to the cage. As the Englishman told it, he waited for Hall, telling him when he arrived, "I am ready to open it when you say so." Moreover, he claimed Hall told him, "Wait a minute, wait a minute, don't open that door."[12] But Hall denied telling Watkinson that or anything to that effect.

Once Baldwin and Little reached the cage gate, Hall was out of sight due to a combination of dense smoke and not being able to physically keep up with them. However, they testified to hearing Hall farther down the first tier ordering unspecified inmates to open windows any way they could to let in fresh air. Hall recounted his actions in opening the windows, offering this as evidence that he was not delayed in reaching the cellblocks. "My first thought when I got to the burning building was to get air to the men, and then get them out. I did not see who opened the gate but supposed it was Watkinson since he was the only man with a key." Curiously, Hall would note that he thought he told Watkinson to "try and get the prisoners out." At this point in his testimony he was either confused or playing loose with the truth. His recollections were often given less than full credence, particularly when some prisoners testified that Hall said, "I don't give a damn if they do die there." When confronted with his own words, Hall protested, "I don't talk like that."[13]

Baldwin and Little testified that Hall fell farther and farther behind on their way to the cellblocks, reaching the cage gate and Watkinson five minutes after they did. Hall insisted that he was never that far behind them and caught up to the guards in less than a minute. This assertion clearly conflicted with the guards' claims that they passed him in the hall leading to the cell and never saw him again and was a linchpin in the cage-gate saga.

Most evidence supported the claim that five to nine valuable minutes were wasted while Watkinson was deciding whether to relinquish the keys. Baldwin gave up pleading with the reluctant guard and began looking for something to break down the cage door. He recalled running around looking for some iron, hoping that plumbers working on the I&K blocks might have left some out after they left for the day. But he could find nothing. Baldwin couldn't resist explaining that that was probably because "that is one thing we watch pretty close around here,"[14] referring to the policy of not leaving around objects that could be later used for nefarious purposes by inmates.

After more than five minutes had passed, Watkinson was about to hand over the key when Little jerked it out of his hands and opened the gate. Watkinson disappeared from the vicinity very quickly, and by 7 p.m. that night he had been suspended by the warden. The Englishman claimed that once the door was opened and rescuers ran past him and up the tiers, he began directing men out the door but "had to get out or die myself."[15] No one argued with this claim, since he disappeared almost as soon as he opened the cage. Little led the rescue up the ranges, but collapsed on the fourth tier. Baldwin found him there and with the help of three or four inmates carried him out.

Another source of contention was Hall's apparent reluctance to let the prisoners out on the first tier as he tried to catch up with Baldwin and Little. Most accounts agreed that sometime during these terror-fraught minutes, Hall ordered convicts to either bust out windows or prop them open with sticks. He was reported to have said (to no one in particular), "Never mind the men, leave them there for the time being and get the air to them first." Convict Roy Williams, caged on the first tier, said he last saw Hall as he was going down the line of cells on his range. He recalled watching the old captain's antics with other inmates and commenting, "Look at that damn silly old SOB. . . . One minute he would say, knock out the windows to let the air in,"[16] and then in the next minute "tell them to close them."

Hall had earned a reputation for cruelty over the previous years, so inmates were not inclined to be charitable in interpreting his actions. When inmate Edward Dolan was released into the yard after the first-tier cells were opened, he was overheard telling other convicts within earshot of Captain Hall (who was also getting fresh air in the quadrangle), "There is a man that is captain of this institution at night time." Dolan claimed that Hall "killed one man here in 1927 or 28 cold turkey, he killed him, left him in his cell when the cell was on fire." Dolan continued to berate the captain, telling the assembled convicts that it was of "no interest to [Hall] how many men in there are dying" and "You don't see him trying to help." Hall had finally heard enough and told Dolan to keep his "mouth shut or you will find self in solitary."

If anyone doubted Dolan's saga, convict Frank Moore confirmed Dolan's accusation at the inquiry, recounting that he was in the actual cellblock where "Hall let the man burn to death" several years earlier. Moore said, "Whether he was crazy or not, there were two guards stationed in front of his cell—didn't have the keys—Cap Hall came up and said, "Oh, leave him burn up," and then told the burning inmate, "What did you set this afire for." Inmate Bobby Hunt was never brought to the hospital and succumbed to his burns. It is doubtful, however, that Hall actually meant for the inmates to die in the fire. More probably his intentions were misunderstood, as can be inferred from the testimony of inmate Dolan, who noted that Hall told the men on the first tier, "You will get out after a while." "A while" probably meant as soon as he was able to get fresh air into the cellblock.

Another important focus of the inquiry was the chain of command when the warden and deputy warden were not physically present. As a captain, Hall should have been the ranking officer, at least according to Deputy Woodard. But Hall told the investigators that as night captain he did not have any jurisdiction over the day guards unless given orders directly by his two superiors. Moreover, there was no day captain on duty. So until his shift began at 6 p.m. he did not feel he had the clout to tell anyone what to do. However, Deputy Warden Woodard would contradict Hall, telling BOI investigators that Hall was third in line that night. Hall's riposte was "They won't take my orders; I wouldn't give them because they would refuse to take them."[17] He still insisted that only the warden or deputy warden could let the men out.

Shortly before the 2 p.m. recess on the first full day of testimony, the warden added to the controversy over the handling of the cell keys when he announced, "I have written a book of rules wherein keys are always to be, where there is detention, are [sic] to be handled by officers." He specifically mentioned rule 15: "Locks in prison, as elsewhere are for protection. They are no protection if anyone has the key. Officers in charge of this prison therefore are the only ones to handle the keys." The warden may have had a rulebook, but it was apparently never shared with anyone else and has not been found in any archive or chronicle of the Ohio Penitentiary during his era. Observers would have been forgiven if they found some humor in what was probably the biggest understatement of the inquiry, when he said, "Watkinson didn't exhibit good judgement" when he vacillated over releasing the cage-door key.[18]

Later that evening, the questioning of inmate George "Cleveland" Johnson revealed just how punitive the Ohio justice system had become since the new minimum sentences were introduced in the early 1920s. When asked by Assistant Attorney General Snively "how long a term are you serving?," Johnson answered, "Five–ten years sir. I am back as a parole violator now." Snively followed up, "Well, what are you in for?" Cleveland succinctly replied, "Perjury." He was rewarded with a round of applause "for his apparent sincerity in this case and for his heroism." An incredulous Hal Griswold couldn't stop himself from adding, "I didn't know they could sentence a man for ten years for perjury." This must have surely been an educational experience for the assembled reporters, convicts, and other observers in the makeshift courtroom.

After an afternoon and evening of testimony several facts had been established. Most disconcerting were the actions of Thomas Watkinson, who had refused to hand over the key to the cage for more than five minutes, until Little wrested it from him. His insistence that he must wait for orders defied credulity. Assistant Attorney General Godown asked him, "Do you mean to tell me you were waiting for orders from Captain Hall in the face of advancing fire?" Watkinson replied, "Certainly. I had to obey orders or be suspended."[19] Secondly, the warden had gone outside to direct security measures, assigning Deputy Warden Woodard to take command inside the walls. By all accounts, personnel had never been given instructions in case of an emergency, and the warden could not remember the last time there had been a fire drill during his seventeen years on the job.

By early Wednesday morning the revolt by groups of convicts in the prison yard began to quiet down. But it wasn't long before inmates in the idle house, where most of the locks had been broken, demanded to be released into the prison yard. For a short time they were mollified with seven hundred gallons of hot coffee.[20] Plans had already been discussed to release some of the soldiers on duty outside, but these were rescinded quickly and additional troops were called in when the unruly leaders in the idle house, other cellblocks, and the yard urged convicts to make a break for it.

It was only when Deputy Warden Woodard, described as the "one man who can make them behave when others have difficulty,"[21] diplomatically intervened that inmates stood down and renounced threats of violence. The convicts made four demands: the commutation of the death sentence for John Richardson, due to be electrocuted that Friday night;[22] the removal of the board of clemency; the provision of an unlimited supply of tobacco; and the removal of Warden Thomas. The last was perhaps the most quixotic.

In response, Attorney General Bettman announced that he would propose the warden's suspension to the governor, with the caveat that "no immediate action would be taken." The warden called the proposal "a giving away on the part of the regularly constituted government to the Red Shirt elements," possibly insinuating that beneath the threatened violence there was communist subterfuge. Moreover, the warden argued that only 10 percent of the inmates "wanted his head."

Between 1:30 and 4:20 Wednesday afternoon a special meeting was hastily convened in the governor's office to discuss Bettman's proposal.[23] The attorney general insisted that the investigation should continue right away and hoped to complete the examination of the day's witnesses in a night session so that the report would be in the governor's hands by Saturday. Following the meeting, Cooper issued a statement forcefully asserting that every "possible effort in the maintenance of order and discipline within the walls of the penitentiary" had been made, but gave no indication that the warden would be suspended.[24] Before the day was out the warden emphasized to the inquiry that he had the full support of Deputy Warden Woodard, who was held in the highest regard by the inmates.

The governor also stayed abreast of the casualty reports, checking to see how the injured were faring at the prison hospital. He ordered a detailed report to be sent to him from the head physicians on site.[25] Cooper also took steps to halt the flow of prisoners into the institution, routing them to local jails until conditions had been restored closer to normal. His instructions were issued after a day of inmate revolt, which had resulted in the transfer of more soldiers to the prison. Tensions seemed to cool when a spokesperson for the convicts made it clear that they would only be engaged in "passive resistance," and by 6 p.m. all was quiet and the convicts began to return to their normal routine of a late afternoon meal before retiring to their cells.

The convicts got to add their voices to the proceedings on Thursday, as relatives of the dead continued to remove the bodies of their loved ones from the temporary morgue at the fairgrounds. A number of remains were still unclaimed, and plans were to bury them the next day during a mass funeral service. All of the inmates who testified declared that more than a half hour elapsed between the discovery of the fire (5:20 p.m.) and the unlocking of the cells (6 p.m.). They also were all of one mind when it came to casting blame on Captain Hall for the loss of life. Most mentioned the fact that Hall had ordered guards to open windows and let in fresh air while keeping the inmates locked up. It didn't help that Hall's strategy backfired when the air rushed in at the bottom level and created a draft that forced the smoke upward, where the convicts on the top two tiers were already dying from the toxic smoke and heat.

Going into the night's session, the theory that an electrical short-circuit had caused the fire was discussed. Chief engineer F. L. Rike, however, pointed out that a short-circuit would have blown out all the fuses and thus cut off the power, which clearly did not occur.

Next to the revelations of staff incompetence and the lack of emergency training, the most damaging testimony had nothing directly to do with the fire and everything to do with the brutal conditions inside the Ohio Penitentiary. Reports came out of the investigation that the warden ruled his charges "with cruelty."[26] Reporters capitalized on the continuing resistance in the prison yard to weigh in on the punitive conditions, which gave convicts a rare opportunity to unite against what they saw as a dictatorial regime.[27]

On Friday, April 25, the last two convicts whose deaths were directly attributable to the fire succumbed to injuries, making the total 320. (Two more deaths would be added after two inmates were accidentally shot in the stockade in the following days.) Although scores still languished in the hospital, no more of them succumbed.

By Friday the mutiny had subsided. Guards were amazed how the demeanor of the men had changed from a "howling mob" that refused to follow orders just the day before. Another about-face in the campaign of passive resistance occurred when eight convicts volunteered to relieve twenty inmates who had been shoveling coal to keep the power house going since the beginning of the fire.

No more inmates testified on Friday, the last scheduled day of testimony, but the guards rehashed their previous statements. A bit of startling new information did come out when guard Hubert L. Richardson, who had been stationed in the upper tiers of the damaged cellblock, testified that the cage door at the center of recriminations was never kept locked. According to Richardson, "the door to the ranges was always kept open until 6 p.m. when night guards came on duty.[28] If this was true, the door had to have been locked *after* the fire broke out, leading to the altercation between the guards. This claim, like many others, was never fully substantiated.

The warden asked to present several witnesses who would refute the charges of brutality leveled against him over the preceding days. Attorney General Bettman, in response, made it clear that the investigation was solely focused on the fire and that the board had no interest in hearing any inmate testimony related to brutality and other fringe issues that had come up from time to time during the inquiry. The warden's son and lawyer, Donald Thomas, a Dayton attorney and former municipal court judge, would have none of it, insisting on refuting the allegations made by various witnesses. The attorney general and Director Griswold relented, agreeing to hear some final witness testimony on Saturday.

On Saturday, Donald Thomas conducted the examination of the witnesses. The first witness was Ray W. Humphreys, editor of the local magazine *Columbus This Week*, who chronicled in detail what he saw from outside the walls from a journalist's perspective.[29]

The next witness, Deputy Warden Woodard, was the first to be grilled about accusations of officer misconduct. He explained the protocol requiring guards to report any acts of violence, whether between guards and prisoners or between inmates. However, he said, it was rare for a prisoner to report another convict for fighting. The prison subculture had strict rules about collaborating with the screws, so Woodard could only answer questions on cases that were reported to him. He supported the warden's contention that unnecessary violence was rare under the current administration.[30]

Woodard was followed by A. T. J. Jenkins, superintendent of the Ohio Reformatory. Thomas asked him how many times he had attended meetings of the

American Prison Congress, and he responded, "Five." It was obvious where this line of questioning was heading. Queried whether, in any conversations that he had had with the heads of various state penal institutions, any of them to his knowledge had fire drills, he replied, "No, sir."[31]

As to the punitive predilections of the warden and the roots of inmate hostility toward him, longtime Ohio Penitentiary prison guard Earl Hofstetter testified that while he had heard prisoners discuss trying to escape from time to time, except for resentment at being confined behind bars, they did not have any great animosity toward the warden.[32] Hofstetter's tenure at the prison had begun a year before Thomas's. He testified that convicts considered the former warden, T. H. B. Jones, in the same manner that they did Thomas.

So close to the end of the proceedings, Hofstetter startled the BOI with his unsolicited testimony that there was actually "a man on fire watch," explaining, "There are two sergeants every night that inspect the buildings, every building in there, where they have been at work. On the night of this fire, there was a special guard on out there besides all those others."[33] In this instance the guard Hubert Richardson was on duty above the G&H blocks. Hofstetter added, "There have been always fire watches on hand." But the question whether there was or was not a specific fire watch was more a semantic debate than reality. Richardson and others were never officially specified as being on *fire duty*. Rather, they had only been tasked with keeping their eyes on the I&K construction as well as any suspicious activity that might portend an escape attempt.

Finally, it was up to Donald Thomas to examine his father, hoping to rebut the damning testimony against him and clarify some of his earlier answers. The warden began his testimony with an expression of "heartfelt sympathy" for relatives and friends of those who perished in the fire, but insisted to the investigators that he had done everything humanly possible to prevent the disaster.[34] Battered by accusations of cruelty and under the threat of suspension, Warden Thomas wasted no time in blaming the legislature for his plight. He insisted that he had been asking for legislation to improve prison conditions since he took over as warden in 1913. More specifically, Thomas asserted that the deaths in G&H blocks were the result of inmates being "quartered in one of the fire traps which the State lawmaking bodies for twelve years have refused to remove." Thomas also heaped criticism on the state's refusal to build new prisons and the 1921 minimum sentence laws enacted by the general assembly "over his objection," which continued to flood the prisons with inmates.[35] He noted that at the last American Prison Association meeting in Toronto, Canada, a resolution was passed that no prison should house more than thirteen hundred prisoners, almost three thousand fewer than he had at the time of the fire.

The warden went to great length defending his prison's preparation at the time of the fire. "I have been attending prison congresses for seventeen years, and I have never heard the matter even broached or spoken of. And if there was ever a place that needs orderly procedure, it is in prison, and that is why we do not yell fire, and start a riot." As he continued, his defensive posture seemed less and less convincing, especially when he suggested that "we have fire drills three or four times a day." He clarified by explaining that the military-style marching of prisoners in and out was ample preparation for responding to an emergency: "I think [it] is about as orderly as you could find."[36]

The BOI established that the administration of Warden Preston Thomas clearly lacked any plans for fighting a prison fire, short of calling on the local fire department. Thomas admitted, "We depend almost entirely on the Columbus Fire Department because we never had a fire here." He added, "They were here in about two minutes." He then probably thought better of his response, admitting to having had "previous fires in the shops," which were protected with "barrels of water with buckets" and extinguishers. The warden insisted that he recently "gave orders" to chief engineer Rike to equip all shops considered fire dangers with the type of extinguishers recommended by the Columbus Fire Department. This had been done before the fire. The fire department had objected to previous extinguishers, "claiming it was hurtful to the eyes," so the warden made sure to conform to its regulations.[37]

Attorney General Bettman asked the beleaguered warden whether any precautions had been taken in advance in case a fire broke out after the convicts were locked up for the night. The warden conceded that despite the measures taken in the industrial and factory buildings, none were made in the cellblocks, which remained wholly dependent on the city fire department. Thomas noted that even in his own residence he didn't have fire extinguishers and depended on the fire department, but he had to admit that obviously, unlike the convicts, he was not locked inside.[38]

Bettman continued to prod the warden as to whether there had ever been a firefighting brigade in the prison. Thomas offered that "We had a few hose and an old wagon, a truck, two wheeled, and we tried to use it on several occasions, and it made the firemen very angry, because they said that they were in the road; they had to take our hose off and put theirs on and it simply stopped them in their work." As a result, the fire department had forbidden the prison staff from using city hydrants, and "they make visitations to the prison for the purpose of inspection of these hydrants."[39] In further questioning, Thomas was asked what exactly happened to the prison fire company. He responded, "I think the wagon broke down several years ago and it became junk—never replaced it . . . it was only a loafing place for prisoners."[40]

It was here that the attorney general missed a chance to examine the decline in safety in the prison over the past half century. Warden Thomas must have known that there had indeed been an organized firefighting brigade years earlier. In fact, a quarter century before the fatal fire, the Ohio Penitentiary fire department was held in enough esteem to be chronicled in one of Ohio's leading newspapers.[41]

Thomas admitted there had never been any discussion on how to get the men out in case of a fire, adding that he had "never heard of a penitentiary or prison having fire drills."[42] He was well aware that other prisons had systems where all cells could be unlocked at one time in a given cellblock, and that there were other types as well, rattling off the double-block, snap-lock, and key-lock systems. He offered that, in any case, a lever-control system would be too expensive for the Ohio prison system. The warden also claimed to have visited more than a dozen prisons, which all had general locking systems with old-fashioned keys and front tumblers.[43] Sing Sing, he noted, still used the old single locking system. It seems, from his testimony and other conversations related to prison-locking devices, that Thomas never really explored any new locking devices and systems.[44]

The questioning of Columbus fire chief A. E. Nice by the BOI offers some valuable insight into the relationship between the fire department and the prison's nonexistent fire-safety program. The report paints an unflattering portrait of the city fire department. Chief Nice recounted having visited the prison many times since he took charge of the Columbus Fire Department in 1926. On these occasions he usually focused on fire-hydrant inspection, but admitted having "not done it in a while." Defensively, Nice told the Board that the state did not always pay attention to recommendations, although, as it turned out, he had never made any himself, saying that he "couldn't remember making any as chief." Furthermore, while he had inspected hydrants, he admitted having never inspected any buildings.[45]

The fire chief was asked whether he thought the institution was a safe place to keep over four thousand men locked up. He responded in the negative, stating that he had known for some time that the "buildings are old and of an inflammable nature." Asked whether prison fire drills might have come in handy, he said it would have been a good idea, "if you could find someone to drill." It was at this point all parties agreed that while there had once been a prison fire company inside, there was none at the time of the fire. Nice continued to parry with the investigators, telling them that he was "never instructed to go inside the building or inspect any part of it—only hydrants, to see which ones were in working order and not blocked."[46]

Most inmates expressed some trepidation before testifying. It was a long-standing tenet of prison culture that convicts did not cooperate with the authorities or testify against fellow convicts. Others worried that testifying against any prison authorities might negatively influence future parole possibilities. Pat Mullins, who had been locked up for fourteen months and still had another six to seven years to go, told investigators that because he had a short sentence he was wary of testifying, particularly if he had to return to his cell "without protection."[47] A Canadian, Mullins, who had his family in town and expected to go before the clemency board, said he was "under the impression" he might get a break and be sent back to Canada. Facing the prospect of testifying, Mullins was damned if he did and damned if he didn't. Testifying against prison officials could set back his release date. Moreover, if he testified he might be treated as a snitch when he returned to prison, thereby facing the wrath of a prison subculture that looked harshly on any type of collaboration with authorities.

Reporters had mentioned that during the fire inquiry and in previous probes into conditions, convicts were told they could "speak right out. There is nothing to fear. Speak as freely as you want." However, these promises usually proved false. According to one source, "This mealy mouthed assurance was given five years ago." Journalists who went back and searched the convict records found that those who spoke freely "did not fare well" and were punished for serious breach of rules. "Silly convicts who followed this advice" found themselves in "standing up cages" and had their food portions cut.[48]

Many of those following the inquiry were curious why Warden Thomas did not personally attend the hearings of other witnesses. However, it could be easily explained by the fact that it was recognized that witnesses might be less than truthful in their testimony if they saw the warden in the courtroom. Many blamed the attorney general for this decision, but at the end of the inquiry Director Griswold took responsibility, figuring the warden's presence might put "undue influence on the witnesses, guards or other prisoners."[49] His reasoning was sound, and the warden had agreed to go along with it.

The BOI revealed some interesting exchanges between the warden and guards Little and Baldwin in the early morning hours following the fire. The warden was probably well aware that his regime and leadership would be questioned in the days to come. He met this head on, lining up favorable testimony from Little and Baldwin, hoping to ensure they would testify that he had ordered the guards to let the prisoners out at the first hint of fire.

Sometime before dawn on the Tuesday after the fire, as Little was preparing to go home, he was called up to the warden's office by the warden's son Don, who congratulated him for his work. Don told him, "This is a terrible thing, wasn't it?" Little said yes, but couldn't resist adding that he would "never would know how bad it was unless he was up there and actually saw it." The only response the warden's son could muster was "No, I guess not."[50] Little was told to sit down, that that the warden wanted to see him. Shortly afterward the warden came in and told him he wanted to shake his hand for the good work, and how glad he was that he "had a man that could hold his head and do a little bit."

Five minutes later Little was joined by William Baldwin, who had been told after his release from the hospital that the warden wanted to see him as well. The warden asked Baldwin how his lungs were, and he responded, "I am alright with the exception that I'm afraid of pneumonia is all."[51] Investigators asked him whether he was afraid of losing his job over telling the truth, and he replied, "No." In fact, after being fired on questionable grounds the prior year, Baldwin told them that he "would never cover up for the warden."[52] Baldwin recounted that Thomas congratulated him for his actions before asking him whether he "heard me when I told you to get keys and release those men?" Baldwin said he did. This must have pleased the warden, who told him, "Fine work."[53]

Curiously, when Baldwin and Little later testified before the inquiry, Little contradicted Baldwin, telling the investigators that he never heard the warden ask Baldwin about the keys and releasing the men. This was never explained, but perhaps when they testified later in the week their memories were a bit murky, especially after they had both survived near-death experiences.

The investigators were concerned that the guards might have been coached by someone from the warden's office on how they should testify. Both were asked how much time they spent in the warden's office, as well as what was said. There was some debate over how long they were in the warden's office, with times ranging from ten to thirty minutes. Little was sure it wasn't more than fifteen minutes. He said he just sat there and smoked. "I don't force conversation with anyone I am working for at no time."[54] He was also sure than Baldwin came in five minutes after he got there. The warden was in the room only briefly. The guards left together and were met at the bottom of the stairs by some photographers who wanted to take their pictures. This done, they went to Deputy Woodard's office and changed into some dry clothes. Until 7 a.m. they "rambled around" looking at "the ruins" and taking in what had transpired just the night before.

The warden made a forceful argument for his decision to position himself outside the walls during the fire, insisting that the governor of the state and the warden of the penitentiary "should not be inside the prison" during these types of events. Indeed, he noted, "they are the only two people who can order the gates opened" and let prisoners outside the walls. He cited examples of inmates taking wardens hostage to start breakouts at other institutions, including the case of Warden Jennings of Auburn Prison, who had to be rescued by state troopers and was badly injured. Likewise, at Colorado Prison the warden was outside the walls during the bloody 1929 riot, when inmates took guards hostage and demanded the gates be opened, but were refused and killed their hostages. There were always plots and schemes for "delivery," or escapes.[55]

On Wednesday, April 23, two days after the fire, the warden finally ventured into the prison yard, walking first across the yard to Deputy Woodard's office and then to the chapel, which had recently lodged dozens of dead inmates. He must have kept up a swift gait as he was greeted with jeers and derisive catcalls. At one point something was said that "brought the warden's head erect." He watched the prisoners for a moment and, with a word of encouragement from one of the chaplains, continued his walk across the yard.

Beginning on April 22, the BOI met in almost continuous session for ten days (five days hearing witnesses). During the final days of the month, the members prepared their final report for the governor on the fire's origins and the massive loss of life. Anyone who expected earth-shattering revelations would have been sorely disappointed by the board's findings.

On May 1, 1930, the BOI submitted its final report to Governor Cooper and Director of Public Welfare Hal H. Griswold. Although it had failed to establish directly the cause of the fire, the board asserted that "there was no evidence which leads the Board to the conclusion that the fire was either of incendiary or spontaneous combustion origin."[56] Moreover, there was "strong circumstantial evidence that the fire was caused by defective wiring."[57]

The BOI summarized its findings in four strongly worded conclusions. First off, it suggested that the "probable cause of the fire" was the result of "temporary lighting arrangements installed on the day of the fire" on the I&K cellblocks, which were regarded as "improper and dangerous both as to type and manner of installation."[58] Deficient construction security practices came under scrutiny, particularly with the revelation that it had become customary to leave the lighting equipment on after construction ended on I&K. Once construction ceased for the day, there was no policy for providing guards or patrol until the crew came back the following day. This omission was compounded by the fact that not only was there no fireproof partition between I&K and the eight hundred men in G&H, but an inflammable wooden roof replete with wood-supporting timbers extended over the entire block. Magnifying the potential for disaster was the fact that except in prison factories, there was no firefighting equipment in any of the cellblocks.

The second finding pointed at the fact the electrical current had not been turned off, despite an absence of oversight or security once the workday ended. Especially biting was the charge that there was no general plan of organization to meet an emergency of fire. The warden had admitted that rather than depending on some general plan, he relied on the guards "to use their common sense." Moreover, there were no established fire rules for the organization of guards or instructions in event of emergency.[59]

The third finding blasted the "failure after the emergency arose to place someone in command of the situation at the cell house which was on fire." It went on to focus on the lack of an organized plan to respond to a fire in a cell house and the delay in transmitting the fire alarm, as well as confusion over how to handle prisoners—all of which contributed to loss of life.[60]

The fourth finding noted that the "failure to designate someone after the emergency arose to take command of situation at burning cell house . . . directly contributed to cause the loss of life."[61]

Missing from the final report were any references to the claims of brutality brought by inmate witnesses against the warden and his regime. During the hearings several inmates brought up tangential information regarding the poor stewardship of the warden, tales of administrative brutality and the general conditions of the prison. However, the investigators were unwilling to take the bait and would later comment that the inquiry was focused on "fact finding, not administration." The closest the board came to casting judgment was recognizing "the deplorable inadequacy and antiquated condition of the penitentiary," and that "comprehensive remedial steps are imperative." The BOI members explained that they were providing the governor with a "narrative summary of evidence setting forth circumstances, conclusions on its causes," and any findings of negligence. Ultimately, they would leave it to the governor to make any recommendations and to apportion blame.[62]

But this strategy did not put these accusations to rest. Thanks to reporters who covered the hearings and had spoken to a number of the inmates, prisoners hoped they would relay their complaints to the proper authorities and to the public. The BOI chastised the convicts for speaking to the press. Officials felt that this only confused the issues and offered a "false equivalency between their actions and the deficiencies of the penitentiary." Moreover, the BOI did not want their findings of negligence to be confused with aiding prisoner demands to have the prison closed.[63]

In its final comments to the governor, the BOI recognized that it was not a technical board. Perhaps this was the stumbling block that kept the committee from discovering the direct cause of the fire. But it was more likely that no direct cause was found because there was no direct evidence linking the fire's origins to any specific cause, whether incendiarism, spontaneous combustion, or defective wiring.

MUTINY IN WHITE CITY

The War is Over.

　—*Governor Cooper, Tuesday, April 28*

No one can see weakness much quicker than the man in gray.

　—*"James Winning"*

　　　In the twenty-four hours following the fire, one reporter noted that "the penitentiary yards resembled an armed camp after a pitched battle."[1] A prison mutiny was indeed under way, but officials were confident they could suppress it using what were described as "persuasive methods." However, sporadic threats of mass violence convinced Warden Thomas that the only way to control any form of inmate insurrection was with force.

　　　The increasing pandemonium within the walls was only made worse by the release of thirteen hundred convicts locked up in the whitewashed ABCD cell-blocks, better known as "White City." Once out of their cells, the prisoners were joined by several hundred G&H survivors, who had formerly been housed in the prison chapel (which lacked any door-locking mechanisms). Making matters worse was the release of almost eight hundred convicts from the E&F dormitory. This meant that nearly twenty-four hundred convicts were running loose inside the prison walls.[2]

As previously noted, at approximately 8:30 on Monday night, incendiary devices went off in the cotton mill, in a dormitory, and then in the chapel, just nine hundred feet from the site of the original G&H blaze, which was now under control. The secondary fires were quickly extinguished. At 8:45 p.m. a company of regular infantry from Fort Hayes entered the prison as rescuers and other volunteers continued to rush into the prison compound carrying oxygen tanks and medical supplies. But it would take until midnight for a combination of the Ohio National Guard, army troops, police, and prison guards to establish a semblance of order.

With so many angry inmates roaming the prison grounds, the forces of order stayed on duty throughout the night. By 9:45 Monday evening, conditions became so tense that Columbus police chief Harry E. French ordered all female staff, which now included a large number of female nurses, to leave the grounds immediately "to insure their safety."[3]

By 4 the next morning, except for several hundred inmates wandering the corridors of White City, most of the convicts seemed to have worn themselves out and gone to bed. Officials were soon made aware of rumors traveling through the prison grapevine of a mass breakout set for 6 a.m. By then, it was hoped there would be plenty of reinforcements. More than seven hundred National Guard troops en route to Columbus from southern and central Ohio were expected to arrive by daylight, augmenting the force already on guard.[4] They would be needed. Additional guardsmen were stationed and machine guns mounted at the wagon and railroad stockade gates. But 6 a.m. passed uneventfully, and another rumor had been safely put to rest.

It had been four days since the night of the fire and passive resistance in White City continued, invigorated by calls to remove Warden Thomas. By most accounts the resistance became more organized over those days, with one observer conceding, "The organization conducting [the resistance] was strengthened with the naming of a convict committee and the announcement of rules and bylaws, which emphasized that there would be no vengeance or escape plot."[5]

A committee of more than one thousand convicts elected a "Committee of Forty for Facts" in an attempt to jumpstart "an agenda of prison reform."[6] Under the direction of the Committee of Forty, chosen, according to one Ohio prison historian, "for brains, not brawn," the mutinous convicts agreed not to escape or riot, to eschew violence, to decline being locked in their cells "until they were convinced they would be safe from fire," to stop shaving, and most importantly, to work together toward the removal of the warden.[7]

When the governor announced on Thursday that he would support the warden, it sapped the committee of its vigor, and on Friday the inmates accepted the governor's judgment and the prisoner mutiny ended for the time being. But the rumor mill was still active, keeping authorities on their toes. Prison officials received a letter from a former convict claiming that a small group of prisoners had been smuggling in gasoline for some time. The fire marshal investigated the claim but found there was nothing to it.[8] That same day the death count rose from 318 to 320.

At least forty unclaimed victims were buried in three local cemeteries on April 26. The coffins were transported to the burial sites in a funeral procession accompanied by the 13th Battalion of the Columbus Naval Reserve. As passive resistance continued inside the prison complex, two thousand mourners paid their last respects to the dead. Each grave was "marked by a metal disc" bearing the convict's accounting number retrieved from prison records.[9] That same day, the BOI had finished hearing witnesses and was preparing its findings for the governor's office. Meanwhile, the mutiny continued among some segments of the convict population through Saturday evening, April 26.

By Sunday, April 27, almost a week since the fire, it was a time for reflection. Memorial services were held for the fire victims at the Ohio Penitentiary's Catholic and Protestant chapels and Jewish synagogue. With thousands of prisoners still on the loose, separated from downtown Columbus only by the prison walls, local residents were becoming increasingly anxious. This did not prevent curious throngs of locals from traipsing toward the old pen to observe the activities of their presumed protectors, which now included the National Guard, Naval Reserve troops, and local police officers.

Later in the day, convicts got wind of a plan to increase the number of guards on Monday in hopes of stemming the passive resistance to oust the warden. Once the prisoners in White City heard this, they unleashed their rage on their cells, destroying locks and tearing off cell doors. The mutiny was quickly subdued by a combination of coaxing and quantities of coffee. However, it soon became clear that total order in White City would not be restored until the locks and doors had been repaired. Most of the locks were inoperable, having been crammed with paper, tobacco, and other products, or just completely torn off.[10]

Well into Sunday evening, Warden Thomas convened a meeting with Colonel Robert Haubrich of the National Guard, Chief of Police Harry French, Deputy Warden Woodard, new night captain H. E. Laukart, and William Duffy, the Columbus service director. Filling in for seventy-one-year-old Captain John Hall, Laukart had visited the prison sporadically in recent days and reported that except for White City, the institution had returned to the conditions that existed before the fire.[11]

Throughout the weekend and into Monday, with most of the leaders of the mutiny transferred to the London Prison Farm, the prisoners seemed to have settled down, and few expected a rerun of the past week's mayhem. As it turned out, the resourceful convicts "apparently found new leaders." Still seething at the past week's events and the continued presence of the warden, inmates revolted again early on Monday. Officials supplemented their forces by rushing a detail of 150 Columbus policemen into the prison yard. Meanwhile, National Guardsmen mounted machine guns on the walls outside, and the newly identified "leaders of the revolt were gathered up and either placed in solitary confinement or transferred to other institutions."[12] Tear gas bombs and gas masks were then delivered inside the walls for emergency duty, and forty-four new men were added to the staff of guards and others. The most recalcitrant inmates went without breakfast and were threatened with missing more meals if they did not get back to their normal routine.[13]

The daily troubles at the Ohio Penitentiary were a continued source of worry for Columbus residents, one of whom, local attorney Orville R. Carson, wrote the governor a week after the fire, offering the services of a group of veterans "for the duration of the 'Passive Resistance War.'" Carson assured the governor that "all our comrades have had war experience and I assure your honor that no prisoner can issue to them any orders nor can any prisoner spit in the face of any, if said prisoner's orders aren't fulfilled, without some very serious opposition. These boys have taken many prisoners in war against tremendous odds. They can again do it." The four veterans who signed the letter included Carson, a chiropractor, an examiner for the city civil service, and a sign painter.[14] The governor expressed his gratitude for the offer, writing back, "We feel that our officers in the National Guard and the officers at the Penitentiary have established a mandate of the State in the control of the prisoners and that additional service will not be necessary." He added, "Nevertheless, I am very grateful to you and we will keep your offer in mind in case an additional emergency should arise."[15]

By late Monday afternoon "the forces of law and order" seemed to have gained control again, the prisoners having apparently worn themselves out once more during the long hours of tumult. The convicts who had been permitted to eat breakfast returned from the mess hall and "either fell into their bunks or sought diversion in card games."[16]

Warden Thomas held firm in his insistence that inmates get back to work as soon as possible; none had done so since the fire. But the convicts held their ground as well. They said they would return to the shops, but working was out of the question. "They can kill us first," they said.[17]

As Monday wore on, the convicts in White City seemed to become more intimidating. The warden conferred with Colonel Haubrich, who declared that he would recommend to state Director of Public Welfare Griswold that the unruly cons be removed from the idle house and either sent to other institutions or confined in some type of stockade nearby until the damaged cell doors and locks in White City were repaired.[18] Apparently this leaked out to inmates, further antagonizing the more mutinous among them. Some suspect that this perhaps contributed to the attack on the guardroom the following morning. Outsiders and those unfamiliar with the prison might not have realized that most of the cells had a working radio. This meant that on the night of the fire they would have been listening to local WAIU. Not only did it help them the night of the fire, but in the following days it would reveal what were supposed to be clandestine plans byand contribute to the mutiny that followed.

When the mutiny began Colonel Haubrich figured he could control information by refusing to allow the convicts to have newspapers. As one reporter put it, Haubrich "did not want them to know of plans that were being formulated for their separation and transfer to other prisons. The convicts in White City originally barricaded themselves in their cells and were probably glued to their little radios. If they were, then "they had advance knowledge on everything," since WAIU continued to broadcast from inside the prison. One of the unexplained aspects of the mutiny is why officials allowed it to continue to broadcast (to the convicts) during the two weeks following the fire. But radio broadcast technology was just one more new device that prison administrators would have to contend with in the years to come.[19]

During the day, the administration complied with several requests from the inmates in exchange for improved comportment. The first demand was that the police detail be removed from the prison yard; they refused to eat until this was done. Thomas relented and had the "bluecoats withdrawn." However, the inmates' promised tranquility "was not forthcoming," as they became "more disorderly than ever." To make matters worse, the inmates in the White City idle house demanded to be served their afternoon meals in their cells. Ever the disciplinarian, the warden responded "that they could starve in their cells if they would not obey orders." It took the more practiced hand of diplomacy of Deputy Warden Woodard to coax the prisoners into keeping quiet and taking their meals in the Ohio Penitentiary mess hall. The convicts asked for assurance that they would be returned safely to their cells after their noon meal, which Woodard granted. Perhaps an ulterior motive for getting them out of their cells was to give officers an opportunity to search their cells for weapons and other contraband or for any evidence of "portending escape plots" while the cons were busy eating.[20]

Early Monday evening, Warden Thomas announced that there would be no more bargaining with the convicts.[21] Observers expected that night's activities to "bring about a showdown." Plans were in the offing to finally clamp down on the White City resistance. Various types of protective equipment, including maces, were delivered to the administrative building in the event they were required for crowd control. One observer claimed to have witnessed the warden packing a brace of pistols as he returned to his offices after the long day of meetings. It was common knowledge that his daughter Amanda was not averse to carrying a "six shooter" or at least making sure to be within arm's reach of one while working in her father's office.[22]

On Monday night, thirty-one National Guardsmen carrying loaded rifles and tear gas bombs were sent into the Ohio Penitentiary to subdue the inmates in a tunnel that connected the White City cellblocks to the prison's power house. Officials were alerted to this turn of events after the convicts managed to cut of the power supply to the lights in White City.

Seven soldiers, led by Colonel Haubrich, made their way into the tunnel as the rest of the guardsmen positioned themselves in the guardroom with fixed bayonets. It turned out that the convicts had managed to cut through a concrete wall to reach the tunnel, but they were gone by the time the soldiers arrived. The warden issued a final ultimatum, asserting that "there will be no more bargaining" with the convicts, and issued a "shoot to kill order."[23] As he met with Colonel Haubrich and several other prison officials, word came that the inmates had apparently made it back into the tunnel. With the cellblocks plunged into darkness, firemen cut two holes in the roof above, allowing them to lower down floodlights that shone over White City.

Anger continued to fester among the inmates into Tuesday morning, April 28. The White City rebels had apparently become "emboldened by the fact that they had disregarded all prison rules and orders for a week" as they decided to "suddenly mutiny."[24] Sometime between 10 and 10:15 a.m., violence broke out, with scores of prisoners bombarding the guardroom adjacent to the White City cellblocks with bolts, nails, and anything else that could be turned into a missile.[25] The guardroom was a strategic target for the prisoners, since it was the only thing separating the rampaging White City inmates from the main entrance to the prison. Surrounded by heavy steel bars, the room's glaring weakness was the glass-and-wood wall partition that separated the guards from the hell-bent inmates in the White City idle house.

Club-carrying mutineers shattered the glass in the guardroom door and its small windows, slightly injuring guard Willis Floyd. The convicts then began to batter down the door leading from the idle house to the guardroom. Tearing their cell doors from their hinges, they used them as battering rams to break down the door leading from the cell block. Newspaper reporters had a field day dramatizing the confrontation at the guardroom door that followed. One account described how "prison guards rained bullets into the prisoners' ranks and ended the attack on the barred doors of 'white city.'"[26] Another reported that "guards sent 200 bullets down the cell block runway."[27] In actuality, when the guards did fire at the onrushing convicts, they were deliberately shooting warning shots over their heads. While an estimated two hundred rounds were unleashed on the unruly inmates, most were fired blindly down the cell-block runway. Following the first volley, by most accounts, the convicts dropped to the floor, then regrouped for a second rush at the guardroom. Guns blazed once more, with some guards exhausting their ammunition pouches.

A local resident named Forrest Richmond, who had come to the prison to see if he could be of any service, just happened to be in the guardroom when the attack took place. Soon after the skirmish, he would write a letter to Governor Myles Cooper, giving his perspective of the recent mutiny. He recounted that after the guards got low on ammunition he had been asked to run to the warden's office for "amunation" for a .38 Special, "only to learn they were out of that size." His ears perked up when he "heard a trusty handing out shot gun shells tell another guard they were out of 44's" as well. By Richmond's account, the guards took turns running into the office to grab a handful of shells "at a time."[28] It is hard to reconcile his account with such a short-lived event, but it should be remembered that the warden's office was close to the guardroom and that he only made one run to get ammunition.

Within a half hour the so-called "uprising" or "mutiny" was over. Miraculously, no inmates or guards were killed, but inmate George Tonoff, serving three to fifteen years for burglary, was shot in the right lung, and Jewell Joffa, doing a seven-year stretch for larceny, took a slug in the leg.[29]

To the uninformed the sequence of events might seem like a spur-of-the-moment decision to escape from the idle house through the guardroom adjacent to the main prison entrance (located on the west side of White City). In actuality, radio broadcasts and inmate rumors had lit up the prison grapevine over the past couple of days, informing residents of the idle house that they were to be transferred to other jails or temporary facilities while their lodgings were being repaired. The inmates, however, were not privy to the fact that this plan had been rejected as unfeasible. But nonetheless, they chafed at having to vacate the idle house, even temporarily. Other inmates heard rumblings of another plan, one in which the prison baseball diamond and a warehouse was being converted into temporary stockades.

There were several reports of an inmate firing a revolver at the guards during the attack, though this was never substantiated. Forrest Richmond's letter to the governor, sent April 30, contains interesting details related to this claim. Richmond informed the governor that he had gone to the Ohio Penitentiary at 6 a.m. Tuesday morning to see if he could be of service. He stayed there throughout the day and evening. He reported, "I was, as far as I know, the only civilian in the Guard room when the so-called riot took place." He remained there until order was restored, "except for two trips I made for amunation [sic]." He was certain that "there was no shooting from the prison block, either before or after the guards were shooting."[30]

Richmond's account challenges several of the accepted versions of the White City crisis. He claimed that he had been pressured by several journalists "to insist" that he witnessed National Guardsmen firing at the inmates. However, he stuck to his story, maintaining that the only people firing from the guardroom were "four guards in the room [who] took positions against the West wall of the room, facing the trouble armed." He also noted that there was no machine-gun fire and that the machine gun was only brought into the room after all firing had ceased. Moreover, contrary to assertions that two guards had been taken hostage, Richmond said that "the two unarmed guards in the White City at the time were not held as hostages. They came running out from their cells into which they had gone at the lower end of the block, and ran to the gate."

Casting further doubt on the official version of the events in White City, Richmond also commented that there had been "no second charge of the prisoners." If there was any action that resembled a second charge, it was probably "the few [convicts] who broke part of the glass out, and then a large group made a rush towards the open place. Guards broke much of the glass out to get a better shooting location, and seemingly to save cutting their hands."[31]

Contrary to the warden's claim that he had issued orders during the fracas, Forrest insisted, "Neither Warden Thomas or his son [Don], or any other person, gave any orders within my hearing during the fiasco." Moreover, he lauded the guards for their preparation "for a real attack as they were during the fire. Each used his own judgment." Despite little or no command structure, they were able to repel the convicts, leading the witness to comment, "During the shooting no one person was in direct charge of any one of the three gates leading out."[32]

After less than a half hour the inmates figured their escape would never work, especially considering that they would have to surmount a perimeter of well-armed National Guard, police, and prison guards if they made it through the guardroom to the outside. Colonel Haubrich next went to the idle house doorway and spoke with several convicts. He found that most had returned to their cells and reported all was quiet. On his arrival at the guardroom, Colonel Haubrich, bringing in reinforcements and a machine gun, ordered "no more firing [by the guards] unless attacked direct." He ordered all of the guards out and placed his men at the three gates. They were under strict orders not to fire their weapons "under any circumstances, unless ordered to do so."

During the mutiny in the White City, inmates took advantage of the situation to free seven condemned men from the death house. After having a brief taste of freedom, by Tuesday night all seven had been recaptured and transferred to the city jail for safekeeping.[33]

Reinforcements rushed to the penitentiary included four more companies of guardsmen: Company A from Marietta, Company B from Marion, and Company L from Athens, and a howitzer platoon from Ironton, armed with one-pounders and a trench mortar for good measure. They would join the five hundred guardsmen already at the Ohio Penitentiary.

Less than two hours after the shooting ended, convicts were marched in "orderly fashion" between lines of state troopers and guardsmen to the mess halls. Meanwhile, a machine gun mounted on the chapel building surveyed the marching inmates. Here Colonel Haubrich established the National Guard headquarters inside the chapel.

Although martial law had not been declared, the governor placed control of the prison in the hands of Colonel Haubrich and his five National Guard units. While the warden remained in office, he was merely a spectator. This probably cheered up the mutineers, who had demanded his ouster since the night of the fire. Governor Cooper had asserted in no uncertain terms that "the control of the Ohio Penitentiary will not get out of hand again." Haubrich relayed the message to anyone listening that "we are going to run things here. We intend to take the revolters out to eat shortly; and then they will return to their cells."[34]

In the aftermath of the White City mutiny it was decided that it might be safer to relieve the much-detested prison guards from duty and allow the guardsmen to take over operation of the prison. Within days they would finish erecting a tent stockade and surrounding the auto tag building with barbed wire. By nightfall a detachment of seven hundred guardsmen controlled the situation and officially pronounced the scene quiet, with the caveat that the institution "still seethed with the spirit of mutiny."[35]

A number of observers described the recent turn of events at the Ohio Penitentiary as "a situation without precedent in Ohio." Once the mutiny had ended on Tuesday, April 29, officials could survey the damage to the cellblocks. It was estimated that it would take at least thirty days to repair the locks and doors. Once the prison and the White City were secure, soldiers completed the building of the barbed-wire stockade on the prison baseball field. Eighteen-foot telephone poles would be sunk into the ground and wrapped with barbed wire; machine-gun crews would be placed to protect the barricades.[36]

Once the convicts agreed to vacate their building, the location of the earlier mutiny, the prison seemed engulfed in rare silence. Although the barred windows of the edifice fronted a busy Columbus street, one reporter noticed there "was no sound" coming from this usually rowdy group of inmates, who "could be seen packing their little valises with toilet articles and other belongings."[37] At 5 p.m. the inmates were ordered to come out of the building. Covered by armed guards, several minutes passed before they came out carrying their valises. "In their uniforms of sheddy [sic] gray they strode quickly across the yard to the mess hall."[38] Once they were out, the door to the now empty idle house was locked behind them.

The building might have been vacated for the time being, but few observers could miss "two banners with crude drawings of pigs that were stretched over the bars of the ancient cell block of the crumbling old prison." On one of them inmates used charcoal to print "P. E. Thomas, Murderer." The other said "Stop-Fed WAIU Lies," which contemptuously targeted the aforementioned local radio station that broadcast weekly from the prison and that prisoners felt gave biased coverage of the "progress of the mutiny."[39]

On Tuesday night militiamen preparing the stockade on the baseball field could be seen swinging hammers and wielding shovels "as if in preparation for war."[40] The plan was to build two enclosures. Eight hundred of the "well disposed" prisoners would be lodged in tents in the major stockade on the baseball field, or transferred to other state prisons,[41] while almost seven hundred of the worst malefactors, still "in rebellious spirit," would be moved to an old automobile tag warehouse, around which a barricade would be erected. Once completed and enclosed with barbed wire both locations would have "deadlines," where the National Guard marked lines that prisoners were forbidden to cross under penalty of death.[42]

On Wednesday night, under the direction of the National Guard, the more compliant inmates were marched to the completed stockade after their evening meal. There were no incidents. Each convict was checked for weapons; only several penknives were confiscated. Once WC was emptied, prison guards uncovered the beginning of a hole in the basement leading toward the warden's residence. Near the hole was a six-inch crowbar.[43] Clearly, the inmates had been working overtime on tunnels as the pandemonium outside covered their activities.

Inmates were promised they would be allowed to return to their old quarters once the cells had been repaired. But officials made it clear that they would need to conduct themselves according to regulations or "take their chances of going to a morgue."[44] Plans were for the guardsmen to stay on duty until the White City cellblock was under control, which was estimated to take from two weeks to a month. Once the militiamen entered the prison, the regular prison guards were withdrawn, but they were kept on standby, ready to return to their posts temporarily when it came time to feed the prisoners after dark.[45]

Once the convicts had been removed from White City, prison officials could finally get a good look inside. They found a scene of "wanton destruction and wild disorder." However, they also found out that not all of the 1,050 convicts held in its 484 cells had taken part in the rebellion. The inspectors found that several inmates, after their cell locks had been torn off by mutinous inmates, had locked themselves into their own cells using bits of chain and padlocks "obtained somewhere in the institution."

Visitors to White City, several of whom were expecting to view antiquated buildings, were surprised to find that every cell "had plumbing facilities" and was well lighted and ventilated, and that the cell doors were made of "grilled iron instead of sheet metal." After observers witnessed the cellblock's stopped sewer drains that flooded the cellar, plumbing fixtures smashed with brass latch bars, and the stripping off of most of the doors in the lower tiers, one judged that the "inmates must have been impelled by what prison workers call 'jail madness.'"

The remnants of attempts to carve out several escape tunnels did not really amount to much. Any attempt to tunnel through the basement was hindered by flooding, although inmates piled mattresses on the water in an attempt to soak it up. Higher up in the ranges, inmates had cut their way through a quarter-inch-thick steel sheet in the back of a cell in the fifth tier. The tunnel was supposed to reach an airshaft leading to the slate-and-wood roof. Evidently it was here that the most progress was made. One account described how a drill and saw had been utilized to cut three sides of a two-foot square into the metal wall, which was then pried back so that it was wide enough for inmates to pass through. However, this tunnel was never used. The escape artists recognized that once they passed through the hole "rifles would have spoken at the first show of a head."

As the transfer of prisoners and the final touches to the stockade were completed, authorities offered evidence of the potential for bloody violence over the past week. In the chapel, where prisoners from the "worst sections" of the prison were initially confined, they had found a number of improvised weapons, including sledgehammers, knives, picks, and several screwdrivers. All were exhibited for reporters and officials. Investigators searching through White City also found a motley collection of rudely crafted weapons, including knives, bludgeons, and blackjacks. Most had been fashioned from locks and wires. While inspecting the Idle House, Ohio National Guardsmen also uncovered a still, "containing two gallons of potent liquor," hidden in a radio cabinet. One reporter suggested that "this is where the prisoners received much of their 'courage' in defying the guards."[46]

Quiet prevailed in the prison complex for several days. On Saturday, May 3, the inmates were described as "still sullen and stubborn" but "submissive to the military rule invoked."[47] Almost five hundred convicts had returned to their normal work schedules by then, and the numbers were increasing. Though there was still an undercurrent of unrest in the prison, the resistance seemed to have petered out.[48]

On Monday, May 5, the "construction of a steel-reinforced concrete slab roof over G and H cellblocks" was proceeding under the watchful eye of Hal Griswold, state director of public welfare. Griswold announced that work had also started on rebuilding the I&K cellblocks. He made sure that everyone knew that the new reinforced roof, once completed, would extend over the four cellblocks.

One of the many construction firms offering bids to build the new roof and fix the cellblocks was the Fries and Son Steel Construction and Engineering Co., out of Covington, Kentucky. Governor Cooper deemed their bid too high, saying that the expenditures quoted would be "an amount in excess of additional cost of the entire block." The governor cited alternative strategies, such as utilizing "the cell fronts as now intact and proceed[ing] with the lock repairs on the individual basis, rather than the modern unit system, such as was contemplated in the bids."[49] It was fairly clear that the governor was more inclined toward saving money than modernizing the facility, and that once again, if possible, older buildings and infrastructure would be repurposed in lieu of substantial new construction.

Of the greatest concern at this point was replacing the roof. The George Rackle and Sons Company, one of the firms that placed a bid, had a reputation as the leading company in the area in the manufacture and erection of artificial stonework. But the governor rejected their bid, saying that it seemed "wise to construct the roof of pre-gypsum tile, in place of concrete." Doing this would enable "the use of lighter steel and [give] what is considered to be the same protection at a lesser cost."[50]

The convict leaders of the postfire mutiny were still housed in the tent city. Sixty-six mutineers who had refused to work were in solitary confinement on a bread-and-water regimen.[51] Late Wednesday night (May 7) and into the wee hours of Thursday morning, smoke once more filled the air. Convicts had begun burning an estimated fifty tents in the stockade. Prisoners on the periphery of the stockade "stood outside the barbed wire fence and laughed as their canvas cells were licked up in flames." Apparently not a lot of thought had gone into this action. Prison officials decided against trying to put it out, fearing a prison break if the gate was opened to let fire apparatus into the walls.

In response to the arson, a machine gun was moved to a more strategic location in case inmates tried to break out. According to one reporter, unruly convicts ran amok within the tent city, armed with "paper firebrands" as they set fire to the rest of the "canvas shelters." It didn't take long for eighty-seven of the eighty-eight tents to be consumed by fire as "surly convicts stood by and watched." The cons refused to help until the National Guard threatened them.

The stockade remained quiet until around 6 a.m. Thursday morning, when the sound of gunfire broke out. Bullets from a machine gun mounted in front of the chapel "carried death and injury into the dormitory through a barred window." A guardsman, not realizing the weapon was loaded, accidentally fired it while he was working on it.[52] Initially it was thought that only one man was wounded—African American inmate Ernest Warren, who was expected to recover. However, it turned out two other African American convicts, Albert Freeman and James W. Ross from Cuyahoga County, both serving long prison terms, had been killed as they slept in the dormitory, "where the better element of prisoners were confined."[53] The two men had been injured and narrowly escaped death in the Easter Monday fire and had been released from the hospital several days earlier. There were evidently no repercussions for the guard, who commented that he "regretted the shooting very much," but noted that such accidents "cannot be helped.'"[54] The deaths of Freeman and Ross increased the number of deaths attributed to the fire to the accepted final count of 322.

On Thursday night, May 8, the tent arson left scores of convicts who had been housed in the eighty-eight tents, pending repairs to their cellblocks, with "only ground cover." Some inmates used their ingenuity to create shelters of improvised "pup tents," made from "sections of burned tents, blankets and other bed clothes." But prison officials had little sympathy for the convicts, who had first destroyed their cells and now their tent encampment, and had no plans to replace the tents. The prisoners would have to sleep in the open until the cellblocks were repaired.

Prison authorities and National Guardsmen had a devil of a time figuring out the identities of many of the stockade prisoners. When asked to identify themselves, "prisoners for the most part refused to answer." Many had swapped shirts during the recent disorders, making shirt tag numbers of little help. The best chance for figuring out who was who was by checking fingerprints.[55]

Work on White City was finished on Friday, May 9, ahead of schedule. By the end of the day, the tent city stockade had been emptied and the prisoners ensconced back in their cells. Searching the empty stockade, authorities uncovered more than two hundred eighteen-inch-long iron clubs and several knives.

On May 12, the regular prison guards resumed duties, and over one thousand inmates returned to their jobs. Prison officials wasted no time in introducing and enforcing a crackdown with rules designed for both guards and prisoners. As the Ohio Penitentiary settled back into a semblance of normality, construction continued on the new roof over fire-ravaged cellblocks G, H, I, and K.

On May 19, the number of National Guardsmen was reduced from 700 to 125, mainly to serve as an emergency force. On the following day, the first complete check of the prison population was taken since before the fire. It revealed that at least six convicts had escaped, or at least were unaccounted for.[56] A week later, on May 27, 1930, the remaining guardsmen were withdrawn. The regular prison guards, who had been patrolling outside the prison for some time, were surely relieved to be returning to their jobs. Warden Thomas would later report that "the entire discipline and detention of the prison was taken over by the officers of the Ohio Penitentiary, and good discipline [had] been secured and maintained, due in large measure to the increased force of officers."[57] Hal H. Griswold, director of the Department of Public Welfare, noted in his annual report "that no lives were lost in the period following the fire except for an unfortunate accident with a machine gun," a testament to the "calmness and good judgment of the officers of the National Guard and the officers of the prison."[58]

Observers were quick to draw comparisons between the riotous behavior following the fire and the previous year's rash of violent prison riots that had occurred throughout the nation. The riots were blamed on the usual factors, ranging from overcrowding and poor nutrition to unsanitary conditions and correctional brutality. However, one factor was little mentioned—the fact that the prison uprisings of this era could be attributed to "the utter failure of un-trained personnel to depart from rule and tradition in coping with an acute crisis."[59] It was the very lack of training, or better yet, lack of imagination and ability to think outside the box, that led to the breakdown in command that kept guards from unlocking the cell doors when the fire began. The *New York Times* was just as scathing in its observations, blaming the millions of dollars of property destruction in seven major prison riots over the previous nine months on housing conditions, feeding overcrowding and the "loss of hope and mass treatment."[60]

Later in May, another victim could have been added to the fire death list, but because his death took place outside the Ohio Penitentiary walls, it was considered to be too indirect to be counted. Inmate Sam Mazello was among the forty-seven disruptive inmates transferred to the London State Prison Farm from Columbus after the fire. Thirty years old and a member of the so-called Company K bad men section, Mazello was serving a one-to-twelve-year term for burglary. He was evidently no master criminal. He had entered the Ohio Peni-tentiary in 1925 and was paroled the following year before returning on another violation in 1928. Apparently his behavior did not improve at the prison farm. On May 30, he was shot down by guards as he tried to break out along with other former Ohio Penitentiary convicts and was mortally wounded in the head and heart. The shooting came as a climax to forty-eight hours of unrest preceding the convicts' attempts to "batter" their way to freedom. The prison farm lacked a wall, and if they had made it out it would have been a major operation to round them back up.

Mazello and his comrades had destroyed most of the cell furnishings and seemed on the verge of storming the prison gates when Superintendent W. F. Amrine ordered the guards to fire their weapons. As soon as Mazello fell dead, the other convicts returned to their cells and settled back into their routines. Amrine then proclaimed he would brook "no foolishness."[61] At this point the prisoners must have believed him. The county coroner ruled Mazello's death as "due to accident."[62]

Initially, six Ohio Penitentiary prisoners were unaccounted for. All but one were located quickly on the prison grounds. Only one inmate escaped during the tumultuous weeks of the fire and its aftermath. Michael Dorn, thirty-three, serving a fifteen-year sentence for burglary, was a trustee working in the prison hospital when the fire started.[63] After nursing some inmates the night of Easter Monday, just before dawn he "put on a hat and doctor's white coat, slung a stethoscope around his neck and picked up a medical case," and then walked across the prison quadrangle and through the main gate unimpeded. According to Rose, he finagled a ride downtown from several doctors, hopped a bus, and met up with some friends in Toledo. Having traded his doctor's whites for civilian clothes, Dorn took a two-week vacation through several states with his girlfriend. His vacation ended sooner than expected when he was captured in a Cleveland hotel. On May 3, he was reunited with the warden back in Columbus. To his great surprise and relief, the warden let his adventure slide, noting that the trustee had been a "good convict," and "laughed it off as just a matter of 'young love.'"[64]

The pseudonymous convict writer James Winning suggested that a mutiny in one form or another was bound to occur during the pandemonium that ran through the end of April. When there is "no semblance of discipline, the stage is set for insurrection." Indeed, it was "bickering among prison administrators, wrangling between political bosses and parties, and a general state of apathy in reconstruction" that "lent vigor to a revolt trend that has seethed for years." In the end, "No one can see weakness much quicker than the man in gray [i.e., a convict]."[65]

THE ARSONISTS

United States prisons have the built-in disadvantage of having high rates of arson.

—*Gilda Moss Haber*

The actual cause of the fire may never be known.

—*Ray Gill, Ohio state fire marshal*

Conjecture was the rule of the day in the weeks and months that followed the fire and the Board of Inquiry. Despite three fire investigations by the beginning of May,[1] there was no hard evidence pointing to the source of the fire. Explanations of the fire's origins rested on four principal theories: an incendiary device (arson), defective electric wiring, a gasoline or acetylene torch left burning on the job, or spontaneous ignition. From almost the beginning there were strong indications that the fire was caused by an incendiary device, but as in most arsons, any direct evidence was burned up in the inferno. Moreover, arson investigation was still a developing component of forensic science. Doubts were cast on the electric wiring theory when it was determined that all of the "permanent circuits in the burned section" were still intact. The gasoline or acetylene torch theory was ruled out simply because there was absolutely no evidence to support it. Likewise, those who favored the spontaneous ignition theory could find no evidence to back it up.

The first indications that the fire was incendiary in origin came from state fire marshal Ray Gill, who was certain that the fire originated "either in the wood roof or wood forms" near the northwest corner of the new cellblocks I&K or was set in several places simultaneously in the construction materials. Other fire department officials agreed with Gill, particularly when it became known that the fire began under the cellblock roof near the spot where inmates worked during the day with an oil preparation to repair the roof. They believed that an oil-soaked cloth may have been used to start not just the blazes in the cellblock, but the three subsequent fires as well.[2] The pragmatic fire marshal admitted, however, that the "actual cause of the fire may never be known."[3]

It seemed as if everyone had an explanation. Guard Thomas Little, for example, said he "was positive the fire was not started with an incendiary device but was either triggered by spontaneous combustion or defective wiring."[4] Another guard posited a more outlandish theory. He said that convicts on the day of the fire had been carrying paper sacks of cement all day, and that several had complained that the sacks were so hot they had a hard time handling them. The sacks had been piled on top of each other close to where the fire started. The sacks may have caused the fire, he said. Or possibly it was the temporary wiring that had stretched all over the building during construction work.[5]

In one of the earliest published accounts of the fire, the authors suggested that the fire could have started innocently enough, perhaps when an inmate used a primitive method for eradicating the swarming pests, the "bed bugs, cockroaches and other vermin" that made "their lives a living hell." "Prisoners lucky enough to have matches" would grab some scrap papers and rumple them into a makeshift torch, "holding the blazing paper near the chinks in the partitions and blowing the flames over the cells and into the crevices" in an attempt to "destroy the merciless vermin and their nits."[6]

The fire marshal's original fire report was followed by a more substantive special report by fire investigators issued a week later, on April 29.[7] It concluded that the "investigators believe this fire was of incendiary origin" and enumerated in great detail its reasons for that conclusion. It also pointed out the similarity of the Ohio Penitentiary fire to the incendiary fire at the Brick Plant at Junction City in October 1928, which resulted in numerous fatalities.

On May 1, the Board of Inquiry released its conclusions. Many of them mirrored the findings in Gill's fire reports.[8] Despite the fire marshal's report, the board failed to conclusively establish the cause of the fire, but agreed it had to be either incendiarism, spontaneous ignition, or defective wiring, none of which could be ruled out at that point. The investigators' biggest challenge was that the location of the fire's origins had suffered "complete destruction." Without any chance of developing a theory based on hard evidence, the general feeling was that any final conclusions would have to rely solely on circumstantial evidence. After the board had interviewed forty-four witnesses and fire investigators had taken several cracks at solving the case, the board went into great detail to support what members thought was "strong circumstantial evidence that the fire was caused by defective wiring."[9]

As the end of the summer of 1930 approached, four months after the Ohio holocaust, there was still no resolution as to the origins of the fire. Opinions were still mixed between defective wiring and incendiarism. In August, Warden Thomas revealed that at least two convicts had been placed in the Columbus city jail for questioning related to the fire deaths.[10] According to several papers, he gave their names as Bernard K. Campbell and James H. Yeager, both of Cuyahoga County. They had been transferred from the penitentiary after an exhaustive investigation by Deputy State Fire Marshal Joseph D. Clear, who had been on the case since April.[11] The New York Times offered a somewhat different account, reporting that the names were not actually disclosed and that they had been transferred to the city jail under "great secrecy . . . brought out of the cell blocks under cover of night, placed in trucks in the prison yard and taken to jail under heavy guard."[12] These revelations gave new life to the prison rumor mill as to the origins of the fire. Neither Campbell nor Yeager was mentioned again as a suspect, and it is unclear how their names came up.

The first big break in the case came on August 19, when thirty-year-old inmate James Raymond, aka Paul Sullivan, serving ten to fifteen years for burglary and larceny and incarcerated since 1923, notified Warden Thomas and Deputy Fire Marshal Clear that he wished to speak with them about the fire. He claimed that it was set to further an escape plot and named his fellow conspirators as Hugh Gibbons and Clinton Grate.[13] Grate was serving twenty to twenty-five years for a Dayton gas station holdup, and Gibbons was serving ten to fifteen years for a Cleveland fur heist. Raymond claimed to have provided the candles used in three previous failed attempts and that another convict, Jimmy Maloney, was responsible for providing the candles used in the Easter Monday fire.[14]

Fearing that other convicts might kill him to prevent him from snitching, Raymond requested some form of protective confinement as the investigation continued. But any hope of making a case on his testimony was dashed when Raymond hanged himself in the hole on August 21, 1930. He had fashioned a rope from strips of cloth torn from his cell mattress and tied it to the top bar of his cell. Reportedly, he couldn't shake the images of long rows of blackened bodies stretched out across the prison yard.[15]

According to Deputy Fire Marshal Clear, before Raymond took his own life he shared with him all of the information he needed to go forward with a case, except for the name of the convict "who touched the match to the slow burning fuse." As Raymond told it, the fuse was supposed to reach a quantity of gasoline and combustible material soaked with gasoline in the I&K cellblocks. Concrete had been poured there recently, and the arsonists expected the primed scaffolding and "false work" to burn. If it had gone as planned the fire would have started at dinner. The plotters hoped that a large number of convicts would join them and begin a riot that could lead to a "wholesale prison delivery."[16]

Without Raymond on the witness stand, the warden and fire marshal had to come up with a plan for gaining confessions from Gibbons and Grate. The first step was to put both in solitary confinement. Gibbons, who was regarded as the weaker of the two suspects, was purposely placed in the same cell where Raymond had committed suicide. Officials also left Raymond's improvised scaffold made from stacked blankets as well as "the rope Raymond had fashioned and hanged himself with," still connected to an "overhead bar," along with his shoes. The very same stacked blankets that Raymond had stepped off beneath the rope would be a constant reminder as Gibbons contemplated his choices.[17]

Grate was held in the cell directly above Gibbons. It was hoped that they might try to communicate with each other, and revelations might be gleaned by nearby guards. According to one source, the warden was counting on Grate to find some way to contact and encourage the weaker Gibbons to hang himself. If Grate was able to do that he would eliminate the only remaining witness who could identify him. In preparation for such a sequence of events a trustee was posted near Gibbons's cell to cut him down before he killed himself. The warden's intuition proved spot on, and the following morning he could report to the deputy fire marshal that Grate had indeed motivated Gibbons to take his own life. According to Rose, Gibbons actually attempted to hang himself three times that night and would have succeeded on the third attempt if he had not been cut down. During one of his failed attempts he tried using his shirt as "the noose and rope," but it could not support his weight and came apart.[18]

On Saturday night, August 16, 1930, BOI investigators shared their findings with reporters. It was revealed that "a delay in the operation of a fuse" had led to the fire disaster. A handful of convicts had planned to set fire to I&K blocks while their comrades dined in the mess hall. Once the fire ignited, they were hoping to escape in the resultant confusion. It was first reported that at least a half-dozen prisoners were involved in the plot, one of whom perished in the flames. If everything went as planned, the convicts hoped to seize a ladder from the responding fire companies and scale the walls. But not only did the fire not start while the prisoners were out of their cells, the firemen did not enter the prison until it was surrounded by National Guardsmen and regular army troops, forcing them to call off the escape.[19]

The escape plot was supposedly conceived as far back as November 1929. "A flickering taper" lighted by convicts was timed to detonate a can of highly volatile fluid while inmates were at dinner. On August 16, 1930, officials sketched out in more detail the failed escape plot to reporters after it became known that two of the convicts responsible were lodged secretly in the Columbus city jail.[20]

Organized societies have always taken a dim view of the crime of arson, almost without exception treating it as a serious if not a capital crime. Most research suggests that the crime is "rarely committed on the spur of the moment,"[21] but typically, as in the case of the Ohio Penitentiary plotters, involves a fair amount of planning and premeditation. It is probably the "easiest crime to commit and the most difficult to detect,"[22] as was made abundantly clear when the board failed to come to a consensus on the cause of the fire.

According to one authority, based on extensive interviews with wardens, staff, and prisoners in eight American prisons, "United States prisons have the built-in disadvantage of having high rates of arson." Those prisons had on average one fire each month.[23] The threat of arson is a "built-in contradiction for prisons," since during fires the staff must evacuate prisoners from the fire area "but not let them escape."

In March 1931, prison officials received another major break when twenty-six-year-old inmate Jimmy Maloney, doing time on a robbery charge, alerted prison officials that he had information to share about the fire. He admitted to having supplied two of the candles stolen from the Catholic chapel, after Grate and Gibbons told him they needed them for a soldering project. Maloney led off his admission with the caveat that he had been told to keep mum by the admitted arsonists unless he wanted to be implicated in the disaster. He was now afraid to go back into the population. Maloney said that Grate had already made several attempts to kill him, and asked for some type of administrative segregation. The warden consented to his request and had Maloney transferred for safety to a jail in Junction City.[24]

Initially, Grate and Gibbons admitted setting the blaze to cover up an escape attempt, but for some unknown reason added another motivation—they objected to building new cells for additional inmates in the overcrowded institution. But their admissions became their undoing and "aided materially in solving the mystery."[25]

The interviews with Maloney and the late James Raymond would seem to have clinched the case against Grate and Gibbons, who had yet to admit their roles. But after conferring with the Franklin County prosecutor, Donald Hoskins, Warden Thomas and Deputy Fire Marshal Clear were told there was still not enough evidence for a conviction. Hoskins described Raymond's confession as "hearsay," and therefore not admissible in court. And Maloney's testimony was sure to be refuted by Gibbons and Grate. It was decided that a Franklin County grand jury should conduct an investigation into the fire's origins, with testimony beginning on Wednesday, March 25, 1931. Over the next week, Deputy Fire Marshal Clear, Warden Thomas, and several guards and inmates testified.[26]

As in the past fire investigations, inmates who testified were concerned about their safety once they were back behind bars. Authorities promised to take steps to avoid publicity. "No subpoenas were issued," and inmates were brought in before the grand jury individually, "before the next witness came in." As a result, inmates never saw each other, no record was kept of who testified, and their testimony was supposed to be kept secret.[27]

The investigation turned up few if any leads, and if not for the accidental interpretation of a note, or "kite" in prison parlance, passed between Grate and Gibbons, the case might never have been satisfactorily resolved.[28] During the final investigation instigated by Maloney's testimony, Grate was afraid that his fellow conspirator Gibbons might crack. He trusted inmate Frank Mills, the "prison kite runner," to deliver a note to Gibbons that read, "Keep your mouth shut—or else! But if you decided to talk, I want to know. When you get back to mess hall nod your head if you're going to talk. If you are going to keep still shake your head when I look at you. But whatever you do, let's stick together."[29]

According to Mills, after Gibbons read the note he put it in his jacket pocket and entered the mess hall. The ever-curious Mills followed Gibbons into the chow hall and waited for him to hang his jacket up and proceed into the dining hall.

With the coast clear, Mills lifted the kite out of the jacket pocket, read it, and in short order delivered it to the deputy warden's office. A typewritten copy was then made, and the note was secreted back into the jacket pocket before Gibbons finished lunch.[30] The copy of the note was taken to Warden Thomas and Deputy Chief Clear before being placed in the hands of Prosecutor Hoskins.

Grate appeared before the grand jury on March 30, unaware that his kite to Gibbons had been compromised. Under questioning by Assistant Prosecutor Eugene Carlin, Grate denied any knowledge of the fire's origins. Carlin then sprang his trap, showing him the copy of Grate's note. Likely nonplussed, Grate said he would only continue his testimony in front of Hoskins, who happened to be absent attending a funeral. Hoskins eventually would get to confront both men in the coming days, but for now Grate faced Assistant Prosecutor Carlin, Clayton Rose,[31] Henry Holden, Franklin County investigator Vincent Martin, Columbus chief of detectives Shellenberger, and city detectives Otto Phillips and Otto Kaffits. Grate admitted, "I split the kindling, Gibbons lit the match."[32]

On the night of April 1, 1931, a little less than one year after the tragedy and just hours after the county grand jury concluded its investigation, Franklin County prosecutor Donald J. Hoskins announced that two men, Clinton "Cotton" Grate and Hugh "the Jew" Gibbons,[33] had confessed to setting the Easter Monday fire. Both were charged with first-degree murder and almost certainly faced a date with the electric chair if convicted. Their admissions came after an intensive night of questioning, with both men interrogated separately in his office. What sealed it for Hoskins was that except for some minor details, both inmates told identical stories and admitted three previous failed attempts to ignite the oil-soaked concrete forms in the I&K cellblock.

Initially, Grate and Gibbons admitted setting the fire as a protest against having to aid in more prison construction, endeavoring to hamper the building of another cellblock to house inmates. Like the rest of the inmate construction gang working on I&K, Grate and Gibbons were housed in the fatal G&H blocks. Unlike so many others, they escaped before smoke and fire overtook them. Both expressed regret but denied setting the fire in pursuance of a prison break.[34] They also denied that any other inmates knew of their plans for the three previous plots.

According to the two cons, on their first attempt, in December 1929, they placed candles stolen from the chapel in the wooden forms piled in the prison yard near the chapel. Gibbons described the other plots, including the final attempt on Easter Monday: "Cotton fixed it up and he fixed it up pretty good, and put the shavings all around it and he took a little pan and we filled it full of oil and put the shavings in it . . . and he set a candle in there and put some sticks around it." Gibbons explained, "I was in on that because I looked while Cotton went and tried to build the fire. . . . We didn't use gas or anything like that, used a candle I got off [James] Raymond." The next step was to pour the oil, a mixture of straw oil and kerosene, over the kindling and the sides of the forms near where a fuse was set. Adjoining woodwork was soaked in oil as well.[35] Gibbons then said, "It is all set now, so let's light it," and watched while Grate attempted to kindle the flames, no small feat in the cold and wind. Impatient with Grate fumbling around with the matches, Gibbons told him, "You've been unlucky three times [previous three attempts]. . . . Let me light it," and Gibbons lit the candle.[36]

The two men then joined their doomed cellblock mates in the mess hall before being locked up for the night. An hour after setting the device, the arsonists figured that this attempt had failed just like the others. They were stunned when they heard a muffled explosion, followed moments later by flames and oil-laden fumes permeating the G&H blocks. When they heard the cry of "Fire" at 5:21, they knew their timing had gone disastrously awry.[37]

In order to pursue the capital case against the two arsonists, specific first-degree murder indictments were needed. It was decided by county prosecutor Hoskins to have the case hinge on the murders of three local Columbus victims, auto thief Howard Brashear and lifers Benjamin Scanlon and Robert Stone. The indictments against Grate and Gibbons, two counts each, were returned by a Franklin County grand jury the next day, April 2,[38] and both men were transferred from the Ohio Penitentiary to the Franklin County Jail for safekeeping. There were more than a few inmates in the penitentiary who would have liked to inflict their own brand of justice on the arsonists.[39]

Once their names were made public, on Friday April 3 Grate and Gibbons, who were at the Franklin County Jail, told prosecutor Hoskins and a group of reporters that they would plead guilty, but only if the prosecution would guarantee they would be sentenced and executed in short order. Both convicts admitted almost simultaneously, "Under the circumstances, what else can we do."[40] Neither inmate wanted to return to the pen. Having served almost a decade each, they knew "what it's like." Asked whether they feared the other inmates, they replied that it was the officials they feared most.

The Ohio Penitentiary fire investigations had lasted nearly a year, but the final inquiry into the fire's origins would have probably come to naught if not for the accidental interception of a note passed between the two conspirators the previous week. Though both said they preferred death to serving a life sentence,[41] their executions were not to be. Gibbons and Grate pleaded guilty in common pleas court to charges of second-degree murder on May 26, 1931, and were sentenced to life in prison. Judge Cecil J. Randall and Hoskins agreed to accept the pleas after a conference call a few minutes before the state closed its case. The prosecution announced that the pleas were acceptable in that "there was some doubt about the Ohio arson law covering penal institutions in cases where deaths occur."[42] Both men had gone into the arraignment under the premise that there had been no premeditation in starting the fire. All they wanted to do, according to Grate and Gibbons, was to prevent the construction of L block and the addition of forty-eight new solitary confinement cells.

On January 15, 1933, confessed arsonist Clinton Grate, who had helped split the kindling for the Easter Monday fire three years earlier, was found hanging from a bar across his cell ceiling by a guard making his morning rounds. The Virginia-born Grate had completed nine years of his sentence. The "conscience-stricken" man had twisted a noose from a sheet so soundlessly that none of the other inmates in the so-called bad-boy block knew of his demise.[43] By some accounts. Grate's partner in crime also tried to kill himself several times in prison, but managed to hold on until July 23, 1973, when he died "a broken and haunted old man."[44]

One would have thought that the question of how the fire was started had been settled. But in the 1950s, Sugar Bill Baliff, a bank robber doing fifty years at the Ohio Penitentiary, told an interviewer, "Well, the recap was that they said two men set the fire; but according to the grapevine of the institution, this isn't so. It was poor wiring that caused it."[45] Rumors die hard.

AFTERMATH

The heavy toll of life in the Columbus fire directed attention as no other fire has done to the fire hazards of prisons.

—*Horatio Bond, 1932*

Overcrowding is not a new thing in American prisons, but apparently at no time in the history of the country has it been so serious as at present.

—Handbook of American Prisons and Reformatories, *1929*

The Ohio prison fire meant death for 322 convicts. However, it meant life for several prisoners on death row, at least for a few more weeks. The first execution following the fire was that of John Richardson. He had been scheduled to die on April 25, but thanks to the riot and inmate demands, his execution was delayed until May 26. Lee Akers, who had murdered a Cleveland man during a gas station holdup, had his date with the electric chair pushed back from May 2 to June 13.[1]

In the fire's aftermath, public opinion as to who should be blamed for the loss of life was rather mixed. More often than not, critics targeted Warden Thomas, or in some cases Governor Cooper. In June 1930, Thomas came under fire from longtime nemesis William B. Cox, the secretary of the National Society of Penal Information. Cox denounced the warden for threatening to cause the defeat of Governor Cooper in the upcoming governor's race if he dared to interfere with his rule. The warden denied saying this, but Cox claimed he had made similar remarks to him during past fact-finding missions at the Ohio Penitentiary. In 1925 and 1928 he reportedly told Cox that "no Governor would dare to remove him or he would uncover the whole rotten graft of the state's system of prisons."[2]

Governor Myers Y. Cooper had a more plausible response for critics who accused him of not responding to the mutiny more forcefully: "Some people seem to think I should have taken steps to put down the rebellion as soon as it started instead of letting it go for nine days without interference." He reminded his detractors, "They forgot that locks on cells had been ruined in the fire and [there was] no place to lock up men." Moreover, "To drive them out of White City, when we had no other place for them would have been folly and might have led to serious consequences. Instead, we made our plans and went about the business with coolness and common sense. As soon as the stockade was ready [we] broke the rebellion as we had planned—and that, mind you, without a shot being fired or a blow being struck."[3] The governor also responded to the criticism that he should have removed the warden, commenting that he "did not consider him letter perfect," but he could not "give in to the convict ultimatum because it would mean that in the short time we would be faced with a mutiny and fresh demands for another warden."[4]

Once the BOI had completed its work, it was up to the governor to decide the fate of Warden Thomas. On April 28, reports filtered out of the state capitol building that Cooper "would make no change in administration personnel." Moreover, the governor would "express approval of the manner in which the warden handled the situation during the fire." It turned out that the only explanation the governor could muster for keeping the warden on was that the prisoners never made a concerted effort at an organized break during the days of confusion.[5]

One letter stood out as a venomous rant at the governor. A George Jackson from Baltimore, Maryland, sent the governor a sketch clipped out of a Baltimore newspaper showing a prison cell labeled "Inhuman Prison System." With a blazing fire in the background, the stripe-clad arms of prisoners reach out from between the bars. At the top of the clipping Jackson had handwritten, "I hope you go this way . . . if possible."[6] Jackson wrote, "You and your warden have a great deal to answer for. You know what Thomas is and how those men under him for years have suffered." Suggesting that his animus was very personal, he said, "I do for I lived in Ohio. All I can say is to hope that the rest of your life will be a hell on earth . . . and when you die you may suffer the anguish these men suffered and forever after in hell." Jackson couldn't resist adding, "I knew none of them or I would go right there and finish you and Thomas."[7] It is doubtful Governor Cooper could count on Jackson's support in the next election.

Cooper was halfway through a two-year term that, except for the Easter Monday disaster, would prove relatively uneventful.[8] While the slumping Ohio economy probably played a major role in his losing reelection that fall, there is some evidence, as the following sample of letters to the governor shows, that the tragic fire may have been a contributing factor as well.

One correspondent, identified only as "G. J.," wrote the governor on behalf of a lady friend who took exception to the implication that the convicts were to blame for the fire. "You are trying now to say your victims set the fire. *You would.* The men there should [*sic*] that they were heroes and brave men, not moral cowards. That is what your warden and guards are with a very few exceptions." She wanted the governor to know that she had spoken to a number of friends, and promised him, "you will *never* get another office from Ohio people."[9] She was rather prescient; the governorship was the last office he ever held.

Cooper received a handwritten letter from a victim's family several days after the fire. Its heading began, "Father of son [Raymond McAlier] who lost life." The father wrote the governor that he was proud to be a native-born Ohioan, that is, until "the awfully [*sic*] Murder that has been brought on it By [*sic*] the mistakes of a warden and his dirty Gards [*sic*]. . . . I had a boy that was in this fire and lost his life." The father could be forgiven for his vitriol, especially considering that he initially received a telegram informing him his boy was okay, before finding out otherwise.[10]

To the governor's credit, he wasted no time in responding to the bereaved father. He began by expressing his sympathy and his intention for the investigation "to determine if there was culpable action on the part of anyone in connection with this tragedy." When he wrote, he had yet to receive the final report. But he attempted to put the disaster in historical context: "I think you also realize that no matter what may be done there are times when tragedy comes, and in this regard the situation at the Penitentiary is not altogether unlike the Iroquois Theatre fire in Chicago, the Collinwood School fire, and others in which many lives have been lost."[11] He then detailed how the mix-up occurred.

> All of us regretted the necessity of sending telegrams informing parents of death, in cases where prisoners had previously been thought to be alive, but conditions which existed in the Penitentiary made it impossible, as yet, to make a check of the men who are alive; and as the work

on the bodies of the dead went along, men who were thought to be alive were found among the dead. It developed that in numerous cases the clothing on the dead bodies was not the clothing properly belonging to such person. I think you will agree that when it did become apparent that your son was among the dead you should have been notified.

The letter ended, "With sincere sympathy, I am Yours very truly, Governor."[12]

     —————

While prison and state officials were most often denigrated in the press and in letters to the governor, the Ohio Penitentiary convicts came in for their share of contempt as well. A Mrs. Heath from Bellefontaine, Ohio, wrote Governor Cooper, "We think it is a great mistake to spend the hard earned money of good citizens to better the conditions of worthless convicts." She warned that if the state gave in to demands for prison reform, prisoners would just ask for more favors. Moreover, she asked, "Why should conditions be made pleasant for convicts? They won't mind going to prison if conditions are pleasant." She went on to blame the convicts for the fire: "it is perfectly clear that they set it afire in order to escape and are mad because they didn't succeed. The guards," she said, "did perfectly right in not letting them out any sooner of course." As for the surviving convicts, "Their pretended grief over their buddies [was] in anger more than anything else over not being able to escape from the prison." Mrs. Heath insisted that many of the dead convicts would have "gone back to the same deeds of robbery and murder" if they had lived.[13]

The governor received letters from all segments of society, from families of the victims to businessmen. Cleveland architect Frank W. Bail supported Cooper, writing, "I am not at all in sympathy with the newspapers which are demanding that you take immediate action by starting construction of a new penitentiary."[14] What is most striking about this letter is Bail's knowledge of prison design and current correctional strategies in Italy, Cuba, and France. Bail suggested that it would not be possible to build one's way out of the current prison crisis: "the problem goes far deeper than the simple matter of housing and requires a careful study of the whole system of treating criminals." He reserved particular disdain for the "psychology of the cell block," which he regarded as "very harmful to the corrective treatment of the criminal."

Clearly a critic of the big house prison model, Bail asserted that what was really needed was better classification of inmates and much more space for housing thousands of inmates. Surely security was paramount in any prison, but unlike the Ohio Penitentiary, prisons in Vicenza, Italy, Is-sur-Tille, France, and the Isle of Pines in Cuba had successfully confined large populations of convicts "in

areas from a thousand to two thousand acres by military methods." Rather than
traditional prison cells, convicts were housed in dormitories. Bail suggested that
other forms of prison construction were cheaper to build than modern penitentiaries, and that the American preference for the cellblock design was the result
of lobbying efforts from "the enterprise of cell block manufacturers." Bail offered
his assistance to the governor, but there is no evidence that Cooper ever considered breaking with traditional prison design.[15]

Warden Thomas was not without his supporters, such as the Ohio Daughters of the American Revolution (DAR), who, in a time of rising fears of global
communist expansion, referred to the mutiny in White City as "the recent 'Red'
uprising." While the organization abhorred the human losses from the recent
disaster, the Daughters were fervent supporters of the administration, declaring
"that the best interests of the state and society are being magnificently served
by Governor Myers Y. Cooper and Warden Preston E. Thomas." DAR chapter
officials extended their support and appreciation for the governor's "fairness in
dealing with Warden Thomas and others of the official family at the big prison."[16]

Similarly, in early May the president of the Kiwanis Club of Southern Columbus, Ohio, sent Governor Cooper a letter expressing "its faith in the integrity and
efficiency of Warden P. E. Thomas."[17]

During the second week of October 1930 members of the American Prison
Association convened in Louisville, Kentucky. Among the speakers was Mrs. Bal-
lington Booth, from the Volunteers of America, who commented on the recent
spate of riots and the Ohio Penitentiary fire. She considered herself a big supporter of "our riot Wardens—if I may call them such," and made a big effort
to restore the reputation of Warden Preston Thomas. "Shortly before the Ohio
trouble," she said, "I heard the great prison population at Columbus cheer Warden Thomas to the echo. We all know how very quickly in a prison crowd hissing
and murmurs are forthcoming if the men have a grudge or grievance against an
individual. The men in Ohio for years have known their Warden was doing the
best he could for them under terribly adverse circumstances."[18]

Booth repeated a litany of justifications for the spate of prison violence, including the fact that Thomas and other wardens had been turned down for appropriations to keep pace with increased population, improve buildings, and provide
better food and adequate work. Prison troubles, she continued, "can be traced to
poor and inadequate food, overcrowding, impossibility of segregating prisoners,
lack of work and any action of the law that tends to steal away their hope for
the future, such as abolishing good time and merit system, the constant turning

down of men apparently eligible for parole, or the long and hopeless sentences imposed, with no chance of liberty in sights."[19]

She argued in conclusion that no matter how you looked at Columbus, it was

> an absolutely different riot from Leavenworth. . . . Although [in Columbus] the overcrowding and the wretched old buildings proved the fundamental difficulty, remember the riot took place after the fire! It was a panic riot—a very natural result of physical fear born of the ghastly disaster. No one could control the terror-stricken men, penned in behind walls where hundreds of their fellows had died. Free men under such circumstances would have acted the same way. Then, as ever, the small, lawless, evil element of the prison had its chance in that vast frightened crowd to influence the weak and ignorant.[20]

She continued, "Warden Thomas, I am sure, will tell you that the majority of his men were orderly, heroic and helpful, . . . Writing to me on the subject of the riot," she related, Thomas noted, "The pity of the whole thing is that prison riots are seldom participated in by more than one tenth of the population, leaving ninety percent who have not rioted to bear the burden of adverse public opinion."[21]

In the year following the fire the Ohio legislature passed a raft of new laws that undeniably "had their origin in the Ohio fire a year earlier." Observers predicted that the new legislation, designed "to lessen the severity of society's revenge on wrongdoers" by addressing the rampant overcrowding and lengthier prison sentences, would have a "sweeping effect" on the state's courts and prisons.[22]

The Weber Bill doubled the state parole board from two to four members and gave it the power to increase the number of parolees released from prisons and reformatories. In October 1931, the state replaced the Board of Clemency by creating a Board of Parole, consisting of four members within the Department of Public Welfare. Members were appointed by the director of public welfare (with the approval of the governor) for terms of four years, ensuring some continuity in policy making, at a salary of $6,000 per year (just over $99,000 in 2018 dollars). Each member was expected to devote his entire schedule to official duties. The new board was also empowered to hire all personnel required to carry out investigation, preparation, and supervision.[23]

The Ackerman Bill reinstituted the indeterminate sentencing system, repealing the current policy of allowing judges in criminal courts to fix minimum sentences. Most inmates would now finish their sentences in a year or less. Moreover, sentencing power was shifted back from the judges to "prison and parole officers[, who] are the best judges of a prisoner's fitness for society." What's more, prisoners serving life sentences for crimes other than treason or first-degree murder, or a minimum sentence longer than fifteen years, would now be eligible for parole at the expiration of fifteen years (less statutory allowance for good behavior).[24]

The Gillen Bill allowed for the shortening of prison sentences for good behavior. A sentence of five years could be cut down to as little as three years and six months.[25]

The sponsors of the bills asserted that their reasons for reverting to earlier strategies was, for the most part, a response to the "alarming increase in the number of inmates and consequent unrest in practically every penal institution in the state."[26] Although some of the new provisions were opposed by prominent Ohio lawyers, during a discussion at the American Prison Association meeting that focused on the conditions of the state's prisons, most members agreed that the persistence of long-term sentences had helped cause the penal disaster at Columbus.

In 1931, Ohio also introduced the new Bureau of Examination and Classification of prisoners, a new central parole board, and a Good Time law intended to restore the statutory minimum for sentences in state prison. The effect of these laws was to reduce the harshness of the penal system, which had greatly increased between 1922 and 1925.[27]

The Ohio prison catastrophe, not surprisingly, was a subject of much discussion among penologists and corrections officials during the proceedings of the 62nd Annual American Prison Congress held in 1932. Attendee Horatio Bond, an engineer with the National Fire Protection Association (NFPA) out of Boston, started things off by telling his audience, "In April 1930, the Ohio State Penitentiary, a typical prison, was visited by a fire which resulted in 320 deaths and 133 injuries."[28] He ticked off the names of some earlier conflagrations, beginning with one at the State Reform School at Mariana, Florida, in November 1914, in which ten inmates burned to death. And others had already followed the Columbus tragedy, such as the "cremation of eleven negro convicts" in a North Carolina county jail in March 1931. Few would have argued with him when he pronounced that "the heavy toll of life in the Columbus fire directed attention as no other fire has done to the fire hazards of prisons."[29]

Bond had spent a year visiting prisons, analyzing fire hazards at each, completing a five-hundred-page report replete with tables and maps. He and two other engineers were assigned by the NFPA to work out a strategy with the Bureau of Prisons to make prisons as fire-safe as possible. The NFPA included members representing a wide array of backgrounds, all linked in a campaign to reduce fire losses. The organization also served as a clearinghouse for information on fire prevention and protection and maintained a field staff to assist municipalities, organizations, and the public with fire-related issues.

Bond was not the first to point out that "the fundamentals of prison operation and fundamentals of life safety from fire represented two absolutely opposite purposes." Ultimately, while it was the aim of fire-protection engineers to make sure buildings can be exited safely, "prison is a place of custody where the principal objective is to keep the population confined." These goals, he said, might seem "diametrically opposed," and working out arrangements that "reasonably satisfy both sets of conditions" near impossible.[30]

Bond went into detail on the conundrum of ensuring both inmate safety and prison security. He began with a description of how the conventional prison design increased life hazards, pointing to the insufficient number of exits in most facilities. Moreover, the traditional cell-block arrangement placed a large number of men in danger of suffocation in the event of a fire, which in fact was the main cause of death on Easter Monday. He next discussed the arrangements of other buildings in the typical prison compound, most of which featured assembly halls with only one exit.

Bond also focused on specific dangerous prison building scenarios. Since the days of silent pictures, prisoners had looked forward to movie night. In the free world, movie theater patrons in the 1930s had been protected through the "universal application of rules which provide for film booths to be properly constructed." However, since prison buildings often did not fall under the purview of municipalities or the state, fire hazards in prison motion picture facilities were rarely contemplated. Often constructed "without proper vents to carry off poisonous and explosive fumes from burning or decomposed nitro-cellulose film," they offered their own set of dangers. Combine this with a lack of exits and the recipe was all there for a potential fire calamity.[31] Bond cited a fire in 1928 Texas State Prison Farm No. 2 near Houston in which several inmates were killed and twenty-three injured. It turned out that the film being projected lacked an appropriate booth and ignited during a performance in a locked mess hall.[32] Foreshadowing the Ohio fire two years later, the Texas inmates flailed at locked doors as officials mulled the potential for a prison break.

Bond encouraged prison officials to make sure there were adequate exits in the event of barred windows and locked doors. He recommended sprinklers as "the most important item," as well as hydrants, standpipes, and fire extinguishers. He also pointed out that the Ohio Penitentiary's neglect of anything resembling emergency drills ensured a poor outcome on Easter Monday. There should have been no question that a big house containing more than four thousand inmates should be required to have a full-time guard devoted to safety and responsible for fire protection, fire brigade drills, and the examination of potential scenarios in order to be prepared with an effective emergency response.

Commenting on the ineffectiveness of relying on telephonic communication during the disaster, Bond asserted that telephones were "unsatisfactory to depend on for the transmission of emergency signals." He noted there were already various signaling systems designed for such emergencies on the market. Many had been adopted by municipalities, large industrial plants, and other institutions; as an added advantage, they were also impossible to put out of service without giving off some type of warning. The mixed verbal signals on the night of the fire demonstrated that reliance on the passage of oral messages was undependable, likely leading to "confusion and error and delay." The telephone should thus serve as auxiliary tool in these situations.[33]

The findings of the National Commission on Law Observance and Enforcement, or Wickersham Commission, published in 1931, devoted an entire volume to America's penal systems.[34] Coming as it did just after the Ohio fire, its conclusions were eagerly anticipated by criminal justice officials and penologists. The American Prison Association unanimously approved the report. A prepared statement by U.S. federal prison chief Sanford Bates and William J. Ellis, who represented the correctional institutions in New Jersey, was less than enthusiastic and more than a little defensive about some of the commission's findings. Bates and Ellis asserted, "We feel in that the report has failed in some respects to credit the programs of many of our penal institutions for their efforts toward improvements. In the last half century we have done much. The ball and chain, the water cure, the striped suits, shaved heads and other practices have been abolished. The report might have stated some of these things."[35]

Former research assistant to the commission Frank Tannenbaum went even further. Speaking at a luncheon before the National Probation Association, he declared that the report, if anything, "suffers by being too conservative, too generous in its estimate of present penal institutions." Tannenbaum could not resist accusing the warden and other Ohio state officials of "political jockeying," asserting that "such tactics made possible conditions that led to riot and fire."[36]

On November 19, 1931, the same year the Wickersham Commission results were published, Ohio Penitentiary nemesis William B. Cox and other investigators from the National Society of Penal Information visited the prison once more.

Indicating the continued siege mentality of the Warden Thomas administration, Cox later wrote that it was the only institution reviewed in the 1933 *Handbook of American Prisons and Reformatories* where the society's representatives did not receive "the fullest cooperation by the prison officials. . . . It was only through the courtesy and personal attention of Mr. John McSweeney, Director of the Department of Public Welfare, that they were able to enter the prison at all, and they were allowed to make only a superficial inspection under the guidance of a subordinate officer."[37] Ultimately, according to Cox, the denial of cooperation at the Ohio Penitentiary resulted in "a meager opportunity for first hand observation," making it "impossible to give a complete report covering conditions at this institution as they existed on the date of the last visit."

This 1931 survey, on which the 1933 *Handbook* above is based, offers a glimpse into the repaired New Hall cellblocks. Cox and his associates found that the two cell houses destroyed by fire had been remodeled and covered with new roofs. Additionally, he reported that good-quality plumbing was installed. In the damaged cell houses there were now 280 cells (5'6" $\times$ 7'8" $\times$ 7') in one cell house, and in the other there were 408 four-man rooms and 34 eight-man rooms. The front of each of the 408 cells was composed of heavy wire, "similar to that used for fences around industrial plants." The whole front of the cells was opened, facilitating better ventilation.[38]

Despite some small advances, not much else had improved at the Ohio Penitentiary in the aftermath of the fire and mutiny. Guards still had no pensions and worked twelve-hour days, five days a week, with only two weeks off for vacation. Except for the nine men equipped with revolvers and tear gas equipment in the "emergency squad," guards were still unarmed.[39]

One major development was the discontinuation of the idle house after the fire. Authorities regarded it a "bad influence," convinced it only furnished inmates the opportunity to plan riots and escapes.[40] But convicts were still lacking any organized vocational training, and there were no provisions for the classification of new inmates. In the prison shops prisoners could earn one cent per day, and married men five cents if they had dependents. Although more and more prisoners could expect written notices of parole, when they were declined, as quite often was the case, "reasons were not always given."[41] Once prisoners were discharged, they were given their earnings, and if those were less than $10 the state would add in the difference. Convicts were then given civilian clothing and transported to the state border.

After the 1931 survey of the Ohio Penitentiary by the Penal Association, the investigators were confident that, despite a lack of assistance, they had obtained enough accurate information, from open hearings and interviews with many

inmates and guards, both present and former prison guards, to paint a portrait
of the postfire conditions. Although the prison population had decreased since its
zenith before the fire, overcrowding remained a serious concern. Major personnel
and administrative reforms were still required. The quality of the guards was of
particular concern. The committee described them as mostly of a "low type of
intellect," selected without any training or experience. Moreover, there was "no
plan or system of instruction or training for new guards."[42] (See chapter 7 on
guards and the training they received.)

The prison administration was remiss in other significant areas as well. The
inspectors found "no coordination between warden and guards," a lack of discipline, and a "great deal of institutional petty politics" that damaged "the morale
of the officers and guards." Although the committee found that fire hazards had
been reduced, the "sanitary and health conditions could be vastly improved." The
committee noted that while many practices "of brutality and inhumane treatment have been eliminated, the practice of placing prisoners in so-called 'dun-
geon cells' still continued." The committee asserted these should be removed
immediately. On the other hand, it gave its support to the use of solitary confinement, as long as it "does not deprive the prisoner of wholesome food, fresh air,
sanitation, and a source of exercise."[43]

The committee of investigators submitted a transcript of its findings to the
director of public welfare. When the conclusions were formally published in 1933,
Warden Thomas still rejected any responsibility for the disaster and sent an acerbic
letter to the *Handbook* authors, accusing them of being "paid knockers [critics]"
representing an association that promoted prisoner rights. Thomas noted, "I do
not wish to be severe with you but rather desire to deal kindly with you and I am
doing so when I realize, after taking a good look at you, that you probably will be
unable to make a living otherwise. . . . I am glad that the final judgment does not
rest with you, and it is my honest belief that no one takes you seriously. Not even
yourself."[44]

While much of the public focus was on the Ohio fire, actual movement toward safer jails and prisons was taking place in other parts of the American correctional system. Just a week after the inferno, the state of Massachusetts pledged
$50,000 to improve safety at Charlestown State Prison.[45] Less than two weeks
later, the seventy-year-old (thirty years younger than the Ohio Penitentiary) Detroit House of Correction, home to sixteen hundred inmates and regarded as a
firetrap for its separate cell locks and other hazards, was abandoned thanks to a
city council "spurred by fire in Ohio."[46]

One day after the fire, the New York State Commissioner of Corrections sent out a general order to all state penal institutions "to exercise extreme vigilance against fire and check all related equipment and discipline of fire services, including squads of prisoners."[47] He suggested particular focus be given to "State Hospitals for the Insane, especially the State Hospital for the Criminally Insane at Matteawan." He added that this was especially timely due to the fact that "pyromaniacs" were "undoubtedly among those confined and might be roused by the Ohio report." He also suggested that since the laundry was not a fireproof structure, patrols in that area should be "quadrupled."[48]

In the wake of the Ohio debacle, particular attention was paid to several New York prisons. The New York State commissioner of corrections, Richard C. Patterson Jr., noted "no fire hazards at our institutions," but conceded several minor fire hazards at Hart's Island and Riker's Island and supported a building program to replace the aging edifices with fireproof replacements. However, plans like these took financing, and budgets across the nation were stretched thin during the Great Depression. So until the funds were available, a temporary plan was conceived to minimize fire hazards in the short term. Emphasis was placed on frequent inspections of pipes and hose lines, with fire drills and detailed instructions delivered at the Prison Keepers School on the proper responses to an emergency. Henceforth, correctional officers were permitted to carry a key to the outside door while on duty, even though it was considered bad prison administration to allow keepers to be locked in with the inmates. Playing the devil's advocate, the commissioner, after considering what occurred in Columbus, decided that this plan was the "lesser of two evils" and chose the chance of escape over mass casualties. Keepers were now instructed to weigh the potential for convict deaths over the potential for escape and to immediately release men in case of fire.[49]

The federal government jumped on the prison fire-protection bandwagon as well, with a Senate committee passing a number of bills within several days of the Ohio disaster. According to the legislation, the attorney general was authorized to obtain sites of not less than one thousand acres each for two new prisons. One was projected as a reformatory located west of the Mississippi River and the other as an institution for "hardened convicts" in the northeast region.[50] However, these reforms were directed only at federal institutions.

In 1936, Federal Prison Bureau of Prisons director Sanford Bates recommended that "a systematic campaign of fire prevention" be undertaken by the bureau. An experienced corps of fire-prevention engineers was sent to each institution. With the cooperation of the National Fire Protection Association, estimates were secured for purchasing the necessary equipment and structural changes, and the central bureau was instrumental in securing the necessary funds for carrying out of all the engineers' suggestions.[51]

What followed was a building campaign that added fire mains, standpipes, fire doors, sprinklers, and an enhanced water supply to existing federal prison structures. In addition, a fire chief was appointed for each institution, and a systematic report of all existing fire hazards was compiled. Likewise, inmates were trained to respond to emergencies, and renewed vigilance was emphasized to all members of the staff and custodial force.[52] Seven years after the fire, the Fire College in Long Island City, Queens, announced that it would begin offering a course on firefighting and prevention to twenty-eight prison guards; two guards from each of the state's fourteen institutions attended. Each was required to sign a waiver absolving the city of any responsibility if he was injured. Fire commissioner John J. McElligott attributed the program to the Ohio penitentiary disaster. Prison guards would be assigned to accompany busy Manhattan fire companies on night duty.[53]

On their first day of instruction, the guards were welcomed by an assistant fire chief, who recounted the 1930 fire, when 320 died at "Ohio State prison." He made a point of stressing that he "did not want anything like that to happen here."[54] The course included lectures by senior fire chiefs of the department along with some sound motion pictures. According to McElligott, "Apparently mindful of the Ohio State Penitentiary fire at Columbus in 1930 . . . [State Correction] Commissioner Edward P. Mulrooney requested that we train prison guards in the most practical manner in order to protect the prisons from fire and to safeguard the lives of the inmates." On completion of the course, the men would report back to their institutions and organize local fire departments. "Every morning the guards will attend the probationary firemen school" and during afternoon attend classes at Fire College. According to the fire commissioner, "this is the first time we have received such a request, and I am gratified we have facilities.[55]

After the fire, "the attention of the entire country was called to the unbelievable conditions" that pervaded the institution in the months and years leading up to the conflagration. In its aftermath, numerous attempts were made to secure funding "through the submission of a bond issue," which required "a vote of the electorate to secure appropriations to build additional institutions and rehabilitate" the Ohio Penitentiary. But these attempts were unsuccessful, and, as so many times before, rather than an improved penitentiary being built, the only action taken was to make improvements on the facilities that had been around for generations.[56]

At the 1939 annual meeting of the American Prison Association, one official noted that the Ohio Penitentiary still only had one part-time physician, and there "was no provision made for the employment of prisoners." However, conditions had improved by 1940 to the extent that both of the previous statements "were inaccurate." Besides three full-time physicians, there was now a full-time psychiatrist as well as "a staff of consulting surgeons and specialists in various fields of medicine." In addition, there were "two fever therapy machines" kept "busy 24 hours of each day" and "six dental chairs" in use during the day by civilian and inmate dentists and technicians. "For many years a part-time dentist did all of the dental work at the Ohio Penitentiary, his principal occupation being the extraction of diseased teeth,—and the inmate, unless he could afford to pay for his dentures, literally 'gummed' his way through his career at the institution."[57] These advances and others were now funded by a "Prisoner Aid Fund," collected "from the charging of admission to those who wish to go through the institution."

Idleness remained a prevalent condition at the Ohio Penitentiary well into the 1930s, as 1,900 "wholly employable men" marked time by marching "around the yards twice a day, and to meals." In 1940, the number of idle men had been reduced to only 211, thanks to "increased manufacturing and sales employment," the development of schools, and additional transfers to the London Prison Farm. By 1940, an estimated 2,655 inmates were engaged in institutional maintenance and the manufacturing and sales unit at the Ohio Penitentiary (which had been in existence for twenty years). At this point the only idle men were those "who are of necessity kept in idleness, such as the infectious syphilitics, perverts, and those who have physical impediments which prevent their working."[58]

By 1940 a classification board had been set up within the Ohio Penitentiary, composed of various staff members tasked with examining all phases of the prisoners' lives. A school system with a curriculum approved by the State Department of Education had also been inaugurated, offering "the incentive for diminution of sentences" for both teachers and pupils who attended or taught at the school, thanks to a statute ordered by the director of public welfare.[59]

According to one Ohio Penitentiary booster at the 1940 American Prison Association meeting in Cincinnati, these and other accomplishments

> are many what might be termed minor improvements, all tending to
> wipe out the long-standing object of scorn which the Ohio Penitentiary
> has been. . . . Those of this Association who have had contact with
> this institution in the last two years, have expressed amazement at the
> perceptible changes in the entire tone of that program. The same walls,
> cells, unsatisfactory location, too large population, have not prevented

definite worthwhile steps toward carrying out a more modern penal program. We invite those of you passing through Columbus on your return to your respective states, to see with your own eyes some of these vast improvements.[60]

If anything, the fire that was started among the detritus of a building improvement effort in cellblocks I&K only served to stall further improvements and renovations. Apparently "discouraged by the loss of the new cell block in 1930, Ohio passed a law forbidding any new building inside the penitentiary—only 'repair and maintenance' work which kept the place in condition to allow more men to be crammed within the walls.[61]

The penological advances at the old Ohio Penitentiary and other Ohio institutions were not enough to prevent a series of prison riots between 1952 and 1993. During an eighteen-month period beginning in April 1952, prisoner idleness, poor housing, and other grievances kicked off forty prison riots throughout the country, more than had taken place during the previous twenty-five years.[62] On October 31, 1952, a familiar litany of issues, including overcrowding, poor food, a stringent parole policy, and restrictive mail privileges, was blamed for a riot that resulted in between $100,000 and $500,000 in property damage. The so-called Halloween riot occurred under the regime of Warden Ralph W. "Big Red" Alvis. A burly former construction worker, state policeman, and football player, Alvis was "one of the few Ohio wardens who could go anywhere in prison without a bodyguard." He blamed the riot on the lack of state funding for the prison. The riot soon reached out into the prison yard, and state and city police were required to "herd" them back to their cells. Six inmates were injured by gunfire, one fatally. The riot was over by November 4, but most of the cell locks had been broken, and a steel shortage caused by wartime exigencies meant that some of the locks were still not fixed a year later. Ohio highway patrolmen were kept on prison duty for three months for security purposes. However, of the twenty-one prison disturbances that took place across the country in 1952, the Ohio Penitentiary riot ranked only twentieth in severity.[63]

In the wake of the 1952 riot, several overdue reforms were passed. The Division of Corrections lobbied the governor to support a bill authorizing $8,500,000 in improvements, which included converting the Mansfield Reformatory into a medium-security prison to help relieve the congestion at Columbus. Construction was also authorized to build a new reformatory at Marion for young first-time offenders.[64] The Ohio Penitentiary continued to operate and for a time was able to offer inmates single-cell confinement. But this would not last long.

In 1954, almost a quarter century after America's worst prison disaster, Ohio Penitentiary Warden R. W. Alvis gave several journalists a tour of the decaying institution. He pointed out that the prison plant was originally constructed in 1831, and since the 1930 fire there "had been very little building or remodeling." He lamented, "We are set up to handle 2,500 inmates. We have 4,700."[65] Judging from his account, the era of the big house persisted into the mid-1950s. He described prison cells that did not meet Ohio standards for air space per prisoner. If this was so, then the warden should be considered the "largest law violator of the state because he has 2,400 men incarcerated in violation of the state law."[66]

In 1968, the Ohio Penitentiary weathered its last two major riots. Since the 1950s, area law enforcement agencies had met and worked out a protocol for dealing with prison disorders. When a disturbance broke out on June 24, 1968, the planning paid off. Bloodshed was averted, but in terms of damage the riot was the worst in the history of the Ohio Penitentiary. At its height over six hundred Columbus police and firemen, state highway patrol officers, and National Guardsmen had been brought in.

Chief of Corrections Maury C. Koblentz lamented several days after the riot that with "less than an acre of recreation ground for the nearly 3000 men," there was little room for convicts to roam and no chance of "separation of different types of criminals."[67] A number of issues dating back to at least the 1930 fire had still not been adequately resolved. The prison was overcrowded, and poor pay meant it was almost impossible to attract qualified staff. Prisoner discontent was often matched by that of the guards, who threatened to strike if their demands for better pay, free meals while on duty, more promotion opportunities, disability compensation, and a better retirement system were not met. By most accounts the institution had become a dangerous tinderbox waiting for the just the right spark.

On August 20, another, much more violent riot broke out. It lasted for over twenty-eight hours and ended with gunfire and shouts of alarm rending the air inside the C&D cellblocks as National Guardsmen used plastic explosives to blast through a wall and the roof to rescue ten guards held hostage. The guards were unhurt, except for one who suffered a minor injury. But five inmates were killed and ten wounded. It would be the last major disturbance in the venerable Ohio Penitentiary. This incident and others were a clarion call to replace the aging facility with a modern prison. It was hoped that the Southern Ohio Correctional Facility in Lucasville would be the answer.

On Easter Sunday 1993, almost exactly sixty-three years after the 1930 fire, a major riot broke out at the new Lucasville facility. On April 11, members of several prison gangs took control of the Southern Ohio Correctional Facility in Lucasville. During the subsequent eleven-day siege, nine inmates and one guard were murdered. It was the "third most lethal disorder in recent penal history,"[68] surpassed only by Attica in 1971 and the New Mexico Penitentiary riot in 1980. It followed in the wake of punitive crime measures that hearkened back to pre-fire sentencing measures, with prisoners being expected to serve "straight time" with no hope for parole. At the time of the Lucasville riot almost 90 percent were serving at least twenty-year stretches for homicide, robbery, and sex offenses. With inmates locked up twenty-three hours a day with no televisions or radios and fed through food slots, high levels of anger and rage were not surprising. By comparison, the inmates in the Ohio Penitentiary in 1930 had access to radios in their cells and could at least march out to the dining hall for meals. Some sources suggest that the major inmate complaint was the requirement that they take part in a tuberculin skin-test program, which many claimed conflicted with their religious beliefs. Others pointed once more to crowding, lack of inmate programs, and increasingly stringent security procedures.[69]

Except for writing writs, inmates had few options to challenge conditions in Lucasville in 1993. The riot supported the conventional wisdom that conditions do not change unless there is a tragedy that results in public opprobrium. In this case it took the death of ten people for the administration to come to the table and agree to inmate demands for more phone calls, fairer commissary prices, and better medical services. Moreover, it led to better training of correctional staff, particularly in how to respond in a hostage situation. Following the riot, inmates were allowed fifteen minutes to eat in the dining hall. Only twenty convicts at a time would be taken out of the cellblocks, with a limit of 160 in the dining hall at one time.[70]

Too often, it takes years, sometimes decades, to learn anything from a tragedy. The farther back in time a disaster takes place, the more difficult it becomes to pass any regulations that might have prevented it in the first place. In 1911, 146 female garment workers perished in the Triangle Shirtwaist fire.[71] This seminal event in the realm of fire safety was given more urgency because the victims were young immigrant women, innocent, and in the prime of life. They had much more palatable bona fides than the 320 convicts who perished on Easter Monday. The Shirtwaist fire caused enough public uproar to stimulate the development of America's first fire safety codes. But it was still sixteen years for the National Fire Protection Association to come to fruition, establishing a building exit code and other safety regulations.[72]

Perhaps a journalist put it best several months after the fire when he commented that the "public is . . . only interested after a tragedy has occurred and not before."[73] Contemporary newspaper editors pointed out that other tragic fires had been followed by vastly improved fire safety initiatives, claiming that "it took the Iroquois theater fire to compel the installation of safety devices in American theaters" and "the Collinwood school fire to make American school buildings safe for children. The disaster at the Ohio pen, let us hope, will result in a similar advance for our prisons."[74]

According to the principal life safety engineer with the National Fire Protection Association (NFPA), however, the Ohio Penitentiary fire did not lead to "wholesale changes in prison construction and fire safety. . . . People I think forgot about the fire very quickly and it took the fires of the 1970s for people to take notice." It would take more tragic fires in the 1970s to complete the safety program promised after the 1930 inferno. Over forty years later, prisons were still hampered in some cases by a lack of keys or by their failure to work under fire conditions.[75] In 1977, forty-two inmates perished at the Maury County Tennessee Jail, followed within a three-week period by fatal fires in New Brunswick and Danbury, Connecticut. In Danbury, five prisoners died while guards searched for keys. Since the 1970s, new prisons have been required to have sprinkler systems and water hoses on each floor, as well as evacuation plans and employee training in firefighting techniques.

A number of lessons were learned in the aftermath of the Ohio Penitentiary fire in 1930, however. As the flood of families and survivors massed outside the prison walls to claim the bodies of their loved ones, the administration was overwhelmed. Although it is not recorded, this must surely have changed the protocol for collecting inmate remains in the event of similar events. Nationally, the American Correctional Association (ACA) has put audit standards into practice designed to improve prison safety, fire safety, chemical and tool control, inmate rights and grievance procedures, food service, prison design, and conditions of confinement. Today, Ohio is one of the few states that requires each corrections facility to comply with ACA standards. Modern prison directors have also placed their stamp on several improvements. As mentioned in chapter 7, Ohio prison director Richard P. Seiter inaugurated a classification system and opened a new training academy in the 1980s, while state prison director Reginald Wilkinson is credited with putting into place a critical incident management system following the Lucasville riot.

Today most modern prisons are no higher than several floors, with cells spread over a much larger footprint than in the previous century. Although the Ohio Penitentiary in Columbus is long gone, the state's other prisons have benefited from the improvements instigated by the 1930 fire. They now have strict fire policies, and each prison employee is expected to attend a fire drill at least four times a year. The state fire code mandates that evacuation plans be certified by outside inspectors and that each prison have automatic fire alarms and portable extinguishers. The code also requires there to be staff members within three feet of each cell area, capable of releasing cell locks for emergency evacuation within *two minutes* of a fire alarm—the same amount of time Warden Thomas expected it would take the Columbus Fire Department to arrive on Easter Monday 1930.

EPILOGUE

Remembering bad things that have happened is more helpful than forgetting

—Dr. Alan Manevitz

No form of popular entertainment captures the zeitgeist of the Prohibition era better than the prison and gangster films of the late 1920s and early 1930s. The Ohio Penitentiary was the focus of what was probably the first prison film, *Convict Life in the Ohio Penitentiary.* This three-reeler, shot in 1912, was produced by America's Feature Film Company of Chicago, thanks to special permission from Warden T. H. B. Jones. It depicts the Bertillon Room, the convict barber shop, and other highlights of the prison. The film was intended by the prison administration to portray the Ohio Penitentiary in the best possible light. Warden Jones believed in educating and elevating the convict, and this was illustrated with footage of the night school, post office, and modern cell houses. Less than twenty years before the big house fire, the film claimed that in no other prison "were the inmates treated with such humane consideration."[1]

In the 1920s, Hollywood produced more than 250 prison-related films. One prison film historian suggests that their popularity "may have been little more than a morbid desire to see what went on behind those cold grey walls and iron bars."[2] The prison culture that developed in the nation's big houses took its cue, to some degree, from the celluloid version. Notoriously brutal and corrupt prison guards became standards of the genre, and unfortunately, are "still living down this depiction."[3]

The prison riots of 1929 gave prison films a boost and led to an intense debate on penal reform. The next year a number of prison films were released, one of which, *The Big House,* stood out as an archetype of the genre. The film was considered a timely release considering the riots of the previous year. One advertisement announced, "See 3,000 desperate convicts in their break for Freedom! Thrills!" What movie fan could resist a film billed as offering "insight into life in a jail that has never been essayed on screen?"[4] Well-crafted and acted, it introduced the "constellation of prison prototypes" instantly recognizable to anyone familiar with penal culture: the informant, or snitch, who occupied the lowest rung of the prison hierarchy; the "well-meaning but ineffective" warden; the "bullying sadistic guards," or screws; and the professional criminal, who continued his activities inside the prison demimonde.[5] It is not difficult to detect the inspirations for many of these stereotypes in the behaviors of the Ohio Penitentiary convicts and staff. If filmgoers did not recognize the real-life inspiration for these stereotypes, they became familiar, through the movies, with the clanging of utensils, the shuffling of convicts in and out of their cells in dreary prison garb, and the protocol of the massive prison dining halls.[6]

When the Ohio Penitentiary fire grabbed the headlines in April 1930, the prison film resonated even more loudly, particularly when it came to the low priority of rehabilitation and the importance of preventing riots. This was made jarringly clear in *The Big House* when the fictional warden described the institution as "3,000 idle men with nothing to do but brood and plot," for after all, "You can't put them all in solitary."[7]

Ironically, none of the close to four thousand inmates of the biggest of the big houses were allowed to see the eponymous film. For that matter, on September 20, 1930, the Ohio Board of Censors formally ruled that no one in Ohio would get to see it, prohibiting the film being shown anywhere in the state. The board declared that it would no longer allow "racketeering and gangland" films, contending that to display such motion pictures would be "harmful to the boys and girls of Ohio."[8]

Henry G. Brunner, the chairman of the State Democratic Executive Committee, charged that the picture had actually been banned because of "fear of possible political effects." Moreover, Brunner stated, "It is more apparent than ever that the State Administration fears the picture would revive interest in the Ohio Penitentiary Fire . . . because it portrays overcrowding and other prison evils involved in that disaster." The fire had become a political football. One critic of the state political machine stated that it was "plain that political expediency" made it "undesirable to direct popular attention to governmental dereliction by releasing a picture that would recall Ohio's prison tragedy" during a political campaign season.[9] Nonetheless, the state censorship campaign against the film had little impact on its success, and *The Big House* went on to earn Oscar nominations for Best Picture and Best Actor (Wallace Beery).[10]

In December 1931, it was time to release the forty alleged ringleaders of the previous year's insurrection from solitary confinement. Their cells had been by no means "dungeons," but were reported as "roomy, well-ventilated and lighted not only by electric bulbs, but by the occasional shafts of dust-flecked sunlight streaming into the 'L' block."[11] It was noted that "some of the prayers of the men could be heard in the corridors at night. They had turned to religion for comfort against the awful silence." As the weeks turned into months, the guards reported that "when a kindness is shown to one of them he weeps."[12] Once this reached the warden, he decided to allow them to have magazines. One by one each sent out word that they were repentant for the revolt and promised to toe the line from that day forward. The warden claimed that all but two of them were sorry, and that he was confident that the prisoners had been punished enough.

Described as "broken and silent," the sullen inmates were led back into the population and permitted "to resume 'normal' life" among their fellow prisoners.[13] One observer described the ringleaders as "silent men [who] appeared burned out in spirit and wrecked in physique." The rioters released from solitary had earned the respect of their fellow cons and became known as the "the forty thieves." But to the guards they remained "the red shirts," the de facto leaders of the rebellion, as they "shuffled from the cell block, their eyes downcast, faces pale, lips closed,"[14] joining the rest of the prison population, whose privileges had already been restored (except for working and eating in the regular mess hall). Two of the forty had already gone mad in stir and been transferred to the Lima State Hospital for the Criminally Insane.

The prison fire continued to claim lives long after the event. In the years leading up to the fire, Father Albert O' Brien had already been suffering from poor health related to some form of "kidney ailment." The events surrounding the fire "caused a terrific strain," contributing to his physical decline and "greatly weakening his physical endurance." His actions aiding fire victims and offering succor and last rites to the dying only worsened his condition. Besides the physical toll, his "sympathizing with the sorrowful parents whose sons suffocated, or burned to death in the prison holocaust" must have taken a psychological toll as well. "All this and more helped shatter his health, and sent him to an early grave."

While traveling by train from Memphis to Columbus on June 28, 1933, the heroic priest became gravely ill and had to be taken off the train in Cincinnati and quickly transported to the Good Samaritan Hospital. Over the next two weeks he clung to life, consoled by the "presence of several Dominican Fathers from Columbus and Cincinnati." His brother, Eddy, managed to arrive from Chicago in time to be with him during his last days. Father O'Brien never left the Good Samaritan Hospital, dying there on the morning of July 9, 1933. His body was then conveyed to Saint Patrick's in Columbus, where it lay in state in the rectory until Tuesday afternoon, July 11. At the request of Ohio Penitentiary prisoners and prison officials, the body was then transferred to the Saint Catherine's Chapel in the prison compound. Out of respect, prison factories closed down at 12:30, allowing some thirty-five hundred convicts to file past his coffin, paying him their final respects. Following the last services, one of the priests commented that the "prisoners' final tribute of farewell" was "the most impressive and soul touching he ever witnessed."[15]

By July 1931, it seemed that Warden Thomas's reputation among the inmates had been somewhat rehabilitated, at least if nicknames tell us anything. George Richmond, the editor of the weekly *Ohio Penitentiary News*, compiled a list of monikers and "colorful appellations." The warden had been dubbed "Good Time" Thomas, evidently referring to his "efforts in behalf of the 'good time' law which allows prisoners with good records to apply for parole."[16] However, not too much should be read into this nickname. His association with the penitentiary fire and his punitive big house regime were just too much to overcome.

Over the next few years, accusations of corruption would dog the warden. The most damaging stemmed from an investigation tying him to the activities of the boss of the notorious Purple Gang, Thomas "Yonnie" Licavoli.[17] Licavoli entered the Ohio Penitentiary in 1934, and almost as soon as he was behind bars he "began asserting his authority, directing his gang on the outside," while enjoying special privileges and favors from prison officials.[18] An investigation into the reciprocal arrangements he made with prison officials revealed that Thomas had granted Licavoli numerous favors, including allowing various known criminals to visit him in the Columbus big house.[19] In another investigation, six inmates testified that Warden Thomas had shown favoritism to certain prisoners, while others had been ruthlessly punished for testifying at previous investigations. Further, a convict asserted that narcotics circulated widely in the Ohio Penitentiary.[20]

On January 26, 1935, with Governor Martin L. Davey (who had recently succeeded Myers Cooper) about to announce that Thomas would be suspended for thirty days (until his current investigation was concluded), the warden met with three lawyers—Henry Ballard, Demus B. Ulrey, and the warden's son, Don Thomas—to prepare a response to the charges included in the governor's order. The warden countered, "Notwithstanding the indefiniteness of the specifications contained in your order of suspension," the warden said, "I hereby deny the truth of each and every specification contained therein."[21]

As whistles announced the noon hour, the announcement came down that Warden Thomas had been suspended. Davey had ordered the National Guard to be on standby for any ensuing disorder. The toots of the whistles were accompanied by jeering, yelling, and boos as "catcalls resounded in every part of the prison" except for the seven men sitting on death row waiting the electric chair. Warden Thomas had to yield his position temporarily to the now acting warden James C. Woodard, who admitted that he "didn't ask for the job." Making his ignominious departure even worse was the fact that the positions of matron and mail censor, held by his wife, Mary E. Thomas, and his daughter, Amanda, were abolished, and the family was forced to move from their living quarters at the prison. For himself, the warden saw the suspension as a mere interruption of his twenty-two-year service at the prison. The governor allowed the Thomas family another three hours after noon to remove their personal items and furniture from their quarters and take them to the family summer home at Buckeye Lake. Pending the completion of the penitentiary investigation, the family would stay in a local hotel.

Thomas was succeeded by his much more popular deputy warden, James C. Woodard. But just four years later, Woodard lost his job, after it was revealed that he had granted special treatment to Licavoli, who was well entrenched in the prison underworld, financially supporting an internal numbers racket and heading narcotics and liquor rings.[22]

The prisoners' joy at the January suspension of Warden Thomas was tempered when, on April 19, 1935, "amid a tempest of charges and counter-charges," the warden won his rancorous fight to gain reinstatement, after appealing seventeen charges filed against him with the State Civil Service Commission. He had emerged victorious again, just as he had from a dozen earlier investigations during his years at the helm of one of America's most notorious prisons. But this would be his last victory, as his return was mostly ceremonial. At sixty-four years of age, he was ready to move permanently to the family home on the lake. He tendered his resignation effective May 1, less than two weeks later. His resignation was accepted by state director of public welfare Margaret Allman without fanfare. Thomas, who had been suspended without pay since January 26, received his full salary over his last weeks in office.[23]

Preston Thomas died in 1952 at the age of eighty at his home in Columbus after a year-long illness.[24] He never spoke publicly about the fire in the years following the disaster. But he would probably have been pleased that after his death memories of the fire continued to dwindle, to the point that most Americans, let alone Ohioans, were unfamiliar with America's worst prison disaster.

Even with the facility in the hands of the new warden, J. C. Woodard, fire safety issues continued to plague the institution in the late 1930s. Perhaps the most public example took place in 1937. Inmate Anna Marie Hahn, who would have a date with the electric chair the following year, was lodged in the prison hospital on her arrival at the prison. Just three days later, Columbus fire Chief Edward P. Welch and the state's assistant fire marshal, Harry Callan, "took prison authorities to task" after a tour of the institution. To the consternation of Warden Woodard, Callan proclaimed the forty-two-year old hospital building a "terrible firetrap." The 1930 Easter Monday fire was still fresh in the minds of anyone connected to the prison, and this warning could not be taken lightly. Woodard soon capitulated to the fire marshal and agreed "that the all-wood hospital building in which Anna Marie resided be abandoned. Planning for a new death row that would include new accommodations for her began immediately."[25]

In 1972, the Ohio Penitentiary ceased to function as a maximum security prison. The following year its designation and purpose were obsolete, after Ohio opened the maximum security Southern Ohio Correctional Facility in Lucasville. Over the next twelve years, few prisoners remained at the Ohio Penitentiary as its buildings served as a combination inmate hospital, convict reception center, a place to discipline troublesome cons transferred from other state facilities.

The Ohio Penitentiary officially ended its storied run in 1984, having received its last inmate the previous year. Ten years later parts of the structure were collapsing, making it a major eyesore and a source of apprehension over potential liability cases. Despite efforts by the local Landmarks Foundation to save the site and structures, between March 1997 and January 1998 the penitentiary buildings were demolished and removed. Even then, the Ohio Penitentiary remained a local curiosity, luring souvenir-seeking Columbians downtown to see what could salvaged. Contemporary newspapers reported that some locals were able to bring home enough bricks from the fallen pen to build patios and fireplaces.[26]

Today the rubble has long been cleared. A stadium parking garage for Nationwide Arena now sits on the site. Without any memorials or plaques to remind modern-day Columbians of what happened on Easter Monday, what should have been a seminal event in the city's history disappeared from the collective memory, except for an occasional reminder in local newspapers on Easter Mondays.

Except for less than a handful of Ohio Penitentiary inmates, such as the writer Chester Himes, the convict victims of the 1930 are forgotten in both life and death. Yet, in Ohio alone, there are numerous memorials marking much less pivotal tragedies. Ohio building fires, most notably the Collinwood school fire of

1908, which left 172 dead, and Cleveland's Our Lady of the Angels fire, fifty years later, which took 95 lives, are both memorialized. After the Our Lady of the Angels fire, Chicago Mayor Richard J. Daley ushered through a raft of school safety reforms, while across the country fire codes "were rewritten, grandfather clauses abolished and older schools retrofitted." Each year, on Sundays before the anniversary of the fire, local parochial schools stopped work at the "approximate time of the fire for prayer." Survivors went on to create an organization and eventually a website "where they and family members found release for bottled-up memories and a means of maintaining deep friendships."[27]

Likewise, visitors to Millfield, Ohio can read the names of the victims and learn about the state's worst mining disaster, the Millfield Mine disaster, which took eighty-two lives on November 5, 1930, just months after the Ohio Penitentiary fire. On the state's myriad country roads, historical signs can be found remembering the fourteen victims of the *Shenandoah* airship crash of 1925; the Xenia, Ohio, tornado of 1974, which left thirty-three dead; and even the "doodlebug" train disaster in Cuyahoga Falls, which took the lives of forty-three passengers in 1940. The long-forgotten train wreck was finally given its monument in 2005 when several seventh graders spearheaded a fundraising campaign. There is no campaign to memorialize the Columbus prison deaths.

Over the past decade, New York City's "Remember the Triangle Fire Coalition" has been raising money to build a permanent art memorial to the victims of the 1911 Triangle Shirtwaist fire. When and if it comes to fruition, a memorial on two sides of the building will extend up eight floors to where the fire began. According to the Coalition website (http://Rememberthetrianglefire.org), it will bear the names of the victims along with engraved text telling the history and consequences of the fire. While many New Yorkers may know nothing about the Shirtwaist fire,[28] it has never really been forgotten. It is in fact probably the best-known, or at least the most studied, building fire in American history. And on every March 25, for more than a century, New Yorkers have commemorated the tragedy by reading off a list of its more than 140 immigrant victims.

The building where it occurred, which for many years housed the New York University biology and chemistry labs, has long been memorialized with several small plaques about the disaster. As he walked through Greenwich Village, author David Von Drehle would stop to read the plaques. Without the plaques, he might never have been inspired to write his best-selling account of the fire, *Triangle: The Fire That Changed America* (2003).

After such a long and winding narrative, the question still lingers: Why is the Ohio Penitentiary fire forgotten, while so many other much less deadly building fires are memorialized and examined in a veritable avalanche of books dedicated to disasters? Perhaps the answer was there all the time, obscured in an editorial buried deep in a May 1930 issue of the *New York Times*. The editorial takes on the notion that convicts represented a lower form of personhood: "There is a very fair, if informal contest of opinion going full blast as to whether convicts in a State prison are 'persons'; whether they should be rescued, or society protected against them, in case the rescue involves social protection."[29]

It took prison journalist George Richmond to unravel this conundrum between man and convict. The mellifluous editor of the *Ohio Penitentiary News* paid homage to his fellow inmates less than two months after the fire, acknowledging that "many men here weathered the storm and came out of it with greater strength, finer courage and more lofty ideals. This storm broke men, but it made men also. It developed latent possibilities long overlooked even by they, who possess them."[30] It took a convict to recognize "that the majority of the men here weathered the storm, stood the test and proved themselves worthy to be called men."[31]

APPENDIX

Ohio Penitentiary Fire Victims

	Name	Age	Race	Marital status	Occupation	POB	Crime	Term	DOB
1	ADKINS, John	24	W	Single	Shoemaker	Kentucky	Burglary & larceny	2–15 yrs	c. 1905
2	ALLEN, Arthur James	23	W	Single	None	Cincinnati, OH	Robbery	15–25 yrs	c. 1907
3	ALLEN, Harold	25	W	Single	Laborer	Cincinnati, OH	Robbery	21–25 yrs	23 Nov 1904
4	ALLMAN, Benjamin	30	W	Married	R.R. worker	San Atio, Mexico	Assault to kill	1–15 yrs	20 May 1899
5	AMES, Fred	28	W	Divorced	Farmworker	Unknown	Burglarizing an inhabited dwelling at night	8–30 yrs	c. 1902
6	ANDERSON, James	36	W	Single	Machinist	Waterbury, CT	House breaking	4–5 yrs	c. 1894
7	ANDERSON, James	37	W	Divorced	Carpenter	Waynesburg, KY	Shooting to kill & wound	19–20 yrs	8 Feb 1893
8	ANDERSON, Joseph	32	W	Married	Drop forge man	Philadelphia, PA	Forgery	2–20 yrs	26 Aug 1897
9	ANDERSON, Robert	33	W	Married	Holland Baking	Ross Co., OH	Cutting to wound	3–20 yrs	9 Oct 1896
10	ANDREWS, James	42	W	Married	Farmer	VA			12 May 1886
11	ANGILAN, Frank	23	W	Married	Mechanic	Louisville, KY	Shooting to kill & wound	19–20 yrs	8 May 1906
12	ANGILAN, Theodore	21	W	Single	Mechanic	Louisville, KY	Shooting to kill & wound	19–20 yrs	8 May 1900
13	ARGABRIGHT, Van	45	W	Married	Machinist	Sidney, OH	Non-support		16 Jun 1885
14	ARMS, Sherman	26	W	Single	Truck driver	Unknown	Burglary	7–15 yrs	c. 1904
15	AXE, Edward	34	W	Single	Laborer	Unknown	Robbery	20–25 yrs	7 Dec 1895
16	BAIS, Paaul (Paul)	55	W	Widower	Laborer	Unknown	Felonious assault		c. 1875
17	BAKER, George	30	W	Single	Laborer	Hamilton, OH	House breaking	4–5 yrs	27 May 1899
18	BAKER, Henry	26	W	Married	Laborer	Corbin, KY	Auto stealing	15–20 yrs	3 May 1904
19	BAKER, Melvin	30	W	Married	Truck driver	Lima, OH	Larceny	2–7 yrs	c. 1900
20	BARNETT, Wales P.	50	W	Divorced	Auto mechanic	Waverly, OH	Robbery	12–25 yrs	c. 1880

	Name	Age	Race	Marital	Occupation	Origin	Crime	Sentence	Date
21	BARTEZKO, Alvin	28	W	Married	Printer	Bridgeport, CT			4 Apr 1902
22	BATES, Sam	37	W	Divorced	Contractor	Ohio	Forgery	1–20 yrs	12 Jun 1822 [sic]
23	BAUGHMAN, Jesse	Unknown	W	Unknown	None	Ohio			c. 1910
24	BEACH, Eugene	25	W	Married	Printer	Hamilton, OH	Receiving stolen property	5–7 yrs	1 May 1904
25	BEERS, Jack	24	W	Married	Trap drummer	Dubois, PA	Robbery		17 Jan 1906
26	BEGLEY, Arnold	39	W	Married	Farmer	KY	Second degree murder	Life	16 Nov 1890
27	BELCHER, Daniel	25	W	Married	Auto mechanic	KY	Forgery	5–20 yrs	c. 1905
28	BENNETT, Wayne	35	W	Single	Boilermaker	Unknown	Burglary	2–15 yrs	c. 1895
29	BERHALTER, Jacob	37	W	Married	Electrician	Unknown	Statutory (rape)	15–20 yrs	c. 1893
30	BILEK, Charles	24	W	Married	Truck driver	Unknown	Assault to rob	1–15 yrs	25 Jan 1906
31	BLACK, Albert	45	W	Married	Decorator	Pittsburgh, PA	Burglary & larceny	1–15 yrs	10 Nov 1884
32	BLACK, Forrest	36	W	Married	Electrician	U.S.	Burglarizing an inhabitedt dwelling at nigh	20–30 yrs	c. 1894
33	BLODGETT, James	35	W	Single	Seaman	Unknown	Burglarizing an inhabited dwelling at nighi	15–30 yrs	c. 1895
34	BONNOUGH, Hugo	49	W	Married	Laborer	Napoleon, OH	Selling liquor to a minor	1–5 yrs	5 Dec 1880
35	BOWMAN, John E.	24	W	Divorced	None	Lancaster, OH			3 Feb 1906
36	BRANNICK, Robert	24	W	Single	Painter	Springfield, OH	Possession of liquor	1–5 yrs	11 Sep 1905
37	BRASHEAR, Howard T.	34	W	Married	Carpenter	Roxbury, OH	Automobile stealing	15–20 yrs	6 Mar 1896
38	BRENNER, Arthur	33	W	Married	None	New York, NY	Fraudulent checks	1–3 yrs	c. 1893
39	BROWN, Albert	33	W	Married	Truck driver	Unknown	Robbery	10–15 yrs	c. 1897
40	BROWN, Dempsey	37	Negro	Married	Houseman	Louisville, KY	House breaking	1 & 1.5 to 5	2 May 1892

	Name	Age	Race	Marital status	Occupation	POB	Crime	Term	DOB
41	BROWN, Ernest	25	Negro	Single	Mechanic	Kenova, WV	Statutory (rape)	1–20 yrs	27 Dec 1904
42	BROWN, Frank	34	W	Married	Butcher	Unknown	Robbery	10–25 yrs	c. 1896
43	BROWN, Roy	28	W	Single	None	Unknown	Robbery	10–25 yrs	15 Jun 1901
44	BROWN, Willie	27	Colored	Married	Tailor	Unknown	Attempted burglary	1 & 1.5 to 5	c. 1893–94
45	BRYANT, Walker	23	W	Divorced	Woodworker	U.S.			2 Nov 1906
46	BUEHNER, John	29	W	Married	Machinist	Unknown	Robbery	10–25 yrs	30 May 1900
47	BUNN, Nile W.	30	W	Married	Fight promoter	Sycamore, OH	Bank robbery		11 Nov 1899
48	BUSH, Harrison	40	W	Single	Farmer	Coshocton, OH	Receiving stolen property	1–7 yrs	4 May 1899
49	BUTLER, Frank (Francis M.)	30	W	Single	None	Munson, PA	Robbery	14–25 yrs	4 Feb 1900
50	CAFARELLI, Pietro	40	W	Married	None	Italy	First degree murder	Life	c. 1890
51	CALLIN, Paul	29	W	Single	Store clerk	Adrio, OH	Robbery	10–25 yrs	14 Nov 1900
52	CAMPBELL, Louis	29	W	Single	Clerk	Chicago	Grand larceny	5–7 yrs	5 Oct 1900
53	CAMPBELL, Louis	30	W	Single	None	Unknown			c. 1900
54	CARMAN, Pearl	39	W	Married	Farmer	Greenfield, OH	Robbery	10–25 yrs	14 Jul 1890
55	CARTER, George	24	W	Married	Laborer	Roanoke, VA	Robbery	10–25 yrs	5 Nov 1905
56	CAYWOOD, Lonnie	31	W	Divorced	Auto mechanic	Valley View, KY	Robbery	10–25 yrs	29 Jan 1899
57	CHEHEY, Alex	35	W	Married	None	Hungary	Auto stealing		c. 1895
58	CHORJEL, George	60	W	Married	None	Zanesville, OH	Statutory (rape)	Life	c. 1870
59	CIBROWSKI, Mike	27	W	Married	Painter	Toledo, OH	Burglary	10–15 yrs	26 Sep 1902
60	CISCO, John	30	W	Married	Truck driver	Unknown	Robbery	15–25 yrs	c. 1900
61	CLAAR, Kenneth	31	W	Married	Machinist	Jackson, OH	Burglary & larceny	1–15 yrs	30 Dec 1898

#	Name	Age	Race	Marital Status	Occupation	Location	Crime	Sentence	Date
62	CLARK, George	31	W	Married	Steam shovel operator	Nashville, TN	Auto stealing	1–20 yrs	17 Mar 1899
63	CLIFFORD, Red [Edward P.]	38	W	Married	Farmer	Arkansas	Shooting to kill	10–20 yrs	13 Dec 1892
64	COATOAM, Ray [Raymond Joseph]	23	W	Unknown	Laborer	Ohio	Burglary & larceny	7–15 yrs	c. 1904
65	COHEN, Harry	24	W	Married	Machinist	Kentucky	Robbery	10–25 yrs	11 Jun 1905
66	COHN, Harvey	33	W	Single	Chauffeur	Cincinnati, OH	Forgery	10–20 yrs	c. 1896
67	COLLINS, Charles	46	W	Divorced	Unknown	Ohio	Burglary	1–15 yrs	c. 1884
68	COLLINS, James	26	W	Single	Laborer	Italy	Larceny	1–7 yrs	5 Jun 1903
69	COMER, Robert Allen	35	W	Married	Trucking business	Bourbon Co., KY			6 Jul 1894
70	CONCLIN, John	38	W	Single	Structural iron worker	Unknown	Burglary & larceny	5–15 yrs	c. 1891
71	COTRAL, Theodore	44	W	Married	None	Ohio	Murder	Life	c. 1887
72	COULTER, Carroll	26	W	Divorced	Machinist	Cheboygan, MI	Bank robbery	Life	5 Sep 1903
73	COULTER, James	32	W	Married	Salesman	Ohio	Forcing entry into a safe	20 yrs	c. 1898
74	CRAMER, Anton J.	32	W	Unknown	None		Auto theft		1898–1902
75	CRAWFORD, Benjamin	34	W	Divorced	Waiter	Missouri	Robbery	10–25 yrs	c. 1896
76	CROUCH, Kenneth	24	W	Married	None	Salem, OH			c. 1906
77	DALBY, Thomas	31	W	Single	Motion picture operator	Wellsville, OH			1 Apr 1904
78	DAVIS, Dave	31	W	Single	Motion picture operator	Cleveland, OH	Robbery	10–25 yrs	3 Mar 1899
79	DAWSON, Gilbert	29	W	Married	Painter	West Virginia	Burglary & larceny	2–15 yrs	c. 1900
80	DAY, Charles S	40	W	Single	Unknown	Unknown	Larceny	6–7 yrs	c. 1890

	Name	Age	Race	Marital status	Occupation	POB	Crime	Term	DOB
81	DEEM, Everett	34	W	Married	Farmer	Parkersburg, WV	Burglary & larceny	5–15 yrs	19 May 1895
82	DASTOY, Steve	39	W	Single	Laborer	Austria	Robbery	10–25 yrs	c. 1891
83	DeWITT, Dorse	30	W	Divorced	Musician	Irvona, PA	Auto stealing	5–20 yrs	16 Oct 1899
84	DILLON, Patrick	64	W	Single	None	Ireland	Burglary & larceny	1–15 yrs	c. 1866
85	DIPPLE, Walter	39	W	Married	Machinist	Unknown	Robbery	10–25 yrs	c. 1891
86	DOE, John	36	W	Married	Farmer	Unknown	Auto stealing	1–15 yrs	c. 1894
87	DOUGLAS, William F.	37	W	Widowed	Farmer	Athens Co, OH	Forgery	1–20 yrs	7 Nov 1892
88	DRAKE, Innis (Ennis)	30	Negro	Single	Laborer	Ohio	Shoot to kill	10–25 yrs	1898–1900
89	DUNCAN, Harry E.	45	W	Divorced	Machinist	Ohio	Robbery	10–25 yrs	c. 1885
90	EARLY, Lawrence	25	W	Single	Mill worker	Ohio	Auto theft	1–20 yrs	c. 1905
91	EBERTH, Homer	38	W	Married	Farmer	Michigan	Robbery	10–25 yrs	5 Mar 1905
92	ECKLER, John	41	W	Widowed	Laborer	Rochester, PA	Burglarizing an inhabited dwelling at night	5–30 yrs	2 Mar 1905
93	EDMONDS, Pierre	40	W	Married	Tool maker	Richmond, IN	Robbery	10–25 yrs	30 Nov 1889
94	EMERICK, Stewart	37	W	Single	Unknown	Pennsylvania	Burglary	7–15 yrs	c. 1893
95	ERNEST, Merle	32	W	Married	none	Kentucky	Robbery	25 yrs	c. 1898
96	EVERSPAUGH, Charles	32	W	Widowed	Farmer	Jackson Co., OH	Second degree murder	Life	8 Sep 1897
97	FARRIS, Floyd	26	W	Single	Barber	Litchfield, OH			31 Dec 1903
98	FEENEY, George Joseph	49	W	Married	Machinist	Unknown	Robbery	1–15 yrs	1882 or 1887
99	FENTON, James AKA Eli LAROQUE	30	W	Married	Cook	Toledo, OH	Burglary & larceny	5–15 yrs	c. 1899

#	Name	Age	Race	Marital Status	Occupation	Location	Crime	Sentence	Date
100	FIDALGO, Manuel	29	W	Divorced	Mechanic + Nurse	South America	Robbery	10–25 yrs	c. 1901
101	FIEHRER, Charles	25	W	Married	Machinist	Hamilton, OH	Robbery	10–25 yrs	28 Sep 1904
102	FISHER, Mike	27	W	Divorced	R.R. worker	Columbus, OH	Robbery	10–25 yrs	c. 1903
103	FLETCHAM, Charles	51	W	Married	Carpenter	New York	Attempted burglary	10–25 yrs	c. 1879
104	FLYNT, Ed	49	W	Married	None	Wellington, KS			25 Dec 1890
105	FORD, Alfred	39	W	Married	Blacksmith	Allen Co., OH	Non-support		28 Jan 1891
106	FORD, Charles G.	34	W	Married	Carpenter	Winamac, IN	Non-support		9 Aug 1895
107	FOREMAN, Harry F.	46	W	Married	Painter	Lancaster, OH	Forgery	7–20 yrs	4 Nov 1883
108	FORKNER, John	55	W	Divorced	Painter	Morrow, OH	Fraudulent checks	1–3 yrs	8 Aug 1874
109	FOSTER, Charles	25	W	Single	Drug clerk	Akron, OH	Auto stealing 2nd offense	15–30 yrs	25 Feb 1905
110	FOSTER, William	27	W	Single	Teamster	Hamilton Co., OH	Burglarizing an inhabited dwelling at night	10–30 yrs	c. 1903
111	FRAZZELL, Sam AKA Oscar FRIZZELL	23	W	Single	Laborer	Columbus, OH	Robbery	10–25 yrs	27 Aug 1906
112	FREMONT, Arol	24	W	Married	Radiotrician	Johnstown, PA	Burglarizing an inhabited dwelling at night	7–30 yrs	c. 1906
113	GARBRY, Robert	25	W	Single	Mechanic	Piqua, OH	Robbery	10–25 yrs	7 Sep 1904
114	GARRISON, William	27	W	Single	Polisher	Columbus, OH	Robbery	15–25 yrs	17 Jan 1903
115	GECSEY, Joe	27	W	Single	Core maker/Farmer	Ohio	Robbery (2 sentences)	20–50 yrs	c. 1903
116	GIBSON, Paul (should be Ralph)	32	W	Single	Chauffeur	Marion, OH	Burglarizing an inhabited dwelling at night	7–30 yrs	c. 1898
117	GLOWATCH, Mike	37	W	Married	Laborer	Austria		Life	May 1893
118	GOOD, Russell	29	W	Single	Farmer	Rushmore, OH	Forgery	2–20 yrs	26 Jul 1900
119	GRAFT, Earl	41	W	Married	Unknown	Ohio	Auto stealing	1–20 yrs	c. 1894

Name	Age	Race	Marital status	Occupation	POB	Crime	Term	DOB
120 HALITSKY, Edward	26	W	Single	Baker	Brooklyn, NY	Larceny	6–7 yrs	1 Apr 1904
121 HALL, Charles AKA Chas. HEALTH	25	W	Married	Welder	Washington Co., OH	Auto theft		c. 1905
122 HANNAH, Pat	31	W	Single	Chauffeur	Cleveland, OH	Robbery	1–15 yrs	29 Jun 1898
123 HARMON, Dale W.	29	W	Divorced	Laborer	Gallia Co., OH	Non-support	1–3 yrs	22 Sep 1900
124 HARPER, Richard	27	W	Single	Farmer	Plain City, OH	Burglary & larceny	1–15 yrs	15 Apr 1903
125 HARRIS, Charles	28	W	Married	Cook	Wheeling, WV	Robbery	11–25 yrs	25 Sep 1901
126 HARROD, Joseph P.	27	W	Divorced	Mechanic	Kentucky	First degree murder	Life	15 Sep 1902
127 HART, Donald	28	W	Unknown	None	Canada			c. 1901
128 HARTLEY, Robert	25	W	Single	Upholsterer	Pennsylvania	Robbery	15–25 yrs	c. 1905
129 HEIN, Fred	28	W	Single	Musician/Machinist	Cleveland, OH	Robbery	24.5–25 yrs	26 Jun 1901
130 HENDERSON, Robert	43	W	Single	Unknown	Ohio	Burglary (Brown Co.)	3–15 yrs	c. 1897
131 HENSON, Carl	30	W	Single	Machinist	Unknown	Robbery	15–25 yrs	c. 1900
132 HESTON, Edward	32	W	Single	Clerk	Cleveland, OH	Robbery	15–25 yrs	23 Jan 1898
133 HEWLING, James	27	W	Single	Truck driver	Covington, KY	Robbery		5 Mar 1903
134 HICKMAN, Montrose	24	W	Married	Laborer	London, OH	Second degree murder	10–25 yrs	c. 1906
135 HICKMAN, Raymond	30	Negro	Single	Laborer	London, OH	Burglary	5–15 yrs	c. 1900
136 HICKMAN, William	32	Colored	Married	Laborer	Tennessee	Robbery	10–25 yrs	c. 1898
137 HILL, Oren	35	W	Married	Blacksmith	West Virginia	Aiding a convict to escape	3–Life	c. 1895
138 HOLLAND, Albert	24	W	Married	None	Fallston, PA	Burglarizing an inhabited dwelling at night	6–30 yrs	c. 1906
139 HOLLENBACHER, Carl	47	W	Single	Welder	Ohio	First degree murder	Life	c. 1882

140	HOSIER, Floyd	30	W	Married	Machinist	Richmond, IN	Larceny	2–7 yrs	7 Oct 1899
141	HUFFMAN, Dorsey AKA Mike SOPKO	35	W	Married	Unknown	Ohio	Burglary	6–15 yrs	c. 1895
142	HUNT, Ernest	26	W	Married	Printer	Canada	Auto theft	4–20 yrs	c. 1904
143	HUTCHENSON, Wm. Arthur	24	W	Single	Machinist	Pennsylvania	Second degree murder	Life	7 Jan 1906
144	JACKSON, James	21	W	Single	Laborer	Somerset, KY	Burglary	10–15 yrs	24 Mar 1909
145	JACKSON, Walter	about 32	Colored	Single	None	Kentucky	Burglarizing an inhabited dwelling at night	5–30 yrs	c. 1898
146	JENKINS, Archie	37	W	Unknown	None	Unknown			c. 1893
147	JENNINGS, Wm.	27	W	Single	Oil contractor	Unknown	Burglary & larceny	5–15 yrs	c. 1903
148	JOHNSON, Hershel R.	21	W	Single	Laborer	Crawford, Texas	Robbery	10–25 yrs	c. 1909
149	JOHNSON, Tom	35	W	Married	Laborer	Bulgaria	Robbery	15–25 yrs	c. 1895
150	JONES, Arthur	26	W	Divorced	Laborer	Iowa	Bank robbery	20–Life	19 Aug 1903
151	JONES, Thomas D.	49	W	Married	Machinist	Thomastown, OH	Forgery	1–20 yrs	c. 1881
152	KELL, Osen D.	27	W	Married	Auto mechanic	Blue Ridgek, GA	Burglary		c. 1903
153	KERN, Fred	28	W	Single	Chauffeur	Unknown	Manslaughter	10–20 yrs	c. 1902
154	KERR, John	24	W	Single	Truck driver	Portsmouth, OH	Robbery	10–25 yrs	20 Aug 1905
155	KERREGAN, Lawrence	29	W	Divorced	Farmer	Mt. Vernon, IL	Auto stealing	1–20 yrs	17 Aug 1900
156	KERWIN, George	42	W	Divorced	Die setter	Rochester, NY	Statutory (rape)	5–20 yrs	30 Jan 1888
157	KIMERLY, Orville	31	W	Single	Laborer	Carey, Ohio	Burglary	4–15 yrs	4 Jun 1898
158	KING, Albert	42	W	Single	Salesman	Asheville, NC	Larceny	7–15 yrs	26 Nov 1887
159	KISNER, William	22	W	Single	None	Swanson, MD	Burglarizing an inhabited dwelling at night	10–30 yrs	14 Sep 1907

	Name	Age	Race	Marital status	Occupation	POB	Crime	Term	DOB
160	KLAYMAN, Frank	29	W	Married	Chauffeur	Russia	Robbery	20–25 yrs	16 Jun 1900
161	KNAPP, Robert	26	W	Married	Telephone worker	Newark, NJ	Assault to rob	10–15 yrs	8 Oct 1903
162	KNOTT, Wilson J.	25	W	Single	None	Maryland	House breaking	1–5 yrs	c. 1905
163	KOONER, Elmer	23	W	Single	Chauffeur	Peasilburg[?], KY		10–30 yrs	7 Apr 1907
164	KOSTIHA, Stanley	23 or 33	W	Married	Painter-decorator	Austria	Burglarizing an inhabited dwelling at night		c. 1897
165	KOWALARSKI, John	37	W	Single	Fireman	Cleveland, OH	Robbery	10–25 yrs	c. 1897
166	KOWALSKI, Felix	21	W	Single	Auto mechanic	Unknown	Robbery	10–25 yrs	15 May 1900
167	KOWALSKI, Joe or Ignacues P.	34	W	Married	Moulder	Cleveland, OH	Robbery	25 yrs	22 Jul 1895
168	KOZAK, Richard	35	W	Married	Truck driver	Cleveland, OH	Burglary		25 Jul 1904
169	KOZMA, Frank	38	W	Unknown	None	Unknown			c. 1892
170	KREYSSIG, Hamilton	30	W	Married	Mechanical shop helper	Haydenville, OH	Auto stealing		31 Jul 1899
171	KRIEGER, Pearl E.	26	W	Single	Mechanic	Napoleon, OH	Robbery	10–25 yrs	c. 1906
172	KRUSE, Walter	29	W	Single	Truck driver	Newport, KY	Robbery	10–25 yrs	c. 1901
173	KUNI, Alex (Alexander)	30	W	Single	Acetylene burner	Unknown	Assault to rape	10–15 yrs	c. 1900
174	KUSO, Harry	40	W	Married	Laborer	Unknown	Second degree murder	Life	c. 1900
175	LAW, William Walter	27	Colored	Married	None	Unknown	Rape	3–20 yrs	c. 1903
176	LAZETTE, James	28	W	Single	Laborer	Sandusky, OH	Burglary & larceny		27 Jul 1901
177	LEE, Bud	39	W	Married	Mechanic	West Virginia	Auto theft	1–20 yrs	5 Apr 1901
178	LEHIO, Erie	67	W	Single	Farmer	Unknown	Manslaughter	10–20 yrs	c. 1863

#	Name	Age	Race	Marital Status	Occupation	Origin	Crime	Sentence	Date
179	LEIBER, Harvey	21	W	Married	Laborer	Defiance, OH	Larceny	1–7 yrs	26 Dec 1900
180	LEMERE, Theodore	39	W	Divorced	Machinist	Minnesota	Statutory (rape)	3–20 yrs	c. 1891
181	LEWIS, Howard	35	W	Single	Machinist	Unknown	Larceny	5–7 yrs	c. 1895
182	LEWIS, Mike	24	W	Single	Plumber	Youngstown, OH	Robbery	10–25 yrs	23 Dec 1904
183	LIGHTNER, William	26	W	Single	Unknown	Limaville, OH	Robbery	10–25 yrs	17 Feb 1904
184	LOVELARE, Edward	41	W	Unknown	None	Unknown			c. 1889
185	LUTHER, Leroy	29	W	Single	R.R. brakeman	Newark, OH	Larceny	1–7 yrs	27 Feb 1909
186	LYONS, Charles	24	W	Single	Blacksmith	Unknown	Robbery	10–25 yrs	c. 1906
187	MACK, Charles	43	W	Married	Carpenter	Walton, KY	Statutory (rape)	3–20 yrs	3 Mar 1887
188	MADDEN, Barney F.	47	W	Single	None	Van Wert, OH	Burglary & larceny	1–15 yrs	c. 1887
189	MANN, Samuel	31	W	Married	Laborer	E. Liverpool, OH	Manufacturing liquor	1–5 yrs	4 Sep 1898
190	MARSHALL, Louis	38	W	Married	Painter	Wayne, WV	Non-support	1–3 yrs	24 Oct 1891
191	MASON, Paul	32	W	Married	Laborer	Baltimore, MD			27 Apr 1897
192	MASSO, Peter	43	W	Widower	None	Italy	First degree murder	Life	c. 1887
193	McABIER, Raymond	26	W	Divorced	None	Ohio	Auto stealing	7–20 yrs	c. 1904
194	McCOWN, Robert	32	W	Unknown	None	Unknown			c. 1898
195	McINTOSH, Guy	35	W	Married	None	Lilley, PA	Robbery	10–25 yrs	c. 1895
196	McMULLEN, Robert	38	W	Married	Laborer	Ireland	Assault to rob	6–15 yrs	16 Apr 1892
197	McNEAL, Eldon AKA Eldon G. HUDSON	22	W	Married	Painter	Georgetown, DE	Robbery	10–25 yrs	10 Sep 1907
198	McPHERSON, Ivan	22	W	Single	Sailor	Buffalo, NY	Robbery	10–25 yrs	29 Oct 1907
199	McWHORTER, Albert	34	W	Married	None	Ohio	Burglarizing an inhabited dwelling at night		1 May 1895
200	MEADOWS, Edward	33	W	Single	Baker	Kansas City, MO	Robbery	10–25 yrs	13 May 1896

	Name	Age	Race	Marital status	Occupation	POB	Crime	Term	DOB
201	MERACKI, Emil	35	W	Widower	Farmer	Unknown	Statutory (rape)	10–20 yrs	c. 1895
202	MEYERS, Ray	47	W	Single	Carpenter	Belding, MI	Statutory (rape)	1–20 yrs	22 Sep 1883
203	MIHALEY, Pete	21	W	Single	Truck driver	Uniontown, PA	Robbery	10–25 yrs	16 Apr 09
204	MILLER, Earl	23	W	Single	Chef	Murphy, NC	Statutory (rape)	10–20 yrs	5 Aug 1897
205	MILLER, Joe	44	W	Divorced	Waiter		Burglarizing an inhabited dwelling & concealed weapon	8–33 yrs	c. 1886
206	MONNETT, Emerson	46	W	Single	Laborer	Kirkersville, OH	Felonious assault	5–10 yrs	14 Mar 1882
207	MONTGOMERY, Eddie	31	Colored	Single	Laborer	Unknown			c. 1899
208	MULLENIX, George, Jr.	29	W	Married	Cook	Piqua, OH	Auto theft	1–20 yrs	25 Jun 00
209	MULLENIX, Guy	29	W	Married	Unknown	Highland Co., OH			c. 1901
210	MURDOCK, William	22	Colored	Married	Teamster	Mt. Pleasant, TN	Burglary	1.5–15 yrs	30 May 07
211	MURPHY, Andrew	42	W	Divorced	Auto mechanic	Co. Carlow, Ireland	Auto stealing	1–20 yrs	7 Feb 1888
212	MURRAY, Charles J.	45	W	Married	Pipefitter	Unknown	Robbery	15–25 yrs	c. 1885
213	MYERS, Archie	30	Negro	Married	Farmer/Laborer	Springfield, OH	Burglary	3–15 yrs	c. 1900
214	MYERS, John	32	W	Single	Laborer	Unknown	Statutory (rape)	1–20 yrs	c. 1898
215	NAGLE, jr, Edward	35	W	Married	Chauffeur	Unknown	Shooting to kill	10–20 yrs	c. 1895
216	NANCE, Robert	38	Colored	Single	Laborer	Unknown	Burglary	10–15 yrs	c. 1892
217	NERI, Harry	43	W	Single	Moulder	Monterrey, Mexico	Burglary & larceny		11 Sep 1885
218	NEUBAUER, Frank	34	W	Married	Truck driver	Ohio	Robbery	10–25 yrs	c. 1896
219	NEWBAUER, Edward	26	W	Married	Cement finisher	Ohio	Robbery	15–25 yrs	c. 1904

#	Name	Age		Marital	Occupation	Birthplace	Crime	Sentence	Date
220	NICHOLS, Maynard	23	W	Married	Cook	Jackson, MI	Assault to kill	5–15 yrs	6 Jul 06
221	NICICEKI, John	36	W	Married	Storekeeper	Poland	Possession of liquor	1–5 yrs	24 Jul 1893
222	NOLTE, George E.	22	W	Single	Truck driver	Elmore, OH	Manslaughter	10–20 yrs	13 Mar 08
223	NORZINSKAY, John	24	W	Unknown	None	Unknown			c. 1889
224	O'BRIEN, Hobsey	30	W	Married	Salesman	San Francisco, CA	Possession of burglary tools		22 Jul 1899
225	OPRA, Joseph	29	W	Single	Farmer	Austria-Hungary	Robbery	20–25 yrs	c. 1901
226	PAINTER, Bert	48	W	Married	Farmer	Ft. Recovery, OH	Burglary & larceny (Cuyahoga?)	1–15 yrs	19 Jul 1891
227	PEDRO, Joe	20	W	Single	Section hand	Tiffin, OH	Attempted burglary	1–15 yrs	c. 1910
228	PENDLETON, Herman	23	W	Married	Molder	Springfield, OH	Robbery	10–25 yrs	c. 1907
229	PERKINS, Roy	45	W	Married	Laborer	Unknown	Breaking & entering	5–15 yrs	c. 1885
230	PHELPS, Raymond	31	W	Single	None	Hocking Co., OH	Murder	Life	c. 1899
231	PHILLIPS, George	31	W	Single	Marine engineer	Vail, IA	Forgery	1–20 yrs	8 May 1898
232	PHILLIPS, Harold	26	W	Married	Farmer	Ohio	Statutory (rape)	3–20 yrs	8 Jul 1903
233	PINTNER, Emil	31	W	Single	Painter	Cleveland, OH	Robbery	10–25 yrs	c. 1899
234	PLAGEMANN, George	28	W	Single	Bricklayer	Unknown	Operating motor vehicle without owner's consent	1–20 yrs	c. 1902
235	POLLES, John	30	W	Married	Truck driver	Greece	Murder	Life	13 Aug 1899
236	PORZIO, Joseph	38	W	Single	Laborer	Brooklyn, NY	Second degree murder	Life	c. 1892
237	POTTS, Derald	34	W	Single	Laborer	Deshler, OH	Burglary & larceny	3–15 yrs	c. 1896
238	POULIN, Charles	30	W	Married	Auto mechanic	Toledo, OH	Bank robbery	30–Life	4 Aug 1899
239	PRATER, Harry c.	38	W	Single	None	Big Springs, OH	Statutory (rape)	Life	c. 1892
240	REASTER, William	31	W	Single	Carpenter	Toledo, OH	Burglary & larceny	1–15 yrs	11 Mar 1899
241	REICH, Nicholas	33	W	Married	Laborer	Canton, OH	Felonious assault		30 Aug 1896

	Name	Age	Race	Marital status	Occupation	POB	Crime	Term	DOB
242	RENO, Joe	26	W	Single	Orderly at hospital		Robbery	10–25 yrs	c. 1904
243	RICHARDSON, Robert	24	W	Single	Auto mechanic	San Antonio, TX	Robbery	14–25 yrs	27 Jan 1906
244	ROBEY, Laurence	35	W	Divorced	Unknown	Ohio	Possession of liquor	1–5 yrs	c. 1895
245	ROSS, Oakley	21	W	Single	Auto mechanic	Unknown	First degree murder	Life	c. 1909
246	ROTH, Lester	34	W	Married	Farmer	Unknown	Felonious assault	5–10 yrs	c. 1896
247	RUDNICKI, John	27	W	Single	Machinist	Michigan	Pocket picking	4–5 yrs	1 Jan 1903
248	RUNYON, Garland	29	W	Married	Millwright	Ironton, OH	Abandoning child	1–3 yrs	11 Jul 1900
249	SADOWSKI, Walter	40	W	Single	Machinist	Unknown	First degree murder	Life	c. 1890
250	SAFFRAN, Larry	26	W	Married	Unknown	New York, NY			c. 1902
251	SALINAS, Genaro (See similarity below)	24	W	Married	Laborer	Mexico	Felonious assault		12 Sep 1905
252	SALINES, George (No record found)						Statutory (rape)	10–20 yrs	
253	SAMS, Frank Zane	34	W	Single	Laborer	Brownsville, OH	Burglary	1–15 yrs	c. 1896
254	SAWMILLER, Clarence	35	W	Married	Cement worker	Allen Co., OH	Larceny	6–7 yrs	23 Jan 1895
255	SCANLON, Benjamin	27	W	Single	Auto repairer	Anderson, IN	Second degree murder	Life	17 Dec 1902
256	SCAPPOLETTI, Joseph	38	W	Married	Baker		Manslaughter	10–20 yrs	c. 1892
257	SCHUCK, Harold	29	W	Married	Grocer clerk	Pittsburg, PA			12 Dec 1900
258	SCOTT, Edward	27	W	Married	Clerk	Cincinnati, OH	Robbery	15–25 yrs	30 Nov 1902
259	SHELPMAN, Charles D.	52	W	Divorced	Laborer	Unknown	Statutory (rape)	25–30 yrs	c. 1878

#	Name	Age	Race	Marital	Occupation	Birthplace	Crime	Sentence	Date
260	SHERMAN, William	35	W	Single	Unknown	Virginia	Burglarizing an inhabited dwelling at night	Life	c. 1895
261	SHERRICK, Charles	21	W	Single	Farmer	Greenfield, OH	Robbery		12 Jul 1900
262	SHERRICK, Thomas	21	W	Married	Tree surgery	Springfield, OH	Robbery		8 Oct 1900
263	SHIPMAN, Lee	38	W	Married	Painter	Dublin, OH	Robbery	10–25 yrs	3 Feb 1892
264	SHIVELY, Jess	34	W	Married	Carpenter	Baltimore, MD	Robbery	14–25 yrs	12 Feb 1896
265	SIBERT, Joseph	43	W	Married	None	Canton, OH			c. 1887
266	SINGLETON, Todd	26	W	Single	Telephone lineman / Pipe fitter	Heaters, WV	Robbery	15–25 yrs	c. 1904
267	SINUTA, Job	55	W	Single	Unknown	Unknown	Statutory (rape)	19–20 yrs	c. 1877
268	SKARKO, John	30	W	Single	Printer	Lithuania	Robbery	10–25 yrs	c. 1900
269	SKEAN, Robert	24	W	Single	Painter	Unknown	Burglary & larceny	3–15 yrs	c. 1906
270	SLAWSON, Sherman	28	W	Single	Structural steel worker	Unknown	Auto stealing	10–25 yrs	16 Feb 1902
271	SMERK, Nicholas	26	W	Single	Laborer	U.S.	Robbery	10–25 yrs	c. 1904
272	SMITH, Edward	32	W	Single	Miner	Kilgore, KY	Shooting to kill	2–25 yrs	9 May 1897
273	SMITH, George AKA Geo.JACKSON	42	W	Single	Clerk	Canton, OH			c. 1888
274	SMITH, Harry	37	W	Single	Mechanic	Auglaize Co., OH			c. 1893
275	SNELLING, Norris	40	W	Married	Laborer	Jacktown, OH	Larceny	1–7 yrs	22 May 1890
276	SOCHA, August	29	W	Single	Cloth cutter	Unknown	House breaking	10–25 yrs	c. 1901
277	SPIRES, John	31	W	Married	None	New York			c. 1899
278	STAYANOTT, Kalio	37	W	Single	Laborer	Unknown	Statutory (rape)	10–20 yrs	c. 1893
279	STETSON, Charles B.	41	W	Single	Carpenter	Marion, OH	Non-support	1–3 yrs	4 May 1898
280	STONE, Robert E.	49	W	Married	Carpenter	Elliston, VA	First degree murder	Life	20 Jun 1880

	Name	Age	Race	Marital status	Occupation	POB	Crime	Term	DOB
281	STONER, Joseph	26	W	Married	None	Austria			c. 1904
282	SUNKLE, Charles	22	W	Married	Garage mechanic	Napoleon, OH	Auto stealing	4–20 yrs	28 Aug 1907
283	SUTLIFF, Alfred	29	W	Married	Welder	Lucas Co., OH	Robbery	10–25 yrs	6 Jun 1900
284	SWEET, Joe	37	W	Married	Laborer	Many, LA	Manufacturing liquor	2–5 yrs	8 Mar 1893
285	TALLEY, Mack	29	Colored	Single	Unknown	Tennessee	Burglary	1–15 yrs	c. 1901
286	TAYLOR, Cleve Orel	41	W	Divorced	R.R. switchman	Limaville, OH	Non-support	1–3 yrs	10 Sep 1888
287	TAYLOR, Faye	23	W	Married	Waiter		Auto stealing	14–20 yrs	c. 1907
288	TAYLOR, Rolland J.	22	W	Single	Clerk	New Lexington, OH	Fraudulent checks	1–3 yrs	20 Mar 1900
289	THOMAS, Harold	25	W	Married	Truck driver	Tiffin, OH	Larceny of an automobile	1–20 yrs	28 Jan 1905
290	THOMPSON, Robert	26	W	Single	None	Tennessee	Forgery	1–20 yrs	c. 1904
291	TIMBLIN, Frank	28	W	Single	Mechanic	Youngstown, OH	Larceny	2.5–7 yrs	2 Feb 1902
292	TISCHLER, Emil	27	W	Single	Laborer	Cleveland, OH	Robbery	20–25 yrs	c. 1903
293	TODOROFF, George	45	W	Divorced	Laborer	Bulgaria	First degree murder	Life	10 Mar 1885
294	TROMBETTI, Mike Lawrence	24	W	Married	Cab driver	Steubenville, OH	First degree murder	Life	c. 1906
295	TYBOR, Joe	26	W	Married	Steel worker	Youngstown, OH	Robbery	20–25 yrs	c. 1904
296	UPCHURCH, Edward	25	W	Married	Machinist	Slick Ford, KY	Larceny		11 Nov 1904
297	VANDERGRIFT, Frank	42	W	Married	None	Indiana	Burglarizing an inhabited dwelling at night	Life	c. 1888
298	VEDOMSKY, Mike	38	W	Married	Laborer	Unknown	Cutting to kill	10–20 yrs	c. 1892
299	VERBATIS, Andy	28	W	Single	Laborer	Unknown	Statutory (rape)	Life	c. 1902
300	VICTOR, Jr., Adam J.	23	W	Single	Truck driver	Latrobe, PA	Robbery	10–25 yrs	3 Jul 1906

#	Name	Age	Race	Marital	Occupation	Origin	Crime	Sentence	Date
301	VINER, Harry	19	W	Single	Blacksmith's helper	Austria	Robbery	10–25 yrs	18 Jan 1911
302	WAGNER, Richard	21	W	Single	Printer	Newport, KY	Robbery	10–25 yrs	29 Aug 1900
303	WAISLOW, Leo	43	Colored	Divorced	Farmer	Unknown	Statutory (rape)	Life	c. 1887
304	WAITE, Clarence	39	W	Married	Steelworker	Fullerton, NE	Burglarizing an inhabited dwelling at night	5–30 yrs	12 Mar 1891
305	WALK, Albert	34	W	Married	None	Ohio			c. 1896
306	WALLEN, Roy	36	W	Married	Machinist	Ohio	Second degree murder	Life	c. 1894
307	WALTERS, Burt	25	W	Single	Mechanic	Norwalk, OH	Burglary & larceny		6 Jan 1905
308	WATERS, Fred	26	W	Single	Printer	Portland, IN	Burglary	1–15 yrs	12 Mar 1904
309	WEBSTER, James. J.	36	W	Married	Salesman	Erie, TN	Robbery	20–25 yrs	30 Dec 1893
310	WEIMAN, Albert J.	38	W	Single	None	Pennsylvania	Robbery	10–25 yrs	c. 1892
311	WEIMER, Lawrence	26	W	Married	Laborer	LeSuer, MN	Felonious assault	8–10 yrs	30 Apr 1903
312	WELLS, Charley A.	38	W	Single	None	Michigan			c. 1892
313	WILLHAM, John	24	W	Married	None	Cleveland, OH	First degree murder	Life	c. 1906
314	WILLIAMS, Charles	39	W	Unknown	None	Unknown			Unkn
315	WILLIAMS, Elisha	30	Colored	Single	Millhand	Unknown	Assault to rob	8–15 yrs	c. 1900
316	WILLS, Edward	32	W	Married	Auto mechanic	Unknown	Larceny	5–7 yrs	c. 1898
317	WILSON, Harry	38	W	Married	Iron molder	Greenville, OH	Larceny	2–7 yrs	c. 1892
318	YOUNG, Earl	26	W	Single	None	Unknown	Auto theft	2–20 yrs	c. 1904
319	YOUNG, W. D.	31	W	Married	Sander	Deshler, OH	Non-support	1–3 yrs	13 Jul 1898
320	ZOLKOWSKI, Joseph V.	22	W	Single	Car repair	Poland	Burglarizing an inhabited dwelling at night	5–30 yrs	27 Aug 1907

NOTES

Introduction

1. The "event ballad" was a staple of popular culture in an era when tragic newspaper headlines were converted into songs, inspired by lurid stories such as the *Hindenburg* disaster and the Lindbergh kidnapping.

2. Mollie C. Cain's *Keys to the Cages: 1930 Ohio Penitentiary Fire* (n.p.: Four Cats, 2013) is a fictionalized account of the prison fire. Donald G. Rose's nonfiction *A Night of Horror* (n.p.: CreateSpace, 2016) is more valuable, being based in part on the participation of his father, Judge Clayton Rose Sr., in the subsequent prison fire inquiries. Unfortunately for researchers, the book contains no citations or attributions outside of a list of several books, newspapers, and documents.

3. Of these, the best account can be found in James Dailey II's chapter, "To What Red Hell," in David Meyers, Elise Meyers Walker, and James Dailey II, *Inside the Ohio Penitentiary* (Charleston, SC: History Press, 2013), 90–102.

4. On the Cocoanut Grove fire, see, e.g., John C. Esposito, *Fire in the Grove: The Cocoanut Grove Tragedy and Its Aftermath* (Boston: Da Capo Press, 2005); Edward Keyes, *Cocoanut Grove: A Spellbinding Account of the Most Famous Fire in American History* (New York: Atheneum, 1984); and Paul Benzaquin, *Holocaust: The Shocking Story of the Boston Cocoanut Grove Fire* (New York: Henry Holt, 1959). The Iroquois Theatre fire has been documented in Nat Brandt, *Chicago Death Trap: The Iroquois Theatre Fire of 1903* (Carbondale: Southern Illinois University Press, 2003), and Anthony P. Hatch, *Tinder Box: The Iroquois Theatre Disaster 1903* (Chicago: Chicago Review Press, 2003).

5. John Barylick, *Killer Show: The Station Nightclub Fire; America's Deadliest Rock Concert* (Hanover, NH: University Press of New England, 2012).

6. David Laskin, *The Children's Blizzard* (New York: HarperCollins, 2004), 2.

Chapter 1: Fire in the Big House

1. "Transcript of Testimony Concerning the Ohio Penitentiary Fire," 1930, Office of the Governor, Ohio History Connection, State Archives series 1144, GR 1573 (microfilm), 201–3. (The Governor's Board of Inquiry, hereafter cited as Transcript.)

2. "Ohio's Prison Horror," *Literary Digest*, May 3, 1930, 9.

3. Transcript, 382.

4. Ibid., 384.

5. Ibid., 398.

6. Ibid., 433–35.

7. Ibid., 490.

8. Ibid., 379. Inmate Murray Wolfe asserted that the 2nd H Company "is supposed to be a nut company. It is supposed to be composed of fellows who are not quite there. They were the ones hollering" (ibid., 554).

9. Ibid., 405.

10. Ibid., 411.

11. Ibid., 551–54.

12. Ibid., 490.

13. Ibid., 88.

14. Ibid., 624.

15. Donald G. Rose, *A Night of Horror* (n.p.: CreateSpace, 2016), 30.

16. Sonny Hanovich, unpublished interview, 1985.

17. Transcript, 43.

18. Ibid., 597.

19. Ibid., 126.

20. Ibid., 602.

21. Ibid., 608.

22. Ibid., 508.

23. Ibid., 587–88.

24. Ibid., 91–93.

25. Ibid., 181.

26. Ibid., 588.

27. Ibid., 589.

28. Ibid., 23–24.

29. Ibid., 2.

30. "Deaths Called Needless in Prison Blaze," *Dallas Morning News*, April 24, 1930, 1.

31. Ibid., 15.

32. Rose, *Night of Horror*, 35.

33. Transcript, 511–12.

34. David Meyers, Elise Meyers Walker, and James Dailey II, *Inside the Ohio Penitentiary* (Charleston, SC: History Press, 2013), 92.

35. Transcript, 581.

36. Ibid., 582.

37. Ibid., 583.

38. Ibid., 693.

39. Ibid., 694–98.

40. "335 Convicts Die in Ohio Prison Fire," *New York Times*, April 22, 1930, 1.

41. "Radio and Flames in Sky Bring Hundreds to Scene of Pen Fire," *Columbus Citizen*, April 22, 1930.

42. Vinson Hunter, "Microphone on Job in Ohio's Jail Fire," *Washington Post*, May 18, 1930, A5.

43. "Tales of Heroism Abound in Stark Pen Tragedy," *Columbus Evening Dispatch*, April 22, 1930, 3.

44. Chester B. Himes, "Crazy in the Stir," *Esquire*, August 1, 1934, 38; also included in *Yesterday Will Make You Cry* (New York: W. W. Norton, 1998), 249, and in *The Collected Stories of Chester Himes* (New York: Thunder's Mouth Press, 1991).

45. Chester Himes, "To What Red Hell?," *Esquire*, October 1, 1934, 100.

46. Transcript, 555.

47. "Entrapped Men Roll in Water," *Columbus Citizen*, April 22, 1930, 11.

48. "Fire Crazed Negro Curses Spectators," *Columbus Citizen*, April 22, 1930.

49. "Ohio's Prison Horror," 9.

50. T. J. Thomas and Dan W. Gallagher, *The Spotlight on Ohio's Black Crime* (Cleveland: Charles Margolian, 1930), 10–11.

51. Peg McGraw and Walter McGraw, *Assignment: Prison Riots* (New York: Henry Holt, 1954), 220–21. If Baliff was telling the truth, after twenty years he probably should be forgiven for his miscount of the corpses. There were 317 deaths the first day and 320 caused directly by the fire. The last two, making the total 322, were the result of a machine-gun accident that killed two prisoners as they slept several days after the holocaust.

52. Horavich, unpublished interview.

53. "Convicts and Guards Vie in Efforts to Battle Fire and Save Endangered Men," *Dallas Morning News*, April 22, 1930.

54. Himes, "Crazy in the Stir," in *Collected Stories of Chester Himes*, 184. The fire is also featured in his novel *Yesterday Will Make You Cry* (New York: W. W. Norton, 1998), the posthumously published first version of his *Cast the First Stone* (New York: Coward-McCann, 1952).

55. John C. Esposito, *Fire in the Grove: The Cocoanut Grove Tragedy and Its Aftermath*, (Boston: Da Capo Press, 2005), 25.

56. Ibid., 83–84.

57. Assistant Fire Chief Osborn estimated it took the firemen two minutes to get from the No. 1 fire house at Front and Elm Streets to the penitentiary. "Tales of Heroism Abound," 3.

58. Transcript, 10.

59. Ohio Bureau of Inspection and Supervision of Public Offices, *Report on the Ohio State Penitentiary Fire, Columbus, Ohio, April 21, 1930*, 3 (hereafter cited as Fire Report).

60. "Guards Didn't Know What to Do, They Tell Probers," *Columbus Evening Dispatch*, April 22, 1930, 2.

61. Dennis Smith, *Dennis Smith's History of Firefighting in America: 300 Years of Courage* (New York: Dial Press, 1978), 62.

62. Charles G. Haywood, *General Alarm: A Dramatic Account of Fires and Fire-Fighting in America* (New York: Dodd, Mead, 1967), 10, 18.

63. "Tales of Heroism Abound," 1–2.

64. Fire Report, 3.

65. Ibid.

66. Howard R. Thompson, "Hero Guards Fight Smoke to Free Locked Convicts," *Ohio State Journal*, April 22, 1930, 1–2.

67. "More Sidelights on Tragedy," *Columbus Evening Dispatch*, April 22, 1930, 3.

68. Edmond Ceslas McEniry, *Hero Priest of the Ohio Penitentiary Fire: Rev. Albert O'Brien* (Somerset, OH: Rosary Press, 1934), 8.

69. Ibid., 12.

70. Ex-Convict 59968, "Chaplain Mingles with Convicts and Calms Disturbers—Saves Prisoner from Electric Chair," *Universe Bulletin*, May 2, 1930, reprinted in McEniry, *Hero Priest*, 15–21.

71. McEniry, *Hero Priest*, 13.

72. Ray H. Coon, "Guard Accused by Survivors," *Ohio State Journal*, April 22, 1930, 11.

73. Kenneth Tooill, "Like War or Hell," *Columbus Evening Dispatch*, April 22, 1930, 1–2.

74. Ibid.

75. This statement is exaggerated. The Iroquois Theater Fire of 1903, which took 602 lives, was the worst single building fire in U.S. history up to 1930. There were also much deadlier forest fires in the years leading up to the Columbus fire. "Convicts Become Heroes in Prison Fire," *Chicago Defender*, April 26, 1930, 2. The rest of the account is taken from this article.

76. "Convicts Become Heroes in Prison Fire."

77. "Ohio's Prison Fire," *Literary Digest*, May 3, 1930, 9.

78. Larry Connor, "Charnel House in Cell Block," *Ohio State Journal*, April 22, 1930, 11.

79. "Warden's Daughter Directs Fight from Office, Calling Help for Him as He Battles amid Flames," *New York Times*, April 22, 1930, 2. The warden should hardly be credited with any heroic activity since he spent the fire and its aftermath outside the prison walls in relative safety.

80. "Daughter of Ohio Warden Is Heroine of Fire," *Dallas Morning News*, April 25, 1930, 1.

81. "Warden's Daughter Directs Fight," 2.

82. "Fire Crazed Negro Curses Spectators."

83. "Convicts Gallant in Ohio Holocaust," *Washington Post*, April 22, 1930, 1.

84. "Convicts Become Heroes in Prison Fire," *Chicago Defender*, April 26, 1930, 2.

85. "Tales of Heroism Abound," 3.

86. Connor, "Charnel House," 1, 11.

87. Coon, "Guard Accused by Survivors."

88. Transcript, 523.

89. See Meyers, Meyers Walker, and Dailey, *Inside the Ohio Penitentiary*, 98.

90. "Guards Didn't Know What to Do, They Tell Probers."

91. Connor, "Charnel House," 1, 11.

92. "Tales of Heroism Abound," 3. The Bertillon system was a complicated identification system of measurements created by Alphonse Bertillon of the Paris, France, police to identify repeat offenders. It would eventually be replaced by fingerprinting.

93. Connor, "Charnel House," 11.

94. Unidentified clipping from what appears to be the *Columbus Citizen*.

95. "Student Herded in with Prisoners Accidentally," *Ohio State Journal*, April 22, 1930, 2.

96. Michel Mok, "The Talking Newspaper," *Popular Science Monthly*, August 9, 1930, 55.

97. "Radio and Flames in Sky," *Columbus Citizen*, April 22, 1930.

98. This technology was still in its infancy in 1930, but advanced enough to transmit photographs over regular phone lines between cities relatively close to each other, such as Columbus and Chicago (under 300 miles). More than 1,000 miles separated Dallas and Columbus.

99. Ibid.

100. There is a short clip of the Ohio Penitentiary fire from British Pathé, without sound, on various internet sites, including https://www.youtube.com/watch?v =1TY4k1XBPnI, accessed August 19, 2017.

101. Mok, "Talking Newspaper," 55.

102. "Journal Man Puts Pen Story on Air," *Ohio State Journal*, April 22, 1930, 11.

103. Hunter, "Microphone on Job."

104. "Relatives Gather."

105. "Caravan of Death Rumbles Out in the Wee Hours of Morning," *Columbus Dispatch*, April 22, 1930, 2.

106. "Wires Taxed," *Ohio State Journal*, April 22, 1930, 11.

107. "Tales of Heroism Abound," 3.

108. "Columbus Radio Announcer Gets Nation's Praise," *Chicago Defender*, May 3, 1930, 10.

109. "Ohio Convict Rewarded," *New York Times*, April 23, 1930, 3; "Talk to the Nation," *Chicago Defender*, May 30, 1930, 8.

Chapter 2: The Fairgrounds

1. Kenneth Tooill, "Like War or Hell, without a Chance Is Convict Story," *Columbus Evening Dispatch* (Morning Extra), April 22, 1930, 1–2.

2. Randall Edwards, "Man Recalls Horror of Pen Fire 60 Years Ago," *Columbus Dispatch*, April 15, 1990.

3. Ibid.

4. Karl B. Pauly, "276 Bodies Listed in Official Count of Pen Fire Dead," *Ohio State Journal*, n.d., 1.

5. "Quiet Follows Night of Horror," *Columbus Citizen*, April 22, 1930, 1.

6. Tooill, "Like War or Hell," 1.

7. Ibid.

8. Ibid.

9. "335 Convicts Die in Ohio Prison Fire," *New York Times*, April 22, 1930.

10. Ray H. Coon, "Guard Accused by Survivors," *Ohio State Journal*, April 22, 1930, 11.

11. "Those Going In Are Alive; Those Going Out Dead," *Columbus Evening Dispatch*, April 22, 1930, 3.

12. Ibid.

13. Tooill, "Like War or Hell."

14. Pauly, "276 Bodies Listed."

15. "231 Victims of Fire Are Held in Hospital," *Washington Post*, April 23, 1930, 2.

16. Ibid.

17. The following interview with Dr. Keil is taken from his testimony to the inquiry, 470–73.

18. "Transcript of Testimony Concerning the Ohio Penitentiary Fire," 1930, Office of the Governor, Ohio History Connection, State Archives series 1144, GR 1573 (hereafter cited as Transcript), 471–72.

19. Ibid., 473.

20. Coon, "Guard Accused by Survivors."

21. Charles L. Roblee, Allen J. McKechnie, and William Lundy, *The Investigation of Fires*, 2nd ed. (Englewood Cliffs, NJ: Prentice Hall, 1988), 125.

22. "Mother, Wife in Record Trip from Cleveland," *Columbus Evening Dispatch*, April 22, 1930.

23. "318 Deaths in Prison Attributed to Laxity," *Washington Post*, April 24, 1930, 1

24. "Moving Bodies Is Slow Work," *Ohio State Journal*, April 22, 1930, 2.

25. James R. Winning, *Behind These Walls* (New York: Macmillan, 1933), 241.

26. "Caravan of Death Rumbles Out in the Wee Hours of Morning," *Columbus Dispatch*, Aprill 22, 1930, 2.

27. "Quiet Follows Night of Horror," *Columbus Citizen*, April 22, 1930, 1; "Convicts, Crazed by Horror, Try to Take Hoses Away from Firemen," *Columbus Citizen*, April 22, 1930, 7.

28. Ibid.

29. "Jack Cannon Aids Embalming Work," *Ohio State Journal*, April 22, 1930, 1.

30. "318 Deaths."

31. Winning, *Behind These Walls*. The writer's identity is still a mystery. What is known about him is that he was sentenced to ten to twenty-five years for robbery while armed in 1924 at age twenty-four. At the time of the publication of his book in 1933 he was living in England. He learned to write while at the Columbus big house, especially during long stints in solitary confinement on a bread-and-water regimen. He apparently compiled a large collection of rejection slips as he improved his writing. Following the fire and the subsequent inmate mutiny, guards took all his manuscripts from him, two novels and forty short stories, and tore them to pieces. See "Book Describing Prison Cruelty and Telling of Fire Linked to Columbus Institution," *New York Times*, May 25, 1933, 22.

32. Winning, *Behind These Walls*, 240–41.

33. "Rows of Blackened Bodies of 317 Fire Victims Await Families for Burial," *Washington Post*, April 23, 1930, 1.

34. "Relatives Gather to Identify Victims," *Columbus Evening Dispatch*, April 23, 1930.

35. Ibid.

36. "Charity Fund Aids, Flowers Donated," *Columbus Citizen*, April 22, 1930, 1.

37. Mary V. Daugherty, "Weeping Women File through Rows of Victims' Coffins," *Ohio State Journal*, April 24, 1930, 2.

38. "Warden Is Called to Testify before Penitentiary Fire Probers," *Columbus Evening Dispatch*, April 23, 1930, 1.

39. "318 Deaths."

40. Daugherty, "Weeping Women," 1.

41. "Caravan of Death."

42. There was no one named Newberry among the dead. This tale probably refers to the brothers Frank and Edward Newbauer, who both perished in the fire.

43. "Caravan of Death."

44. "Jack Cannon Aids Embalming Work."

45. Daugherty, "Weeping Women."

46. Ibid.

47. Ibid.

48. Columbus native Howard Thurston (1869–1936), the self-proclaimed "King of Cards," was a world-famous stage magician. He reportedly "had the largest traveling Vaudeville show" of his era, using more than eight "entire" train cars to transport props and equipment through the United States.

49. "Former Pen Guard Is Reported Dead," *Ohio State Journal*, April 22, 1930, 3.

50. "Cousin of Irene Shrader Dies in Ohio Penitentiary Disaster," *Columbus Evening Dispatch*, April 23, 1930, 1.

51. Irene Schroeder was sometimes misidentified as "Shrader." Among her monikers were "Trigger Woman," "Blonde Bandit," "Tiger Woman," and "Iron Irene." She led a gang on a crime spree that began in 1929 and ended with her arrest the following year. In 1931 she became the first woman executed in Pennsylvania's electric chair.

52. Bruce Catton, "An O. Henry Story in O. Henry's Prison!," *Austin Statesman*, April 28, 1930, 4.

53. "Man in Pen Less Than Hour Dies," *Columbus Citizen*, April 22, 1930, 1.

54. Catton, "An O. Henry Story."

55. Ibid.

56. "Two of Four Brothers Housed in Ohio Penitentiary Are Victims of Fire," *Columbus Dispatch*, April 22, 1930, 2.

57. Catton, "An O. Henry Story."

58. "Rows of Blackened Bodies."

59. "Huge Grave for Unclaimed Victims," *Ohio State Journal*, April 26, 1930, 1.

60. "Columbus Cemetery Receives Prison Dead," *Chicago Defender*, May 3, 1930, 13.

61. Transcript, 725–26.

Chapter 3: Columbus, Ohio

1. B. F. Dyer, *History of the Ohio Penitentiary, Annex and Prisoners* (Columbus: Ohio Penitentiary Print, 1891), 7.

2. Andrew Henderson, *Forgotten Columbus* (Charleston, SC: Arcadia, 2002), 9.

3. Clara Belle Hicks, "The History of Penal Institutions in Ohio to 1850," *Ohio History 33* (July–October 1924): 371.

4. Ibid.

5. Ibid., 376–78.

6. Ibid.

7. Hicks, "History of Penal Institutions in Ohio," 380n37.

8. Norman Johnston, *Forms of Constraint: A History of Prison Architecture* (Urbana: Illinois University Press, 2000), 79.

9. Norman Johnston, *The Human Cage: A Brief History of Prison Architecture* (New York: Walker, 1973), 40.

10. Glen A. Gildemeister, *Prison Labor and Convict Competition with Free Workers in Industrializing America, 1840–1890* (New York: Garland, 1987), 21.

11. Hicks, "History of Penal Institutions in Ohio," 394, cited in Gildemeister, *Prison Labor*, 21.

12. Johnston, *Human Cage*, 40.

13. Paul F. Cromwell, "Auburn: The World's Second Great Prison System," in *Penology: The Evolution of Corrections in America*, ed. George G. Killinger and Paul F. Cromwell (St. Paul, MN: West, 1973), 6–73; Johnston, *Forms of Constraint*; Scott Christianson, *With Liberty for Some: 500 Years of Imprisonment in America* (Boston: Northeastern University Press, 1998); Norman Johnston, *Eastern State Penitentiary: Crucible of Good Intentions* (Philadelphia: Philadelphia Museum of Art, 1994).

14. James B. Finley, *Memorials of Prison Life* (Cincinnati: L. Swormstedt and J. H. Power, 1850).

15. John Phillips Resch, "Ohio Adult Penal System, 1850–1900: A Study in the Failure of Institutional Reform," *Ohio History* 81, no. 4 (1972): 236–37.

16. Dyer, *History of the Ohio Penitentiary*, 10.

17. Charles Dickens, *American Notes: A Journey* (New York: Fromm International, 1985), 192–93.

18. David Meyers, Elise Meyers Walker, and James Daily III, *Inside the Ohio Penitentiary* (Charleston, SC: History Press, 2013), 12.

19. Writers' Program of the Works Projects Administration in the State of Ohio, *The Ohio Guide* (New York: Oxford University Press, 1962), 247 (hereafter cited as *Ohio Guide*).

20. Gildemeister, *Prison Labor*, 22.

21. Henderson, *Forgotten Columbus*, 37.

22. Ibid., 247

23. William B. Cox, F. Lovell Bixby, and William T. Root, eds., *Handbook of American Prisons and Reformatories*, vol. 1 (New York: Osborne Association, 1933), 780.

24. Stephen Cox, *The Big House: Image and Reality of the American Prison* (New Haven, CT: Yale University Press, 2009), 9.

25. T. J. Thomas and Dan W. Gallagher, *The Spotlight on Ohio's Black Crime* (Cleveland: Charles Margolian, 1930), 12.

26. Gresham M. Sykes, *The Society of Captives: A Study of a Maximum Security Prison*, 3rd ed. (Princeton, NJ: Princeton University Press, 1974), 3.

27. *Ohio Guide*, 264.

28. Richard E. Barrett, *Columbus, 1910–1970* (Charleston, SC: Arcadia, 2006), 51.

29. Ibid.

30. Ibid., 108.

31. *Ohio Guide*, 24.

32. Edward Margolies and Michel Fabre, *The Several Lives of Chester Himes* (Jackson: University of Mississippi Press, 1997).

33. "Mother Who Killed Seven Children Dies in Prison," *Chicago Defender*, May 24, 1930.

34. "Kills Seven Children, Then Shoots Herself," *New York Times*, May 7, 1930, 5.

Chapter 4: Ohio Penitentiary

1. David Meyers, Elise Meyers Walker, and James Dailey III, *Inside the Ohio Penitentiary* (Charleston, SC: History Press, 2013), 17–23.

2. Blake McKelvey, *American Prisons: A Study in American Social History Prior to 1915* (Chicago: University of Chicago Press, 1936), 55. A state board of charities is established by law to oversee the charities of a state, including charitable institutions, sometimes private charitable societies and institutions, typically county, city, and state penal facilities. Ohio abolished the board in 1871 and reestablished and reorganized it in 1876 and 1880 respectively.

3. Ohio Bureau of Inspection and Supervision of Public Offices, *Report on the Ohio State Penitentiary Fire, Columbus, Ohio, April 21, 1930*, 6 pp. (hereafter cited as Fire Report). This is considered the first fire report.

4. B. F. Dyer, *History of the Ohio Penitentiary, Annex and Prisoners* (Columbus: Ohio Penitentiary Print, 1891), 15.

5. "Shocking Criminals, Electricity Substituted for Ducking in the Ohio Penitentiary," *New York Times*, November 24, 1878, 2.

6. Richard E. Barrett, *Columbus, 1910–1970* (Charleston, SC: Arcadia, 2006), 108.

7. McKelvey, *American Prisons: A Study*, 153.

8. Barrett, *Columbus, 1910–1970*.

9. Charles L. Clark, *Lockstep and Corridor: Thirty-Five Years of Prison Life* (Cincinnati: University of Cincinnati Press, 1927), 66. The contract system was a form of convict leasing that allowed prison contractors to utilize cheap prison labor for an assortment of projects. Prisoners were required to work behind prison walls, where they were fed and lodged by prison authorities. Thus, the lessor was only hiring labor of convicts behind prison walls. Other states, mostly in the South, used the convict-leasing system, in which inmates were hired to work outside the confines of the prison structure.

10. Cited in David Lore, "Inside the Pen," *Columbus Dispatch*, October 28, 1984.

11. Tremaine E. O'Quinn and Jenny Lind Porter, *Time to Write: How William Sidney Porter Became O. Henry* (Austin: Eakin Press, 1986), 1.

12. Marvin E. Fornshell, *The Historical and Illustrated Ohio Penitentiary* (Columbus: Marvin E. Fornshell, 1908), 9.

13. Fredric C. Howe to *New York Times*, "Ohio's Prison Farm," *New York Times*, December 1, 1913, 8.

14. John Bartlow Martin, *Break Down the Walls: American Prisons, Present, Past, and Future* (New York: Ballantine Books, 1954), 155.

15. Quoted in ibid., 157–58.

16. "Transcript of Testimony Concerning the Ohio Penitentiary Fire," 1930, Office of the Governor, Ohio History Connection, State Archives series 1144, GR 1573 (hereafter cited as Transcript), 347.

17. Fire Report.

18. Austin H. MacCormick and Paul W. Garrett, eds., *Handbook of American Prisons, 1926* (New York: G. P. Putnam's Sons, 1926).

19. Ibid., 17, 15.

20. Ibid., 465.

21. "Found Conditions Bad at Ohio Prison," *New York Times*, April 22, 1930, 3.

22. Ibid.

23. "Fifteen Ohio Convicts Die in Dormitory Blaze," *New York Times*, October 9, 1928, 22.

24. "Fifteen Bodies Removed from Prison Ashes," *Washington Post*, October 9, 1928, 9.

25. "Fifteen Ohio Convicts Die in Dormitory Blaze."

26. Ibid.

27. Ibid.

28. "Fifteen Bodies Removed from Prison Ashes."

29. Ibid.

30. "Destructive Fire at the Ohio Penitentiary," *Columbus Statesman*, October 27, 1857.

31. "Penitentiary Factories on Fire," *New York Times*, August 28, 1889.

32. "A Penitentiary Fire," *New York Times*, October 22, 1886, 3.

33. "Fire in Ohio Penitentiary," *New York Times*, April 3, 1900.

34. Dyer, *History of the Ohio Penitentiary*, 25.

35. Ibid., 42.

36. Ibid.

37. "How Convicts Fight Fire at Penitentiary," *Ohio State Journal*, March 26, 1905, 4.

38. In March 1905 the fire company was made up of William Idiom, an inmate fire chief; James Lee, Indian Territory; Bob Robinette, Circleville; Jacob Lyon, Findlay; Julius Bernstein, Columbus; Harry Scott, Newark; and John B. Brown, Pickaway County.

39. "How Convicts Fight Fire."

40. James V. Bennett, *I Chose Prison* (New York: Alfred A. Knopf, 1970), 56.

41. Ibid., 56–57.

42. The state use system was the result of prohibitions against competing with free-world laborers. A compromise was reached that permitted the manufacture and sale of prison goods as long as they were for the consumption of state agencies.

43. Paul W. Garrett and Austin H. MacCormick, eds., *Handbook of American Prisons and Reformatories* (New York: National Society of Penal Information, 1929), 743–46.

44. Scott Christianson, *With Liberty for Some: 500 Years of Imprisonment in America* (Boston: Northeastern University Press, 1998), 238.

45. Blake McKelvey, *American Prisons: A History of Good Intentions* (Montclair, NJ: Patterson Smith, 1977).

46. Christianson, *With Liberty for Some*, 238.

47. McKelvey, *American Prisons: A History*, 292–93. This was an ongoing struggle. As early as 1801 the free mechanics of New York protested against the unfair competition of prison industries.

48. The passage of the Ashurst-Summers Act in 1935 strengthened the Hawes-Cooper Act by prohibiting transportation companies from accepting prison products for transportation into any state in violation of the laws of the state and provided for the labeling of all prison products shipped in interstate commerce.

49. By 1933, twenty-nine states had passed similar laws restricting the sale of prison products on the open market.

50. Frank Tannenbaum, *Wall Shadows: A Study in American Prisons* (New York: Putnam, 1922), 119.

51. Harry Elmer Barnes, *The Story of Punishment: A Record of Man's Inhumanity to Man* (Boston: Stratford, 1930), 220–21.

52. John W. Roberts, *Reform and Retribution: An Illustrated History of American Prisons* (Lanham, MD: American Correctional Association, 1997), 86.

53. Garrett and MacCormick, *Handbook of American Prisons*, 747.

54. T. J. Thomas and Dan W. Gallagher, *The Spotlight on Ohio's Black Crime* (Cleveland: Charles Margolian, 1930), 13, 15, 25.

55. Garrett and MacCormick, *Handbook of American Prisons*, 747.

56. Roberts, *Reform and Retribution*, 85.

57. Wickersham Commission, *No. 9 Report*, 11–14.

58. "For Bigger and Better Prisons," *Literary Digest*, August 24, 1929, 8–9.

59. Ibid., 9.

60. Ibid.

61. Peg McGraw and Walter McGraw, *Assignment: Prison Riots* (New York: Henry Holt, 1954), 220.

62. Roberts, *Reform and Retribution*, 95.

63. Norman Johnston, *The Human Cage: A Brief History of Prison Architecture* (New York: Walker, 1973), 40.

64. Richard E. Barrett, "Ohio Penitentiary," *Columbus and Central Ohio Historian*, November 1984, 13.

65. Donald G. Rose, *A Night of Horror* (n.p.: CreateSpace, 2016), 25.

66. Various heights have been given for this. The fire inspectors measured it at fifteen feet. Ray R. Gill, "Special Report, Division of State Fire Marshal. Columbus, Ohio, April 29, 1930," 2 (hereafter cited as Gill Report). The Ohio Pen report described it as ten feet. Thomas estimated it to be twenty to twenty-five feet high (77). "Ohio Penitentiary Fire Report, May 1, 1930," MSS 028, box 18, folder 5, item 3, Ohio University, Mahn Center for Archives and Special Collections (hereafter cited as OPFR), 77.

67. Rose, *A Night of Horror*, 2016.

68. Gill Report, 5. Architecturally speaking, the purlin, or purline, is "a longitudinal member in a roof frame for supporting common rafters between the plate and the ridge."

69. Ibid., 6.

70. Meyers, Walker, and Dailey, *Inside the Ohio Penitentiary*, 90.

71. Gill Report, 5.

72. Transcript, 269.

73. OPFR, 3.

74. According to the original Gill report on the fire, the workers had "discontinued operations about 4 pm for the day, or about an hour and a half before the fire was discovered." Gill Report, 2.

75. Transcript, 405.

76. Ibid., 49.

77. Ibid., 99.

78. Ibid., 164.

79. Ibid., 77.

80. Ibid., 385.

81. Ibid., 430.

82. Wickersham Commission, *No. 9 Report*, 14.

Chapter 5: The Big House

1. Ben M. Crouch, ed., *The Keepers: Prison Guards and Contemporary Corrections* (Springfield, IL: Charles C. Thomas, 1980), 5.

2. Fyodor Dostoevsky, *The House of the Dead* (New York: Grove Press, 1957).

3. Crouch, *Keepers*, 5.

4. Irwin, *Prisons in Turmoil*, 1.

5. Ibid., 3.

6. "Our Overflowing Prisons," *Literary Digest*, April 12, 1930, 12.

7. John L. Gillin, *Taming the Criminal* (New York: Macmillan, 1931), 295–96.

8. Frank Tannenbaum, *Osborne of Sing Sing* (Chapel Hill: University of North Carolina Press, 1933), 3.

9. Percy S. Bullen, "America's Overcrowded Prisons," *Living Age*, June 15, 1930, 503. The "Black Hole of Calcutta" refers to one of the iconic events that took place during Great Britain's drive for India. A number of Europeans were imprisoned in a small prison in Calcutta (now Kolkata) in June 1756. An unknown number of them perished from heat exhaustion or were suffocated. Much of this event is shrouded in myth, but it remains part of the British imperial narrative.

10. The most prominent member was Rutherford B. Hayes, an Ohio governor and Civil War general who became president (1877–81). He would conclude his distinguished career of national service as president of the National Prison Association from 1883 until his death in 1893.

11. Samuel S. Desselem, "Convict Clothing," in *Transactions of the National Congress on Penitentiary and Reformatory Discipline: Held at Cincinnati, Ohio, October 12–18, 1870*, ed. E. C. Wines (Albany: Weed, Parsons, 1871), 294–98.

12. Rev. A. G. Byers, Secretary of the Ohio Board of State Charities, "District Prisons under State Control for Persons Convicted of Minor Offences: Size, Organization, and Discipline Suited to Them," in Wines, *Transactions of the National Congress*, 219–31.

13. Indeterminate sentences were a form of sentencing reform in which convicts could earn marks for good behavior, leading to earlier release from prison. It was a precursor to parole.

14. "Declaration of Principles," in Wines, *Transactions of the National Congress*, 541–71; See also Blake McKelvey, *American Prisons: A History of Good Intentions* (Montclair, NJ: Patterson Smith, 1977); Scott Christianson, *With Liberty for Some: 500 Years of Imprisonment in America* (Boston: Northeastern University Press, 1998).

15. Edgardo Rotman, "The Failure of Reform: United States, 1865–1965," in *The Oxford History of the Prison: The Practice of Punishment in Western Society*, ed. Norval Morris and David J. Rothman (New York: Oxford University Press, 1995), 165.

16. Stephen Cox, *The Big House: Image and Reality of the American Prison* (New Haven, CT: Yale University Press, 2009).

17. Lewis E. Lawes, *Life and Death at Sing Sing* (Garden City, NY: Doubleday, Doran, 1928).

18. Cox, *Big House*, 4–5.

19. McKelvey, *American Prisons: A History*, 291.

20. "One Convict Killed, Two Flee in Break," *Washington Post*, November 5, 1929, 3.

21. Ibid.

22. Mitchel P. Roth, *Crime and Punishment: A History of the Criminal Justice System*, 2nd ed. (Belmont, CA: Wadsworth, 2011), 228.

23. Samuel A. Kramer, "The Norwood Law and Its Effect upon the Penal Problem in Ohio," *Journal of the American Institute of Criminal Law and Criminology* 21, no. 4 (1931): 556.

24. Ibid., 565–66.

25. George W. Alger, "Behind the New York Mutinies," *Survey*, September 1, 1929, 586.

26. Hastings H. Hart, "Riots a Result of Many Causes: Old Cell Houses in Use, What Might Be Done," *New York Times*, April 27, 1930, 135. According to Hart, the actual numbers of prisoners committed under this legislation was rather small, maybe two hundred or so, but "its discouraging influence" was tremendous, creating much bitterness.

27. William Helmer and Rick Mattix, *Public Enemies: America's Criminal Past, 1919–1940* (New York: Checkmark Books, 1998), 61.

28. Alger, "Behind the New York Mutinies," 559.

29. Ibid., 584.

30. "Four Convicts Set Blaze That Cost 322 Lives," *Dallas Morning News*, April 2, 1930, 10.

31. Ralph Blumenthal, *Miracle at Sing Sing: How One Man Transformed the Lives of America's Most Dangerous Prisoners* (New York: St. Martin's Press, 2004), 170.

32. Frank C. Wilcox, "Prison Conditions and Penal Reform," in *Editorial Research Reports 1930*, vol. 2 (Washington, DC: CQ Press, 1930), http://library.cqpress.com/cqresearcher/document.php?id=cqresrre1930050800.

33. Paul W. Keve, *Prison and the American Conscience: A History of U.S. Federal Corrections* (Carbondale: Southern Illinois University Press, 1991), 102.

34. *Proceedings of the 60th Annual Congress of the American Prison Association* (New York: American Prison Association, 1930), 112.

35. [Winthrop D. Lane?], *Survey*, September 1, 1929.

36. "For Bigger and Better Prisons," *Literary Digest*, August 24, 1929, 8–9.

37. See Tom Wicker, *A Time to Die* (New York: New York Times Books, 1975), and Heather Ann Thompson, *Blood in the Water: The Attica Prison Uprising of 1971 and Its Legacy* (New York: Pantheon Books, 2016) (winner of the 2017 Pulitzer Prize).

38. Wayne K. Patterson and Betty L. Alt, *Slaughter in Cell House 3: Anatomy of a Riot* (Arvada, CO: vanderGeest, 1997).

39. "The Bloodiest Prison Mutiny," *Literary Digest*, October 19, 1929, 8.

40. *Proceedings of the 60th Annual Congress*, 113.

41. "Desperation Will Out," *Survey*, January 15, 1930, 451.

42. "Lesson from the Auburn Slaughter," *Literary Digest*, December 28, 1929, 19.

43. Cited in "The Bloodiest Prison Mutiny," 9.

44. *Report of the National Commission on Law Observance and Enforcement* (Wickersham Commission), vol. 9, *Report on Penal Institutions, Probation and Parole* (Washington, D.C.: Government Printing Office, 1931), 235.

45. *Proceedings of the 60th Annual Congress*, 111.

46. Ibid., 113.

47. Ibid.

48. George W. Kirchwey, "The Prison's Place in the Penal System," *Annals of the American Academy of Political and Social Science* 157, no. 1 (1931): 13.

49. Harry Elmer Barnes, *The Story of Punishment: A Record of Man's Inhumanity to Man* (Boston: Stratford, 1930), 170.

Chapter 6: The Warden

1. John Philips Resch, "Ohio Adult Penal System, 1850–1900: A Study in the Failure of Institutional Reform," *Ohio History* 81, no. 4 (1972): 236–62.

2. Ibid., 236.

3. *Report of the National Commission on Law Observance and Enforcement* (Wickersham Commission), vol. 9, *Report on Penal Institutions, Probation and Parole* (Washington, DC: Government Printing Office, 1931), 41.

4. Resch, "Ohio Adult Penal System," 238–39.

5. Osman Castle Hooper, "Preston Elmer Thomas," in *History of the City of Columbus, Ohio* (Columbus: Memorial, ca. 1920), 466.

6. "Transcript of Testimony Concerning the Ohio Penitentiary Fire," 1930, Office of the Governor, Ohio History Connection, State Archives series 1144, GR 1573 (hereafter cited as Transcript), 717.

7. Hooper, *History of the City of Columbus*, 467.

8. Chester Himes, *Cast the First Stone* (New York: Coward-McCann, 1952), 87.

9. T. J. Thomas and Dan W. Gallagher, *The Spotlight on Ohio's Black Crime* (Cleveland: Charles Margolian, 1930), 32.

10. Transcript, 441.

11. Wayne K. Patterson and Betty L. Alt, *Slaughter in Cell House 3: Anatomy of a Riot* (Arvada, CO: vanderGeest Publishing, 1997), 1–2.

12. Cited in Diana Britt Franklin with Nancy Pennell, *Gold Medal Killer: The Shocking True Story of the Ohio State Professor—an Olympic Champion—and His Coed Lover*

(Spokane, WA: Marquette Books, 2010), 155. See also *The Murder of Theora Hix: The Un-censored Testimony of Dr. Snook* (Columbus: n.p., 1929), a pamphlet published shortly before the verdict.

13. Britt with Pennell, *Gold Medal Killer*, 155.

14. James V. Bennett, *I Chose Prison* (New York: Alfred A. Knopf, 1970), 55.

15. Ibid., 55–56.

16. Ibid., 57.

17. Ibid.

18. Ibid., 57–58.

19. Walter A. Lunden, *The Prison Warden and the Custodial Staff* (Springfield, IL: Charles C. Thomas, 1965), 31, 36.

20. David J. Rothman, *Conscience and Convenience: The Asylum and Its Alternatives in Progressive America* (Boston: Little, Brown, 1980), 146.

21. Edwin H. Sutherland and Thorsten Sellin, eds., "Prisons of Tomorrow," special issue, *Annals of the American Academy of Political and Social Science* 157, no. 1 (September 1931): 145–46.

22. Ibid., 146.

23. John Lewis Gillin, *Criminology and Penology* (New York: Century, 1926), 475.

24. Wickersham Commission, 23.

25. Ibid., 40–41.

26. Transcript, 708–10.

27. Ibid., 711.

28. Ibid., 50. See chapter 9 for more on the locking systems available at the time.

29. *Proceedings of the 60th Annual Congress of the American Prison Association, October 1930* (New York: American Prison Association, 1931), 110.

30. Transcript, 439.

Chapter 7: The Keepers

1. Jessica Mitford, *Kind and Usual Punishment: The Prison Business* (New York: Alfred A. Knopf, 1973), cited in Dana M. Britton, *At Work in the Iron Cage: The Prison as Gendered Organization* (New York: New York University Press, 2003), 51.

2. www.bankrate.com/finance/jobs-careers/worst-jobs-1.aspx#slide=1, retrieved August 10, 2017.

3. Ted Conover, *Newjack: Guarding Sing Sing* (New York: Random House, 2000), 20.

4. Peter G. Bourne, "Some Observations on the Psychosocial Phenomena Seen in Basic Training," *Psychiatry* 30, no. 2 (1967): 187–96, cited in Conover, *Newjack*, 12.

5. David J. Rothman, *Conscience and Convenience: The Asylum and Its Alternatives in Progressive America* (Boston: Little, Brown, 1980), 145.

6. Frank Tannenbaum, *Wall Shadows: A Study in American Prisons* (New York: Putnam, 1922), 11–12.

7. D. L. Howard, *John Howard: Prison Reformer* (New York: Archer House, 1963); Edgar C. S. Gibson, *John Howard* (London: Methuen, 1901).

8. Howard, *John Howard*; Norval Morris and David J. Rothman, eds., *The Oxford History of the Prison: The Practice of Punishment in Western Society* (New York: Oxford University Press, 1998).

9. In his final testimony to the board of inquiry on April 26, 1930, Warden Preston Thomas claimed that this form of preparation and regimentation was just as effective as any form of prison fire drill when it came to moving inmates quickly and in organized fashion.

10. David J. Rothman, *The Discovery of the Asylum: Social Order and Disorder in the New Republic*, rev. ed. (Boston: Little, Brown, 1990), 106–7.

11. Thorsten Sellin, "Historical Glimpses of Training for Prison Service," *Journal of Criminal Law and Criminology* 25, no. 4 (1934): 594.

12. John Lewis Gillin, *Taming the Criminal: Adventures in Penology* (New York: Macmillan, 1931); Gillin, "The World's Oldest Training School for Prison Officials," *Journal of Law and Criminology* 23, no. 1 (1932): 101–2.

13. Clarence Stewart Peterson, "Prison Officers' Training Schools," *Journal of Criminal Law and Criminology* 22, no. 6 (1932): 896.

14. Sellin, "Historical Glimpses," 599.

15. Cited in Frederick A. Dorner, "The Prison Officer," in *The Prison and the Prisoner*, ed. Julia K. Jaffray (Boston: Little, Brown, 1917), 117.

16. Lewis E. Lawes, *Twenty Thousand Years in Sing Sing* (New York: Ray Long and Richard R. Smith, 1932), 12.

17. Ralph Blumenthal, *Miracle at Sing Sing: How One Man Transformed the Lives of America's Most Dangerous Prisoners* (New York: St. Martin's Press, 2004), 23.

18. Lawes, *Twenty Thousand Years*, 17–18.

19. Dorner, "Prison Officer," 118.

20. Peterson, "Prison Officers' Training Schools," 895–96.

21. John Bartlow Martin, *Break Down the Walls: American Prisons, Present, Past, and Future* (New York: Ballantine Books, 1954), 171.

22. According to Eric Partridge's classic book on criminal argot, *A Dictionary of the Underworld* (New York: Macmillan, 1950), 603–4, the origins of the word "screw," particularly its relationship with prisons, date back to at least 1797, when it referred to a "false key" or "picklock key." By 1904 it was common lingo for a prison guard, and was even used by the keepers themselves.

23. *Report of the National Commission on Law Observance and Enforcement* (Wickersham Commission), vol. 9, *Report on Penal Institutions, Probation and Parole* (Washington, DC: Government Publishing Office, 1931), 44. See also Edgardo Rotman, "The Failure of Reform: United States, 1865–1965," in Morris and Rothman, *Oxford History of the Prison*, 164.

24. Gordon Hawkins, "Correctional Officer Selection and Training," in *The Keepers: Prison Guards and Contemporary Corrections*, ed. Benjamin M. Crouch (Springfield, IL: Charles C. Thomas, 1980), 60; Harry Elmer Barnes and Negley K. Teeters, *New Horizons in Criminology* (New York: Prentice Hall, 1943), 428–29, cited in Hawkins, "Correctional Officer Selection," 60.

25. Frank Tannenbaum, *Osborne of Sing Sing* (Chapel Hill: University of North Carolina Press, 1933), 3.

26. Tannenbaum, *Wall Shadows*, 29.

27. Between 1929 and 1931 the National Commission on Law Observance and Enforcement, chaired by George Wickersham, examined criminal justice in America. Its conclusions and recommendations were published in two volumes.

28. Victor F. Nelson, *Prison Days and Nights* (Boston: Little, Brown, 1933), 118.

29. Benjamin M. Crouch and James W. Marquart, "On Becoming a Prison Guard," in Crouch, *Keepers*, 74.

30. Ibid..

31. Cited in John Phillips Resch, "Ohio Adult Penal System, 1850–1900: A Study in the Failure of Institutional Reform," *Ohio History Journal* 81, no. 4 (1972): 252.

32. Cited in Rothman, *Conscience and Convenience*, 147.

33. "Transcript of Testimony Concerning the Ohio Penitentiary Fire," 1930, Office of the Governor, Ohio History Connection, State Archives series 1144, GR 1573 (hereafter cited as Transcript), 20.

34. T. J. Thomas and Dan W. Gallagher, *The Spotlight on Ohio's Black Crime* (Cleveland: Charles Margolian, 1930), 37.

35. Ibid., 9.

36. Transcript, 494.

37. Ibid., 443.

38. Richard Straw, "An Act of Faith: Southeastern Ohio Miners in the Coal Strike of 1927," *Labor History* 21 (1980): 221–38.

39. Transcript, 87. Amounts in parentheses are 2018 equivalents.

40. Ibid., 6.

41. Ibid., 147.

42. Ibid., 152.

43. State Civil Service Commission of Ohio, Application for Examination, Arthur John Miller, 1935. Ohio State Archives.

44. Thomas and Gallagher, *The Spotlight on Ohio's Black Crime*, 4.

45. Ibid., 21.

46. Transcript, 704–5.

47. Rothman, *Conscience and Convenience*, 146.

48. Britton, *At Work in the Iron Cage*, 52.

49. https://www.nalc.org/about/facts-and-history/body/1929-1949.

50. William Weinfeld, "Income of Lawyers, 1929–1948," *Survey of Current Business*, August 1949, 18.

51. Rothman, *Conscience and Convenience*, 146; see also Wickersham Commission.

52. "The People History," http://www.thepeoplehistory.com/1930.html.

53. Wickersham Commission, 46.

54. Rothman, *Conscience and Convenience*, 147.

55. Ibid.

56. *Proceedings of the 63rd Annual Congress of the American Prison Association* (New York: American Prison Association, 1933), 228.

57. Martin, *Break Down the Walls*, 170.

58. Britton, *At Work in the Iron Cage*, 2003, 52.

59. D. E. Lundberg, "Methods of Selecting Prison Personnel," *Journal of Criminal Law, and Criminology* 38 (1947): 38.

Chapter 8: The Convicts

1. C. Wilcox, "Prison Conditions and Penal Reform," in *Editorial Research Reports 1930*, vol. 2 (Washington, DC: CQ Press), http://library.cqpress.com/cqresearcher/cqresrre1930050800.

2. *Report of the National Commission on Law Observance and Enforcement* (Wickersham Commission), vol. 9, *Report on Penal Institutions, Probation and Parole* (Washington, DC: Government Printing Office, 1931).

3. James V. Bennett, *I Chose Prison* (New York: Alfred A. Knopf, 1970), 55–56.

4. David Meyers and Elise Meyers, *Central Ohio's Historic Prisons* (Charleston, SC: Arcadia, 2009), 15.

5. Charles L. Clark, *Lockstep and Corridor: Thirty-Five Years of Prison Life* (Cincinnati: University of Cincinnati Press, 1927, 66.

6. T. J. Thomas and Dan W. Gallagher, *The Spotlight on Ohio's Black Crime* (Cleveland: Charles Margolian, 1930), 21.

7. Ibid., 32–33.

8. Ibid.

9. Paul W. Garrett and Austin H. MacCormick, eds., *Handbook of American Prisons and Reformatories* (New York: National Penal Society of Penal Information, 1929), 740–41.

10. Himes would be transferred to the London Prison Farm in 1934, six years into his sentence, before being paroled to his mother in 1936.

11. See for example, Chester Himes, *The Quality of Hurt* (New York: Thunder's Mouth Press, 1988), 60; James Sallis, *Chester Himes: A Life* (New York: Walker, 2001), 210.

12. These will be highlighted through his autobiographical works from this time period when appropriate. One of the major enigmas of his 743 pages' worth of memoirs is that only six pages are devoted to the Ohio Penitentiary. More important are his *factionalized* accounts of the prison and the fire in his 1934 *Esquire* story, "To What Red Hell?" In this early work he vividly portrays the prison holocaust. He would later expand it into *Cast the First Stone* (New York: Coward-McCann, 1952), which after his death was published as originally written as *Yesterday Will Make You Cry* (New York: W.W. Norton, 1998).

13. Originally published in Himes, *Cast the First Stone*, 21–24. Cited in Stephen F. Milliken, *Chester Himes: A Critical Appraisal* (Columbia: University of Missouri Press, 1976), 164.

14. Himes, *Cast the First Stone*, 21–24.

15. Himes, *Yesterday Will Make You Cry*, 34.

16. Ibid., 27–28.

17. James Lundquist, *Chester Himes* (New York: Frederick Ungar, 1976), 7.

18. Himes, *Yesterday Will Make You Cry*, 34.

19. Ibid.

20. Edward Margolies and Michel Fabre, *The Several Lives of Chester Himes* (Jackson: University of Mississippi Press, 1997), 31–32.

21. Donald Clemmer, *The Prison Community*, 2nd ed. (New York: Rinehart, 1958), 56.

22. Glen A. Gildemeister, *Prison Labor and Convict Competition with Free Workers in Industrializing America, 1840–1890* (New York: Garland, 1987), 84.

23. Ibid., 84–85.

24. Ibid., 85n21. A comparison of statistics between the various occupations offers an overview rather than a precise accounting of the former occupations of inmates, hampered by the fact that prisoners often had to choose from a list of categories that varied from prison to prison, while some officials just wrote down whatever the convict replied when asked what his former occupation was.

25. Ibid., 85.

26. Ibid., 79.

27. D. J. Bonzo (Parole and Record Clerk), *Annual Statistical Report with Movement of Population of the Ohio Penitentiary, May 31, 1930*: Nativity report, 13; Descent, 18.

28. Lee J. Levinger, "A Note on Jewish Prisoners in Ohio," *Jewish Social Studies* 2 (January 1940): 210–12. As of December 1938, when there were 67 Jewish prisoners and 2,911 white inmates, the most common crimes committed by current inmates were robbery, burglary, and homicide. For Jewish inmates the top three crime started with robbery, followed by burglary and forgery.

29. Bonzo, *Annual Statistical Report*, Balance sheet of nativity of colored men, 34.

30. John Phillips Resch, "Ohio Adult Penal System, 1850–1900: A Study in the Failure of Institutional Reform," *Ohio History* 81, no. 4 (1972): 240–41.

31. Bonzo, *Annual Statistical Report*. In several of these reports dated May 1930 there are some small numerical errors on the original documents, as in sometimes they just don't add up. Most categories give the number of inmates at the end of April and the end of May, the author used the end of April numbers. The figures cited in this chapter speak to the general breakdown of the prison population the week after the fire.

32. White and "colored" inmates were doing life for the same crimes—bank robbery, first-and second-degree murder, rape, and burglary of an inhabited dwelling at night. The only variation was that of the 571 serving life, 219 were white and the rest colored. *Statistical Report*, Balance Sheet of Life Inmates for April 30, 1930, 37.

33. Bonzo, *Annual Statistical Report*, 24.

34. Ibid., 10–11.

35. Ibid., Occupations, 20–22.

36. Ibid., Ages, 26.

37. Ibid., Marital status, 27.

38. Ibid., Dependents, 36.

39. Ibid., Religions, 29.

40. Ibid., Military training.

41. Edgardo Rotman, "The Failure of Reform: United States, 1865–1965," in *The Oxford History of the Prison: The Practice of Punishment in Western Society*, ed. Norval Morris and David J. Rothman (Oxford: Oxford University Press, 1995), 151–77; Scott Christianson, *With Liberty for Some: 500 Years of Imprisonment in America* (Boston: Northeastern University Press, 1998); Mitchel P. Roth, *Prisons and Prison Systems: A Global Encyclopedia* (Westport, CT: Greenwood Press, 2006), 273–74. In the United States the trustee system

has been the subject of court challenges and much diminished by various legislation and administrations averse to allowing prisoners to control other prisoners. It continues to flourish in countries such as Egypt and Thailand.

42. Diana Britt Franklin with Nancy Pennell, *Gold Medal Killer: The Shocking True Story of the Ohio State Professor—an Olympic Champion—and His Coed Lover* (Spokane, WA: Marquette Books, 2010), 161.

43. Jon Daly, "Tacks Latimer," SABR Bio Project, https://sabr.org/bioproj/person/97221cdd.

44. "'Tacks' Latimer Gets Life Term for Killing," *Washington Post*, January 7, 1925, 18. Meyers, Walker, and Daley note that Latimer had been a teammate of Hall of Famer Honus Wagner. See also David Meyers, Elise Meyers Walker, and James Dailey III, *Inside the Ohio Penitentiary* (Charleston, SC: History Press, 2013), 95; Donald G. Rose, *A Night of Horror* (n.p.: CreateSpace, 2016), 121–22.

45. Thomas and Gallagher, *Spotlight on Ohio's Black Crime*, 32; Rose, *Night of Horror*, 122. According to Rose, it was the warden's daughter and not the warden who handed the weapon to Latimer.

46. "Prison Fire Features," *Austin Statesman*, April 22, 1930, 2.

47. Thomas and Gallagher, *Spotlight on Ohio's Black Crime*, 28.

48. Ibid., 32

49. Meyers, Walker, and Daley, *Inside the Ohio Penitentiary*, 95.

50. Thomas and Gallagher, *Spotlight on Ohio's Black Crime*, 9, 74–76.

51. "Hero of Penitentiary Fire Sought in Pal's Shooting," *Washington Post*, May 19, 1933, 1.

52. Victor F. Nelson, *Prison Days and Nights* (Boston: Little, Brown, 1933), 124.

53. Ibid., 125

54. Ibid., 127.

55. Thomas and Gallagher, *Spotlight on Ohio's Black Crime*, 62–63.

56. Juliet Ash, *Dress behind Bars: Prison Clothing as Criminality* (London: I. B. Tauris, 2010), 73. Prison reformer Dr. Katherine Bement Davis, who had been the superintendent of New York's Bedford Women's Reformatory, has been credited as one of the prime movers for the eradication of prison stripes. Not surprisingly, New York's Auburn Prison, in 1904, was the first prison to do away with the iconic stripes.

57. William B. Cox, F. Lovell Bixby, and William T. Root, eds., *Handbook of American Prisons and Reformatories* (New York: Osborne Association, 1933), 784. Even in 2017 one cannot simply send an inmate a book directly, but must have it mailed from the publisher.

58. Ibid.

59. Thomas and Gallagher, *Spotlight on Ohio's Black Crime*, 25.

60. Ibid., 24–25.

Chapter 9: Board of Inquiry

1. "Death Toll in Pen Fire Reaches 319," *Columbus Citizen*, April 22, 1930, 1–2.

2. *The Governors of Ohio* (Columbus: Ohio History Connection, 1954). It is also not mentioned on the Ohio Central History Central website at http://ohiohistorycentral.org/w/Myers_Y._Cooper as of 2017.

3. "Death Toll in Pen Fire Reaches 319."

4. "Transcript of Testimony Concerning the Ohio Penitentiary Fire," 1930, Ohio History Connection, State Archives series 1144, GR 1573 (hereafter cited as Transcript), 42.

5. "Rows of Blackened Bodies of 317 Prison Fire Victims Await Families for Burial," *Washington Post*, April 23, 1930, 1.

6. Louis Sandy Maisel, ed., *Jews in American Politics* (Lanham, MD: Rowman and Littlefield, 2001), 312; https://supremecourt.ohio.gov/SCO/formerjustices/bios /bettman.asp.

7. Donald G. Rose, *A Night of Horror* (n.p.: CreateSpace, 2016), 58.

8. James R. Winning, *Behind These Walls* (New York: Macmillan, 1933), 245.

9. "Ohio Penitentiary Fire Report, May 1, 1930," MSS 028, box 18, folder 5, item 3, Ohio University, Mahn Center for Archives and Special Collections (hereafter cited as OPFR), 1.

10. Transcript, 2.

11. "318 Deaths in Prison Attributed to Laxity," *Washington Post*, April 24, 1930, 1.

12. Transcript, 91.

13. Ibid., 102.

14. Ibid., 143.

15. Ibid., 98.

16. Ibid., 498.

17. Ibid., 659.

18. Ibid., 70–75.

19. "Delay in Freeing Convicts," *New York Times*, April 23, 1930, 1.

20. "Cruelty Charges Made by Convicts Who Revolt Again," *Dallas Morning News*, April 24, 1930, 1.

21. "Gov. Cooper Backs Prison Warden," *New York Times*, April 25, 1930, 1.

22. Later in the day Richardson was given a thirty-day respite by Governor Cooper, since the clemency board had no time to consider the case.

23. Attending the meeting were Governor Cooper, Director of Public Welfare Hal H. Griswold, Director of Finance Harry D. Silver, Attorney General Bettman and his assistants Earl C. Shively and John J. Chester Jr.

24. "Gov. Cooper Backs Prison Warden."

25. These included Columbus physician Dr. E. J. Emerick and the heads of two state hospitals.

26. "Cruelty Charges Made by Convicts."

27. Ibid.

28. "Ohio Prison Guards at Odds on Rescue," *New York Times*, April 26, 1930, 4.

29. Transcript, 693–703.

30. Ibid., 705–6.

31. Ibid., 707.

32. Ibid., 710.

33. Ibid., 711.

34. "Prison Blaze Blame Placed on Legislature," *Dallas Morning News*, April 26, 1930, 1.

35. Transcript, 717–19; "Prison Blaze Blame Placed on Legislature."

36. Transcript, 720.

37. Ibid., 301.

38. Ibid., 301–4.

39. Ibid., 720–21.

40. Ibid., 337–38.

41. "How Convicts Fight Fire at Penitentiary," *Ohio State Journal*, March 26, 1905, 4.

42. Transcript, 309.

43. He saw these locking systems at San Quentin; Stillwater, Minnesota; Sugar House Prison, Salt Lake City; Waupun Correctional Prison, Wisconsin; Michigan State Prison, Jackson, Michigan; Western Penitentiary in Pittsburgh, Pennsylvania; Florida State Prison in Raiford; and Charleston Prison in Charleston, West Virginia.

44. Transcript, 339.

45. Ibid., 292–93.

46. Ibid., 294.

47. Ibid., 449.

48. T. J. Thomas and Dan W. Gallagher, *The Spotlight on Ohio's Black Crime* (Cleveland: Charles Margolian, 1930), 51.

49. Ibid., 724.

50. Transcript, 592.

51. Ibid., 149.

52. Ibid., 616.

53. Ibid., 602.

54. Ibid., 695.

55. Ibid., 722.

56. OPFR, 6.

57. Ibid., 6a.

58. Ibid., 7a–8.

59. Ibid., 8–14.

60. Ibid., 14–16.

61. Ibid., 16.

62. Ibid., 17.

63. Ibid., 18.

Chapter 10: Mutiny in White City

1. "Incendiarism Seen in Holocaust That Traps Felons," *Washington Post*, April 22, 1.

2. Donald G. Rose, *A Night of Horror* (n.p.: CreateSpace, 2016), 78.

3. "Incendiarism Seen."

4. "Guards Didn't Know What to Tell Probers," *Columbus Evening Dispatch*, April 22.

5. "Stories of Prison Fire Are Jumbled," *Washington Post*, April 26, 1930, 2.

6. Lawrence Jackson, *Chester B. Himes: A Biography* (New York: W. W. Norton, 2017), 85.

7. Rose, *Night of Horror*, 84–85.

8. "Ohio Prison Guards at Odds on Rescue," *New York Times*, April 26, 1930, 4.

9. Rose, *Night of Horror*, 88.

10. "Troops Drop Bombs as Ohio Prisoners Start New Revolt," *New York Times*, April 29, 1930, 17.

11. Rose, *Night of Horror*, 90

12. "Mutinous Convicts Pursued in Tunnel," *Washington Post*, April 28, 1930, 1.

13. Ibid.

14. Orville R. Carson to Governor Myers Y. Cooper, April 28, 1930, Governor Cooper Collection, Ohio State Archives.

15. Governor Cooper to Orville R. Carson, May 5, 1930, Governor Cooper Collection, Ohio State Archives.

16. "Mutinous Convicts Pursued."

17. Ibid.

18. Ibid.

19. Vinson Hunter, "Microphone on Job in Ohio's Jail Fire," *Washington Post*, May 18, 1930, A5. In 2018 prisons had still not figured how to prevent cell phone use.

20. "Mutinous Convicts Pursued."

21. "Troops Drop Bombs."

22. Rose, *Night of Horror*, 90.

23. "Mutinous Convicts Pursued"; "Troops Drop Bombs."

24. "Guards Shoot Two Convicts in Ohio Clash," *Washington Post*, April 30, 1930, 1.

25. "Rifle Fire Repels Rush of Convicts in Ohio Outbreak," *New York Times*, April 30, 1930, 1.

26. "Militia Rules Ohio Prison Convicts," *Austin American Statesman*, April 30, 1930, 1.

27. "Rifle Fire Repels Rush of Convicts."

28. Forrest Richmond to Hon. Myers Y. Cooper, Governor, Confidential Memo, April 30, 1930, Ohio State Archives. This account has never been cited in any account of the fire and its aftermath.

29. "Rifle Fire Repels Rush of Convicts"; "Pen Rioters Free Doomed Convicts," *Austin Statesman*, April 29, 1930, 1.

30. Forrest Richmond to Hon. Myers Y. Cooper.

31. Ibid.

32. Ibid.

33. "Pen Rioters Free Doomed Convicts."

34. Ibid.

35. "Rifle Fire Repels Rush."

36. Rose asserts that the stockade fence was only eleven feet high. If this is true, then the telephone posts had to have been placed at least seven feet into the ground. Rose, *Night of Horror*, 101.

37. F. Raymond Daniell, "Revolting Convicts Give up Stronghold to Ohio Militiamen," *New York Times*, May 1, 1930, 1.

38. Ibid.

39. Ibid.

40. "Rifle Fire Repels Rush."

41. "Troops Stay at Ohio Prison Two Weeks," *Austin Statesman*, May 2, 1930, 2.

42. "Rifle Fire Repels Rush."

43. "Troops Stay at Ohio Prison."

44. "Rifle Fire Repels Rush."

45. "Guards Shoot Two Convicts in Ohio Clash," *Washington Post*, April 30, 1930, 1.

46. "Still Discovered in Radio Cabinet in Ohio's Prison," *Dallas Morning News*, May 4, 1930, 1; Hunter, "Microphone on Job."

47. "Quiet Prevails in Ohio Prison," *Austin Statesman*, May 4, 1930.

48. F. Raymond Daniell, "Crowding Menaces Ohio Institutions," *New York Times*, May 4, 1930, 1.

49. Governor Cooper to Daniel Fries, May 17, 1930, Governor Cooper Collection, Ohio State Archives.

50. A. White to Governor Cooper, May 5, 1930; Governor Cooper to P. A. White, May 19, 1930, Governor Cooper Collection, Ohio State Archives.

51. "Concrete to Roof Ohio Cell Blocks," *Washington Post*, May 6, 1930, 3.

52. "Murder Two More in Ohio Pen," *New York Liberator*, May 17, 1930, 1. In this account in an African American newspaper, an editor describes the killings as the result of a machine gun "'accidentally' discharged," the quotation marks seemingly mocking the notion that these deaths could have been anything other than outright murder.

53. "Two Convicts Killed," *Dallas Morning News*, May 9, 1930, 1; "Machine Gun Kills Two Ohio Convicts," *New York Times*, May 9, 1930, 15.

54. "Machine Gun Kills Two."

55. Ibid.

56. "Six Ohio Convicts Missing," *New York Times*, May 21, 1930, 19.

57. P. E. Thomas, "The Ohio Penitentiary," in H. H. Griswold, *Ninth Annual Report of the Department of Public Welfare, State of Ohio for the Fiscal Year Ending December 31, 1930*, 562.

58. H. H. Griswold, "Significant Events: Penitentiary Fire," in Griswold, *Ninth Annual Report*, 36.

59. A Prisoner, "The Prisoner Speaks," in *Prisons of Tomorrow*, ed. Edwin H. Sutherland and Thorsten Sellin, Annals of the American Academy of Political and Social Science 157 (Philadelphia: American Academy of Political and Social Science, 1931), 142.

60. "Again Death Stalks through a Prison," *New York Times*, April 27, 1930.

61. "Shot Halts Break at Ohio Prison Farm," *New York Times*, May 31, 1930, 1.

62. Ibid.; "One Prisoner Slain as 47 Essay Break," *Washington Post*, May 31, 1930, 4.

63. David Meyers, Elise Meyers Walker, and James Dailey II, *Inside the Ohio Penitentiary* (Charleston, SC: History Press, 2013), 100.

64. Rose, *Night of Horror*, 110.

65. James R. Winning, *Behind These Walls* (New York: Macmillan, 1933), 246.

Chapter 11: The Arsonists

1. Ohio Bureau of Inspection and Supervision of Public Offices, *Report on the Ohio State Penitentiary Fire, Columbus, Ohio, April 21, 1930;* Ray R. Gill, "Special Report, Division of State Fire Marshal, Columbus, Ohio, April 29, 1930"; "Ohio Penitentiary Fire Report, May 1, 1930," MSS 028, box 18, folder 5, item 3, Ohio University, Mahn Center for Archives and Special Collections (hereafter cited as OPFR).

2. "Incendiarism Seen in Holocaust That Traps Felons in Cell Block, Disorder Comes in Wake of Flames with 1,500 Soldiers Called Out," *Washington Post*, April 22, 1930, 1; "Hundreds of Prisoners Trapped by Fire Due to Incendiaries," *New York Times*, April 21, 1930.

3. Ohio Bureau of Inspection and Supervision of Public Offices, *Report on the Ohio State Penitentiary Fire, Columbus, Ohio, April 21, 1930* (hereafter cited as Fire Report).

4. "Death Toll in Pen Fire Reaches 319," *Columbus Citizen*, April 22, 1930, 1–2.

5. "Guard's Theory," *Columbus Citizen*, April 22, 1930, 1.

6. T. J. Thomas and Dan W. Gallagher, *The Spotlight on Ohio's Black Crime* (Cleveland: Charles Margolian, 1930), 13.

7. Ray R. Gill, "Special Report, Division of State Fire Marshal, Columbus, Ohio, April 29, 1930" (hereafter cited as Gill Report).

8. OPFR, 6.

9. Ibid., 6a.

10. "To Query Two on Prison Fire," *Dallas Morning News*, August 16, 1930, 1.

11. Ibid.

12. "Ohio Convicts Held in Fire," *New York Times*, August 16, 1930, 17.

13. Gibbons's real last name was actually Gibson. I have used Gibbons for consistency and because most of the contemporary accounts did. According to Rose, his real name was indeed Gibson, but for some reason he was identified as Gibbons when he was checked in and the inaccuracy was never rectified.

14. Donald G. Rose, *A Night of Horror* (n.p.: CreateSpace, 2016), 132.

15. "Four Convicts Set Blaze That Cost 322 Lives," *Dallas Morning News*, April 21, 1931, 10. According to Rose, *A Night of Horror*, he used a stack of blankets as a jerrybuilt scaffold from which to hang himself.

16. "Ohio Prison Arson Traced to Inmates," *New York Times*, August 18, 1930, 3. "Prison delivery" was contemporary slang for "escape" or "breakout."

17. Rose, *Night of Horror*, 133.

18. Ibid., 134. It is unclear how he attempted to kill himself the other time.

19. "Convicts' Ruse Failed; Caused Deaths of 320," *New York Times*, August 17, 1930, 19; "Delay in Convicts' Plot Caused 320 to Die, but Kept Thousands from Escaping, Probers Find," *Dallas Morning News*, August 17, 1930, 1.

20. "Ohio Prison Fire Caused by Ill-Timed Escape Plot," *Austin American Statesman*, August 17, 1930, 1.

21. A. Bruce Bielaski, "Introduction," in Brendan P. Battle and Paul B. Weston, *Arson: A Handbook of Detection and Investigation* (New York: Arco, 1967), xiii.

22. Brendan P. Battle and Paul B. Weston, *Arson: A Handbook of Detection and Investigation* (New York: Arco, 1967), 3; Gilda Moss Haber, "Human Behaviour in Fire in Total Institutions: A Case Study," in *Fires and Human Behaviour*, ed. David Canter (Chichester, UK: John Wiley, 1980), 138.

23. Haber, "Human Behaviour in Fire," 138.

24. Rose, *Night of Horror*, 135.

25. "Four Convicts Set Blaze."

26. Much of the narrative on the March 1931 Franklin County grand jury is based on Rose's *A Night of Horror*.

27. Ibid., 136.

28. "Two Facing Trial for Tragic Fire of Year Ago," *Dallas Morning News*, April 6, 1931, 1.

29. "Man Who Aided Start in Prison Fire Kills Self," *Washington Post*, January 16, 1933, 1.

30. Rose, *Night of Horror*, 137.

31. Clayton Rose was the father of *A Night of Horror* author Don Rose, who based much of his book on the fire on his father's records. Unfortunately, the manuscript lacks any citations or attributions.

32. "Man Who Aided Start."

33. Gibbons was not Jewish. I have not been able to determine where this moniker came from.

34. "Two Convicts Admit Starting Ohio Prison Fire That Killed 320," *Washington Post*, April 2, 1931, 1.

35. It was still not clear how the oil concoction got into the cellblock, nor how the two men were able to spend so much time alone on the fifth tier of the I&K block. But, as already noted, there was no shortage of combustible materials on hand, since construction on a new cellblock was under way just feet away. Nor was it difficult to find an accelerant. Fire investigators later mentioned they were struck by the availability of highly inflammable liquids such as oil and low-grade gasoline cigar lighters and candles.

36. "Two Convicts Admit Starting Ohio Prison Fire," 2.

37. "Four Convicts Set Blaze."

38. "Two Convicts Indicted for Prison Fire," April 3, 1931, *Dallas Morning News*, 12; "Indicts Two Felons in Ohio Prison Fire," *New York Times*, April 3, 1931, 20.

39. "Indicts Two Felons in Ohio Prison Fire," *New York Times*, April 3, 1931, 20; "Two Convicts Indicted."

40. "Felons Ask Death Soon for Prison Fire," *New York Times*, April 4, 1931, 3.

41. "Two Facing Trial for Tragic Prison Fire of Year Ago," *Dallas Morning News*, April 6, 1931, 1.

42. "Two Get Life Terms for Ohio Prison Fire," *New York Times*, May 27, 1931, 56.

43. "Man Who Aided Start in Prison Fire Kills Self," *Washington Post*, January 16, 1933, 1; "Prison Incendiary Ends Life in Cell," *New York Times*, January 16, 1933, 16.

44. Rose, *Night of Horror*, 160.

45. Peg McGraw and Walter McGraw, *Assignment: Prison Riots* (New York: Henry Holt, 1954), 221.

Chapter 12: Aftermath

1. "1930: Lee Akers, after the Ohio Penitentiary Fire," June 13, 2012, http://www.executedtoday.com/2012/06/13/1930-lee-akers-ohio-penitentiary-fire/

2. "Cox Again Assails Ohio Prison Warden," *New York Times*, June 4, 1930, 24.

3. F. Raymond Daniell, "Crowding Menaces Ohio Institutions," *New York Times*, May 4, 1930, N1.

4. Ibid.

5. "Rioting Again Breaks Out in Ohio's Prison," *Washington Post*, April 28, 1930, 2.

6. George Jackson to Governor Cooper, handwritten from Baltimore, no date, Myers Y. Cooper Collection 337, box 18, Ohio Historical Society.

7. Ibid.

8. *The Governors of Ohio* (Columbus: Ohio History Connection, 1954). It is also not mentioned on the Ohio Central History Central website, http://ohiohistorycentral.org/w/Myers_Y._Cooper, of 2017.

9. George Jackson to Governor Cooper, ca. 1930, Myers Y. Cooper Collection, 337, box 18.

10. H. J. McAbier to Governor Cooper, April 25, 1930, Myers Y. Cooper Collection, 337, box 18.

11. Cleveland's Collinwood school fire in 1908 was one of the deadliest school fires in U.S. history, costing the lives of 172 students and 2 teachers. The tragedy prompted a number of school safety reforms across the country. Chicago's 1903 Iroquois Theater inferno left 602 dead, making it the deadliest single-building fire in U.S. history.

12. Governor Cooper to H. J. McAbier, April 28, 1930, Myers Y. Cooper Collection, 337, box 18.

13. Mrs. M. L. Heath to Myers Y. Cooper, April 29, 1930, Myers Y. Cooper Collection, 337, box 18.

14. Frank W. Bail to Governor Myers Y. Cooper, "Re: Problems of Prison Commission," May 1, 1930, 1, Myers Y. Cooper Collection, 337, box 18.

15. Ibid., 2.

16. Ann Simpson Chapter, DAR, to the Ohio Daughters of the American Revolution, May 5, 1930, Myers Y. Cooper Collection, 337, box 18.

17. Kiwanis Club to Gove[r]nor Myers Y. Cooper, May 6, 1930, Myers Y. Cooper Collection, 337, box 18.

18. *Proceedings of the 60th Annual Congress of the American Prison Association* (New York: American Prison Association, 1930), 110.

19. Ibid., 111.

20. Ibid., 113.

21. Ibid.

22. N. R. Howard, "Ohio Adopts Plans for Prison Reform," *New York Times*, April 19, 1931, 57.

23. *Proceedings of the Sixty-First Annual Congress of the American Prison Association* (New York: American Prison Association, 1931), 140.

24. Ibid.

25. Ibid.

26. Ibid.

27. *Journal of Criminal Law* (July 1931); *Proceedings of the Sixty-First Annual Congress*, 365.

28. *Proceedings of the Sixty-Second Annual Congress of the American Prison Association* (New York: American Prison Association, 1932), 418.

29. Ibid.

30. Ibid., 419.

31. Ibid.

32. Ibid., 420.

33. Ibid., 423.

34. *Report of the National Commission on Law Observance and Enforcement* (Wickersham Commission), vol. 9, *Report on Penal Institutions, Probation and Parole* (Washington, DC: U.S. Government Printing Office, 1931.

35. "Penologists Back Wickersham Data," *New York Times*, October 32, 1931, 17.

36. Ibid.

37. William B. Cox, F. Lovell Bixby, and William T. Root, eds., *Handbook of American Prisons and Reformatories*, vol. 1 (New York: Osborne Association, 1933), 780. The 1933 handbook followed three previous ones published in 1925, 1926, and 1929. They are a valuable resource for anyone studying American prison conditions in the 1920s and 1930s. In November 1932, the National Society of Penal Information, Inc. and the Welfare League Association, Inc., both founded by noted prison reformer Thomas Mott Osborne, merged into one association, forming the Osborne Association, Inc. This transition was in part a response to the current economic conditions. By combining forces, both organizations could improve the quality of work and make better use of resources.

38. Ibid., 781.

39. Ibid., 782.

40. Ibid., 785.

41. Ibid., 790.

42. Ibid., 791.

43. Ibid., 792.

44. Ibid., 795.

45. *New York Times*, April 30, 1930.

46. *New York Times*, May 4, 1930.

47. "Orders Safeguards in State Prisons," *New York Times*, April 23, 1930.

48. Ibid.

49. "Most Prisons Here Called Fireproof," *New York Times*, April 23, 1930, 3.

50. "Seven Federal Bills Favorably Reported by Senate Committee, Spurred by Ohio Fire," *New York Times*, April 24, 1930, 32.

51. Sanford Bates, *Prisons and Beyond* (New York: Macmillan, 1936), 210–11.

52. Ibid.

53. "Prison Guards Get Fire Training Here," *New York Times*, April 13, 1937, 2.

54. Ibid.

55. "Two Guards from Every Prison in the State Will Be Trained at Fire College Here," *New York Times*, March 29, 1937, 21.

56. Charles L. Sherwood, "Ohio's Penal Problems," in *Proceedings of the Seventieth Annual Congress of the American Prison Association, October 1940* (New York: American Prison Association, 1940), 19.

57. Ibid., 19–20.

58. Ibid., 20.

59. Ibid., 21.

60. Ibid.

61. Peg McGraw and Walter McGraw, *Assignment: Prison Riots* (New York: Henry Holt, 1954), 221.

62. Bert Useem and Peter Kimball, *States of Siege, 1971–1976* (New York: Oxford University Press, 1989), 10.

63. David Meyers, Elise Meyers Walker, and James Dailey III, *Inside the Ohio Penitentiary* (Charleston, SC: History Press, 2013), 125–31.

64. Blake McKelvey, *American Prisons: A History of Good Intentions* (Montclair, NJ: Patterson Smith, 1977), 325.

65. McGraw and McGraw, *Assignment: Prison Riots*, 219.

66. Ibid., 220.

67. Cited in Meyers, Walker, and Dailey, *Inside the Ohio Penitentiary*, 141.

68. Bruce Porter, "Terror on an Eight Hour Shift," *New York Times Magazine*, November 26, 1995, 42.

69. Reid H. Montgomery Jr. and Gordon A. Crews, *A History of Correctional Violence: An Examination of Reported Causes of Riots and Disturbances* (Lanham, MD: American Correctional Association, 1993).

70. Porter, "Terror on an Eight Hour Shift," 42.

71. See, for example, David Von Drehle, *Triangle: The Fire That Changed America* (New York: Grove Press, 2003); and Leon Stein, *The Triangle Fire* (New York: Carroll and Graf, 1985).

72. Nicholas Faith, *Blaze: The Forensics of Fire* (London: Channel 4 Books, 1999).

73. "Ohio's Prison Holocaust," *World's Work* 59 (July 1930): 19–20.

74. "Ohio Tragedy Jar to Faith in Human Nature," *Austin Statesman*, April 26, 1930, 4.

75. Gilda Ross Haber, "Human Behaviour in Fire in Total Institutions," in *Fires and Human Behaviour*, ed. David Canter (Chichester, UK: John Wiley, 1980), 147.

Epilogue

1. See *Moving Picture World*, June 22, 1922, 1159; Kevin Brownlow, *Behind the Mask of Innocence* (Berkeley: University of California Press, 1990), 240.

2. Bruce Crowther, *Captured on Film: The Prison Movie* (London: B. T. Batsford, 1989), 8.

3. Ibid, 3.

4. James Robert Parish, *Prison Pictures from Hollywood* (Jefferson, NC: McFarland, 1991), 31.

5. Ibid.

6. Ibid.

7. Ibid.

8. "Ohio Censors Bar 'The Big House' Film," *New York Times*, September 21, 1930.

9. Ibid.

10. Ibid. The famous actor Lon Chaney had been scheduled to star in the film but was dying of cancer, so the role went to Beery.

11. "Ohio Rioters End Solitary Confinement," *Washington Post*, December 16, 1931, 1.

12. Ibid.

13. Ibid.

14. Ibid.

15. E. C. McEniry, *Hero Priest of the Ohio Penitentiary Fire: Rev. Albert O'Brien* (Somerset, OH: Rosary Press, 1934), 23.

16. "Compiles List of Nicknames," *Madera Tribune*, July 30, 1931.

17. Detroit's Purple Gang was a major player in the Prohibition bootlegging rackets. It was Detroit's dominant mob faction from the 1930s into the 1950s. See for example, Paul R. Kavieff, *The Purple Gang: Organized Crime in Detroit, 1910–1945* (New York: Harper and Brothers, 2000).

18. Denny Walsh, "Leniency for a Hoodlum, Slush Fund Income," *Life Magazine*, May 2, 1969, 30–32A.

19. Ibid.

20. "Ohio Warden Suspended," *New York Times*, January 26, 1935, p. 11.

21. "Ohio Convicts Boo Departing Warden," *New York Times*, January 27, 1935, 17.

22. Ibid., 31.

23. "Thomas Is Reinstated as Ohio Prison Head," *New York Times*, April 20, 1935, 28.

24. "P. E. Thomas, Warden in '30 Ohio Prison Fire," *New York Times*, October 7, 1952, 29.

25. Diana Britt Franklin, *The Good-Bye Door: The Incredible True Story of America's First Female Serial Killer to Die in the Chair* (Kent: Kent State University Press, 2006), 180–81.

26. Andrew Henderson, *Forgotten Columbus* (Charleston, SC: Arcadia, 2002), 21–23.

27. Peter Steinfels, "A Most Awful Inferno, 50 Years Ago this Week," *New York Times*, December 6, 2008, A14.

28. Steven Greenhouse, "Coalition Pushes for Memorial to the Triangle Fire," *New York Times*, November 20, 2015.

29. "Ohio Is Divided on Prison Ethics," *New York Times*, May 11, 1930, 52.

30. George Richmond, "After the Storm New Strength," *Ohio Penitentiary News*, June 7, 1930, 1.

31. Ibid.

BIBLIOGRAPHY

Archives

Thomason Room, Sam Houston State University Special Collections, Huntsville, TX
Ohio History Connection Archives and Library
Columbus Metropolitan Library

Primary Resources

Application for Guard Examination, State Civil Service Commission of Ohio, [Arthur John Miller], 1935. Arthur Miller Collection, Ohio History Connection, State Archives MSS 1096.

Bonzo, D. J. *Annual Statistical Report with Movement of Population of the Ohio Penitentiary, May 31, 1930*. Ohio History Connection, State Archives series 1796, box 51, 593.

Cooper, Governor Myers Y., Papers. Ohio History Connection, Collection 337, Prison Fire . . . , 1930, box 18; Prison Files A–G, 1929–30, box 24; Prison Files, Letters A–Z, box 27; Prison Files, Pardons A–Z and misc., box 28. Ohio History Connection, State Archives and Library.

Gill, Ray R. "Special Report, Division of State Fire Marshal. Columbus, Ohio, April 29, 1930." 6 pp.

List of Board and Staff Members on Active Duty during Ohio Penitentiary Disaster Apr 21–26, 1930, Franklin County Chapter, American Red Cross. Ohio History Connection, State Archives.

[List of] Embalmers and Assistants from Columbus and Nearby Towns Who Volunteered Their Services at State Fair Grounds. Ohio History Connection, State Archives.

List of Victims of the Ohio Penitentiary Fire with their Death Certificates. http://www.geneologybug.net/ohio_alhn/crime/ohio_pen_fire.html.

McEniry, E. C. *Hero Priest of the Ohio Penitentiary Fire: Rev. Albert O'Brien*. Somerset, OH: Rosary Press, 1934. Ohio History Connection, State Library. Call #922.2 Ob6m.

Miller, J. Notes on Ohio Pen Educational Series of Lectures, November 14, 1939. Arthur Miller Collection, Ohio History Connection, State Archives MSS 1096.

Ohio Bureau of Inspection and Supervision of Public Offices. *Report on the Ohio State Penitentiary Fire, Columbus, Ohio, April 21, 1930*. New York Public Library, control no. 5399621, call no. *Cp.v. 2147.

"Ohio Penitentiary. Amount of Vegetables etc. used in Preparation of Meals for 4000 inmates." 1938. Ohio History Connection, State Archives.

"Ohio Penitentiary Fire Report, May 1, 1930." (OPFR) MSS 028, box 18, folder 5, item 3. Ohio University, Mahn Center for Archives and Special Collections.

Ohio Penitentiary Fire [graphic]. Ohio History Connection, State Archives and Library, SC 762.

Ohio Penitentiary News (microfilm). Ohio History Connection, State Library, FLM 345, roll 1.

Thomas, P. E. "The Ohio Penitentiary" (December 31, 1930). In *Ninth Annual Report of Public Welfare, State of Ohio for the Fiscal Year Ending December 31, 1930*, by H. H. Griswold, 562–76. 1931.

Thomas, T. J., and Dan W. Gallagher. *The Spotlight on Ohio's Black Crime*. Cleveland: Charles Margolian, 1930. Ohio History Connection, State Library, PA box 649 20.

"Transcript of Testimony Concerning the Ohio Penitentiary Fire" (microfilm). Office of the Governor. Ohio History Connection, State Archives series 1144, GR 1573.

Newspapers Consulted

Austin Statesman
Buffalo Courier-Express
Chicago Defender
Chronicle-Telegram (Elyria, OH)
Columbus Citizen
Columbus Evening Dispatch
Connelsville (PA) *Courier*
Dallas Morning News
New York Times
Ohio Penitentiary News
Ohio State Journal
Wall Street Journal, 1930.
Washington Post

Secondary Sources

Prisoner, A. "The Prisoner Speaks." In *Prisons of Tomorrow*, edited by Edwin Sutherland and Thorsten Sellin, 137–49. Annals of the American Academy of Political and Social Science 157. Philadelphia: American Academy of Political and Social Science, 1931.

Ash, Juliet. *Dress behind Bars: Prison Clothing as Criminality*. London: I. B. Tauris, 2010.

Barnes, Harry Elmer. *The Story of Punishment: A Record of Man's Inhumanity to Man*. Boston: Stratford, 1930.

Barnes, Harry Elmer, and Negley K. Teeters. *New Horizons in Criminology*. New York: Prentice Hall, 1943.

Barrett, Richard E. "Ohio Penitentiary." *Columbus and Central Ohio Historian* (November 1984): 2–24.

Bates, Sanford. "Have Our Prisons Failed?" *Journal of Criminal Law and Criminology* 23, no. 3 (1930): 562–74.

———. *Prisons and Beyond*. New York: Macmillan, 1936.

Battle, Brendan P., and Paul B. Weston. *Arson: A Handbook of Detection and Investigation*. New York: Arco, 1967.

Beitler, Stu. "Columbus, OH State Penitentiary Fire Disaster, Apr 1930." February 22, 2008. http://www.gendisasters.com/ohio/5191/columbus,-oh-state-penitentiary-fire-disaster,-apr-1930.

Bennett, James V. "American Prisons—Houses of Idleness." *Survey* (April 1935).

———. *I Chose Prison*. New York: Alfred A. Knopf, 1970.

Bernstein, Arnie. *Bath Massacre: America's First School Bombing*. Ann Arbor: University of Michigan Press, 2009.

Blue, Ethan. *Doing Time in the Depression: Everyday Life in Texas and California Prisons*. New York: NYU Press, 2012.

Bond, Horatio. "The Fire Problem in Prisons." In *Proceedings of the Sixty-Second Annual Congress of the American Prison Association*, 418–24. New York: American Correctional Association, 1932.

Blumenthal, Ralph. *Miracle at Sing Sing: How One Man Transformed the Lives of America's Most Dangerous Prisoners*. New York: St. Martin's Press, 2004.

Bourne, Peter G. "Some Observations on the Psychosocial Phenomena Seen in Basic Training." *Psychiatry* 30, no. 2 (1967): 187–96.

Britton, Dana M. *At Work in the Iron Cage: The Prison as Gendered Organization*. New York: New York University Press, 2003.

Brownlow, Kevin. *Behind the Mask of Innocence*. Berkeley: University of California Press, 1990.

Bullen, Percy S. "America's Overcrowded Prisons." *Living Age*, June 15, 1930, 503.

Butler, Hal. *Inferno! Fourteen Tragedies of Our Time*. New York: Dorset, 1975.

Byers, A. G. "District Prisons under State Control for Persons Convicted of Minor Offences: Size, Organization, and Discipline Suited to Them." In *Transactions of the National Prison Congress on Penitentiary and Reformatory Discipline*, edited by E. C. Wines, 219–31. Albany: Weed, Parsons, 1871.

Cain, Mollie C. *Keys to the Cages: 1930 Ohio Penitentiary Fire*. n.p.: Four Cats, 2013.

Christianson, Scott. *With Liberty for Some: 500 Years of Imprisonment in America*. Boston: Northeastern University Press, 1998.

Clark, Charles L. *Lockstep and Corridor: Thirty-Five Years of Prison Life*. Cincinnati: University of Cincinnati Press, 1927.

Clemmer, Donald. *The Prison Community*. 2nd ed. New York: Rinehart, 1958.

Cole, Charles Chester. *A Fragile Capital: Identity and the Early Years of Columbus, Ohio*. Columbus: Ohio State University Press, 2001.

"Columbus Mental Hospital Harper-McKinley Cemetery." http://www.forgottenoh.com/Asylum/harper.html.

Conover, Ted. *Newjack: Guarding Sing Sing*. New York: Random House, 2000.

Cox, Stephen. *The Big House: Image and Reality of the American Prison*. New Haven, CT: Yale University Press, 2009.

Cox, William B. "Ohio [Penitentiary Fire, Columbus]." National Society Pen Information, New York Bulletin, June 1930, 1:1–4.

Cox, William B., F. Lovell Bixby, and William T. Root, eds. *Handbook of American Prisons and Reformatories*. New York: Osborne Association, 1933.

Cromwell, Paul F. "Auburn: The World's Second Great Prison System." In *Penology: The Evolution of Corrections in America*, edited by George G. Killinger and Paul F. Cromwell, 6–73. St. Paul, MN: West, 1973.

Crouch, Ben M., ed. *The Keepers: Prison Guards and Contemporary Corrections*. Springfield, IL: Charles C. Thomas, 1980.

Crowther, Bruce. *Captured on Film: The Prison Movie*. London: B. T. Batsford, 1989.

Daly, Jon. "Tacks Latimer." SABR BioProject. https://sabr.org/bioproj/person/97221cdd.

"The Deadliest Prison Fire." *National Fire Protection Association Journal* (September /October 1995): 84–85.

Deford, Miriam Allen. *Stone Walls: Prisons from Fetter to Furloughs*. Philadelphia: Clinton, 1962.

Desselem, Samuel S. "Convict Clothing." In *Transactions of the National Congress on Penitentiary and Reformatory Discipline: Held at Cincinnati, Ohio, October 12–18, 1870*, edited by E. C. Wines, 294–98. Albany: Weed, Parsons, 1871.

Devon, James. *The Criminal and the Community*. London: John Lane, 1912.

Dickens, Charles. *American Notes: A Journey*. New York: Fromm International, 1985.

Dorner, Frederick A. "The Prison Officer." In *The Prison and the Prisoner*, edited by Julia K. Jaffray, 115–23. Boston: Little, Brown, 1917.

Dostoevsky, Fyodor. *The House of the Dead*. New York: Grove Press, 1957.

Dyer, B. F. *History of the Ohio Penitentiary, Annex and Prisoners*. Columbus: Ohio Penitentiary Print, 1891.

Edwards, Randall. "Man Recalls Horror of Ohio Pen Fire 60 Years Ago." *Columbus Dispatch* online, April 15, 1990.

Esposito, John C. *Fire in the Grove: The Cocoanut Grove Tragedy and Its Aftermath*. Boston: Da Capo Press, 2005.

Faith, Nicholas. *Blaze: The Forensics of Fire*. London: Channel 4 Books, 1999.

Finley, James B. *Memorials of Prison Life*. Cincinnati: L. Swormstedt and J. H. Power, 1850.

Fogle, H. M. *The Palace of Death*. Columbus: H. M. Fogle, 1908.

Fornshell, Marvin E. *The Historical and Illustrated Ohio Penitentiary*. Columbus: Marvin E. Fornshell, 1908.

Fox, Vernon Brittain. *Violence behind Bars: An Explosive Report on Prison Riots in the United States*. Westport, CT: Greenwood Press., 1975

Franklin, Diana Britt, with Nancy Pennell. *Gold Medal Killer: The Shocking True Story of the Ohio State Professor—an Olympic Champion—and His Coed Lover*. Spokane, WA: Marquette Books, 2010.

Franklin, H. Bruce. *Prison Literature in America: The Victim as Criminal and Artist*. New York: Oxford University Press, 1989.

Friedman, Lawrence M. *Crime and Punishment in American History*. New York: Basic Books, 1993.

Gall, Joe. "Death on a Legend: Book Closing on Another Chapter in Ohio History." *Motive* (November/December 1971). http://www.mrps.org/learn/history/death-on -a-legend.

Garrett, Paul W., and Austin H. MacCormick, eds. *Handbook of American Prisons and Reformatories*. New York: National Society of Penal Information, 1929.

Gibson, Edgar C. S. *John Howard*. London: Methuen, 1901.

Gildemeister, Glen A. *Prison Labor and Convict Competition with Free Workers in Industrializing America, 1840–1890*. New York: Garland, 1987.

Gillin, John Lewis. *Criminology and Penology*. New York: Century, 1926.

Goodman, Ralph. "What Type of Locks Do Prisons Use?" Lock Blog, October 12, 2015. http://united-locksmith.net/blog/what-type-of-locks-do-prisons-use.

Groome, John C. "The Riot Call." *Saturday Evening Post*, January 25, 1930, 6–7, 98 102.

Haber, Gilda Moss. "Human Behaviour in Fire in Total Institutions: A Case Study." In *Fires and Human Behaviour*, edited by David Canter, 137–54. Chichester, UK: John Wiley, 1980.

Hale, George W. *Police and Prison Cyclopaedia*. Boston: Richardson, 1893.

Hart, Hastings H. "Do These Conditions Exist in Your Local Police State, County Jail, or 2 Workhouse?" *American City* 41 (October 1929): 11–12.

Harvey, O. L. "Recommendations for Legislative Reform in Prison, Parole, and Probation." *Journal of Criminal Law and Criminology* 27, no. 4 (1936): 539–44.

Haywood, Charles G. *General Alarm: A Dramatic Account of Fires and Fire-Fighting in America*. New York: Dodd, Mead, 1967.

Headsman. "1930: Lee Akers, after the Ohio Penitentiary Fire." ExecutedToday.com, June 13, 2012. http://www.executedtoday.com/2012/06/13/1930-lee-akers-ohio-penitentiary-fire/.

Helmer, William, and Rick Mattix. *Public Enemies: America's Criminal Past, 1919–1940*. New York: Checkmark Books, 1998.

Henderson, Andrew. *Forgotten Columbus*. Charleston, SC: Arcadia, 2002.

Hicks, Clara Belle. "The History of Penal Institutions in Ohio to 1850." *Ohio History Journal* 33 (July–October 1924): 359–425.

Higginbotham, Peter. *The Prison Cookbook*. Stroud, UK: History Press, 2010.

Himes, Chester. *Cast the First Stone*. New York: Coward-McCann, 1952.

———. *The Collected Stories of Chester Himes*. New York: Thunder's Mouth Press, 1991.

———. *The Quality of Hurt*. New York: Thunder's Mouth Press, 1988.

———. *Yesterday Will Make You Cry*. New York: W. W. Norton, 1998.

History of the Ohio Penitentiary, Annex and Prisoners: A Brief Sketch of Its Origin. Columbus: Ohio Penitentiary Printing, 1891.

Hooper, Osman Castle. "Preston Elmer Thomas." In *History of the City of Columbus, Ohio*, 466–67. Columbus: Memorial, ca. 1920.

Hopkins, Alfred. *Prisons and Prison Building*. New York: Architectural Book, 1930.

Howard, D. L. *John Howard: Prison Reformer*. New York: Archer House, 1963.

Illinois Prison Inquiry Commission. *The Prison System in Illinois: A Report to the Governor of Illinois*. N.p.: State of Illinois, 1937.

Irwin, John. *Prisons in Turmoil*. Boston: Little, Brown, 1980.

Jackson, Lawrence P. *Chester B. Himes: A Biography*. New York: W. W. Norton, 2017.

Jacobs, James B. *Stateville: The Penitentiary in Mass Society*. Chicago: University of Chicago Press, 1977.

Jaffray, Julia K., ed. *The Prison and the Prisoner*. Boston: Little, Brown, 1917.

Jennings, Al. *Through the Shadows with O. Henry*. New York: H. K. Fly, 1921.

Johnston, Norman. *The Human Cage: A Brief History of Prison Architecture*. New York: Walker, 1973.

———. *Forms of Constraint: A History of Prison Architecture*. Urbana: University of Illinois Press, 2000.

Johnston, Norman, with Kenneth Finkel and Jeffrey A. Cohen. *Eastern State Penitentiary: Crucible of Good Intentions*. Philadelphia: Philadelphia Museum of Art, 1994.

Jordan, Philip D. *Ohio Comes of Age: 1874–1899*. Columbus: Ohio State Archaeological and Historical Society, 1943.

Keve, Paul W. *Prison and the American Conscience: A History of U.S. Federal Corrections*. Carbondale: Southern Illinois University Press, 1991.

Killinger, George G., and Paul F. Cromwell Jr. *Penology: The Evolution of Corrections in America*. St. Paul: West, 1973.

Kirchwey, George W. "The Prison's Place in the Penal System." *Annals of the American Academy of Political and Social Science* 157, no. 1 (1931): 13–22.

Kramer, Samuel A. "The Norwood Law and Its Effect upon the Penal Problem in Ohio." *Journal of the American Institute of Criminal Law and Criminology* 21, no. 4 (1931): 553–97.

"Lack of Fire Resistive Material and Fire Protection Cost 320 Lives at Ohio State Penitentiary." *Safety Engineering* 59 (1930): 317–18.

Lane, Winthrop D. "Prisons Where Trouble May Come." *Survey* 61, no. 9 (1930): 399–401.

Lawes, Lewis E. *Life and Death in Sing Sing*. Garden City, NY: Doubleday, Doran, 1928.

———. *Twenty Thousand Years in Sing Sing*. New York: Ray Long and Richard R. Smith, 1932.

Lee, Alfred E. *History of the City of Columbus*. Chicago: Munsell, 1892.

Levinger, Lee J. "A Note on Jewish Prisoners in Ohio." *Jewish Social Studies* 2 (1940): 209–12.

Lindley, Harlow. *Ohio in the Twentieth Century, 1900–1938*. Columbus: Ohio State Archaeological and Historical Society, 1942.

Lundberg, D. E. "Methods of Selecting Prison Personnel." *Journal of Criminal Law and Criminology* 38, no. 1 (1947): 14–29.

Lunden, Walter A. *The Prison Warden and the Custodial Staff*. Springfield, IL: Charles C. Thomas, 1965.

Lundquist, James. *Chester Himes*. New York: Frederick Ungar, 1976.

MacCormick, Austin H., and Paul W. Garrett, eds. *Handbook of American Prisons, 1926*. New York: G. P. Putnam's Sons, 1926.

March, Ray A. *Alabama Unbound: Forty-Five Years Inside a Prison System*. Tuscaloosa: University of Alabama Press, 1978.

Margolies, Edward, and Michel Fabre. *The Several Lives of Chester Himes*. Jackson: University of Mississippi Press, 1997.

Matthews, J. H. *Historical Reminiscences of the Ohio Penitentiary from Its Erection in 1835 to the Present*. Columbus: Charles M. Cott, 1884.

Martin, John Bartlow. *Break Down the Walls: American Prisons, Present, Past, and Future.* New York: Ballantine Books, 1954.

McCarthy, John. "When Ohio Suffered Nation's Deadliest Prison Fire in 1930." *Morning Journal,* May 1, 2005.

McGraw, Peg, and Walter McGraw. *Assignment: Prison Riots.* New York: Henry Holt, 1954.

McKelvey, Blake. *American Prisons: A History of Good Intentions.* Montclair, NJ: Patterson Smith, 1977.

———. *American Prisons: A Study in American Social History Prior to 1915.* Chicago: University of Chicago Press, 1936.

Meyers, David, and Elise Meyers. *Central Ohio's Historic Prisons.* Charleston, SC: Arcadia, 2009.

Meyers, David, Elise Meyers Walker, and James Dailey II. *Inside the Ohio Penitentiary.* Charleston, SC: History Press, 2013.

Milliken, Stephen F. *Chester Himes: A Critical Appraisal.* Columbia: University of Missouri Press, 1976.

Mok, Michel. "The Talking Newspaper." *Popular Science Monthly,* August 1930, 53–55.

"More Prison Outbreaks Predicted." *Science News-Letter,* August 9, 1930, 91.

Morgan, Daniel J. *Historical Lights and Shadows of the Ohio State Penitentiary.* Columbus: Hann and Adair, 1899.

Morris, Norval, and David J. Rothman, eds. *The Oxford History of the Prison: The Practice of Punishment in Western Society.* New York: Oxford University Press, 1998.

National Society of Penal Information. *Handbook of American Prisons: Covering the Prisons of the New England and Middle Atlantic States.* New York: G. P. Putnam's Sons, 1925.

Nelson, Donald Lee. "The Ohio Prison Fire." *JEMF Quarterly* 9 (Summer 1973): 42–45.

Nelson, Victor F. *Prison Days and Nights.* Boston: Little, Brown, 1933.

Newman, Victoria R. *Prisons of Cañon City.* Charleston, SC: Arcadia, 2008.

"The 1930 Ohio State Penitentiary Fire." *National Fire Protection Association Journal* (September/October 1994): 54.

"Ohio Prison Catastrophe." *Commercial and Financial Chronicle,* May 3, 1930, 3059–61.

"Ohio's Holocaust." National Affairs. *Time,* April 23, 1930.

"Ohio's Prison Holocaust." *World's Work* 59 (1930): 19–20.

O'Quinn, Tremaine E., and Jenny Lind Porter. *Time to Write: How William Sidney Porter Became O. Henry.* Austin: Eakin Press, 1986.

Osborne, Thomas Mott. *Within Prison Walls: Being a Narrative of Personal Experience during a Week of Voluntary Confinement in the State Prison at Auburn.* New York: D. Appleton, 1916.

Parish, James Robert. *Prison Pictures from Hollywood.* Jefferson, NC: McFarland, 1991.

Patterson, Wayne K., and Betty L. Alt. *Slaughter in Cell House 3: Anatomy of a Riot.* Arvada, CO: vanderGeest, 1997.

Peterson, Clarence Stewart. "Prison Officers' Training Schools." *Journal of Criminal Law and Criminology,* 22, no. 6 (1932): 895–98.

"Prisoners in Ohio." *Ohio Citizen,* December 10, 1927, 1–22.

Proceedings of the Sixtieth Annual Congress of the American Prison Association. New York: American Prison Association, 1930.

Proceedings of the Sixty-First Annual Congress of the American Prison Association. New York: American Prison Association, 1931.

Proceedings of the Sixty-Second Annual Congress of the American Prison Association. New York: American Prison Association, 1932.

Proceedings of the Sixty-Third Annual Congress of the American Prison Association. New York: American Prison Association, 1933.

Proceedings of the Seventieth Annual Congress of the American Prison Association. New York: American Prison Association, 1940.

Prison System in Illinois, The. A Report to the Governor of Illinois by the Illinois Prison Inquiry Commission. N.p: State of Illinois, 1937.

Report of the National Commission on Law Observance and Enforcement (Wickersham Commission). Vol. 9, *Report on Penal Institutions, Probation and Parole.* Washington, DC: U.S. Government Printing Office, 1931.

Resch, John Phillips. "Ohio Adult Penal System, 1850–1900: A Study in the Failure of Institutional Reform." *Ohio History* 81, no. 4 (1972): 236–62.

Roberts, John W. *Reform and Retribution: An Illustrated History of American Prisons.* Lanham, MD: American Correctional Association, 1997.

Robinson, Louis N. "Jails and Workhouses Breed Crime." *American City* 40 (April 1929): 126–28.

———. *Should Prisoners Work?* Chicago: John C. Winston, 1931.

Roblee, Charles L., Allen J. McKechnie, and William Lundy. *The Investigation of Fires.* 2nd ed. Englewood Cliffs, NJ: Prentice Hall, 1988.

Rose, Donald G. *A Night of Horror.* N.p: CreateSpace, 2016.

Roth, Mitchel P. *Crime and Punishment: A History of the Criminal Justice System.* 2nd ed. Belmont, CA: Wadsworth, 2011.

———. *Prisons and Prison Systems: A Global Encyclopedia.* Westport, CT: Greenwood Press, 2006.

Rothman, David J. *Conscience and Convenience: The Asylum and Its Alternatives in Progressive America.* Boston: Little, Brown, 1980.

———. *The Discovery of the Asylum: Social Order and Disorder in the New Republic.* Rev. ed. Boston: Little, Brown, 1990.

Rotman, Edgardo. "The Failure of Reform: United States, 1865–1965." In *The Oxford History of the Prison: The Practice of Punishment in Western Society,* edited by Norval Morris and David J. Rothman, 151–77. New York: Oxford University Press.

Sallis, James. *Chester Himes: A Life.* New York: Walker, 2001.

Sellin, Thorsten. "Historical Glimpses of Training for Prison Service." *Journal of Criminal Law and Criminology* 25, no. 4 (1934): 594–600.

Short, Oliver C. "The Training and Selection of Institutional Personnel." In *Proceedings of the 63rd Annual Congress of the American Prison Association,* 226–36. New York: American Prison Association, 1933.

Simpson, Harry G. *The Prisoners of the Ohio Penitentiary: The Daily Routine of Their Lives.* Columbus: Hann and Adair, 1883.

Smith, Dennis. *Dennis Smith's History of Firefighting in America: 300 Years of Courage.* New York: Dial Press, 1978.

Stutsman, Jesse O. *Curing the Criminal: A Treatise on the Philosophy and Practices of Modern Correctional Methods*. New York: Macmillan, 1926.

Sullivan, Larry E. *The Prison Reform Movement: Forlorn Hope*. Boston: Twayne, 1990.

Suters, Charles. (1948). "Ohio's Prison Horror." In *Disaster!*, edited by Ben Kartman and Leonard Brown, 220–24. New York: Pellegrini and Cudahy, 1948.

Sutherland, Edwin H., and Thorsten Sellin, eds. *Prisons of Tomorrow*. Special issue, *Annals of the American Academy of Political and Social Science* 157, no. 1 (September 1931).

Sykes, Gresham M. *The Society of Captives: A Study of a Maximum Security Prison*. 3rd ed. Princeton, NJ: Princeton University Press, 1974.

Tannenbaum, Frank. *Wall Shadows: A Study in American Prisons*. New York: Putnam, 1922.

Thomas, Robert D. "Ohio Pen Inferno Called Worst U.S. Prison Fire." *Columbus Dispatch*, November 28, 1993, 71.

Thomas, T. J., and Dan W. Gallagher. *The Spotlight on Ohio's Black Crime*. Cleveland: Charles Margolian, 1930.

Thompson, Heather Ann. *Blood in the Water: The Attica Prison Uprising of 1971 and Its Legacy*. New York: Pantheon Books, 2016.

"Two Prison Mutinies." *New Republic*, August 7, 1929, 302.

Wallack, Walter M. *The Training of Prison Guards in the State of New York*. New York: Columbia University, 1938.

Wheeler, Melinda. "The Final Sentence: Prison Fire Kills 322." *Firehouse* (March 1980): 27–28, 30, 77–78.

Wicker, Tom. *A Time to Die*. New York: New York Times Books, 1975.

Wilcox, C. "Prison Conditions and Penal Reform." In *Editorial Research Reports 1930*, vol. 2. Washington, DC: CQ Press, 1930. http://library.cqpress.com/cqresearcher/cqresrre1930050800.

Wines, E. C., ed. *Transactions of the National Congress on Penitentiary and Reformatory Discipline Held at Cincinnati, Ohio, October 12–18, 1870*. Albany: Weed, Parsons, 1871.

Winning, James R. *Behind These Walls*. New York: Macmillan, 1933.

Writers' Program of the Works Projects Administration in the State of Ohio. *The Ohio Guide*. New York: Oxford University Press, 1962.

INDEX

National Prison Congress, first, 86–87, 105; Declaration of Principles, 86, 105
National Society of Penal Information, 67, 68, 196, 197
Nelson, Victor F., 109, 125

New Hall building, 77
New Jersey State Prison, 60
New York State Commissioner of Corrections, 198; fire hazards in New York prisons, 198
Nice, A. R., fire chief, 15, 22, 148, 157
Noel, William Robert, 14
Norwood Act, 88, 89
"notorious gun woman." *See* Schroeder, Irene
Notre Dame, 44

O'Brien, Albert, Father, 11, 17, 27; death of, 209
O. Henry, 66, 123
Ohio arson law, 187
Ohio Board of Censors, 208
Ohio Board of State Charities, 86
Ohio building fires, 69, 70; previous attempts at Ohio Penitentiary, 186; State Brick Plant fire, 69–70
Ohio Civil Service exam, 111
Ohio Militia, 166th Infantry Militia, 16
Ohio National Guard, 49, 164, 166, 171
Ohio Penitentiary, 2, 54–58, 62–83; arson, 19th century, 70; automobile tag shop, 77; banker's row, 65–66; cell locks, 77, 82, 156, 157; closed down, 212; courtyard, 28; dining hall, 68; doomed cellblocks, 67, 69, 77, 78, 80; drug addicts, 75; escapes from, 88; expansion of, 62; famous inmates, 3; as firetrap, 67; fire department prior to 1930, 71–72; G&H cellblocks, 46; guards, 49, 109; history of construction, 54–58; hospital, 41, 42; Idle House, 74, 116, 197; idleness of prisoners, 57, 68, 73, 74, 75, 76, 201; improvements to, 201; incendiary materials, 78–79; industries, 58; inmate admission protocol, 117; main entrance, 80; motion pictures of, 207, 208; New Hall, 63, 77; overcrowding, 76, 126; punishments, 63–65; renovations, 67; rules and regulations, 125; timber roof, 79; tours of, 65; strategic location of, 59; torn down, 212; tuberculosis, 116; vice, 126; wardens, 57; Wasserman tests, 117
Ohio Penitentiary arsonists, 179–87; capital case against, 186; escape plots, 183; first

break in case, 181; first suspects, 181; Grate and Gibbons admission, 183; incendiary, 179, 180; investigation, 179
Ohio Penitentiary News, 210
"Ohio Prison Fire" ballad, 1
Ohio State Fairgrounds, 44
Ohio State Journal, 36, 49
Ohio State Penitentiary. *See* Ohio Penitentiary
Ohio State Penitentiary, convicts. See convicts, Ohio Penitentiary
Ohio State University, 48, 61; Dr. James Snook, 98
Oliver, Charles, 20
opiates, 43
Orville, R. Carson, 166
Osborn, assistant fire chief, 19
Osborne Society, 126
overcrowding, and federal legislation, 76; Dyer Act, 76; Harrison Narcotic Drug Act, 76; Mann Act, 76

Paley, William S., 37
Paragon Oil, 18
Pathé News, 1
Patterson, Richard C., 198
Peel, Sir Robert, 104
Pennsylvania silent system, 57
physicians, response by, 34
Pi Kappa Alpha Fraternity, 48
Porter, William Sydney. *See* O. Henry
prison cell lock standards and technology, 77
Prison Community, The, 119
"Prisoner Aid Fund," 201
prison guards, 81, 103–14; better training, 200; overlapping shifts, 81; poor training, 81. *See also* keepers
prison labor and industries, 73–74; anti-labor legislation, 73–74; Hawes-Cooper Act, 74; state use system, 73, 74
prison movies, 207–8
prison riots, 90–94, 160, 203; Auburn Prison, 91, 93, 160; Canon City, 91, 92–93; Clinton Prison, 91; Halloween riot, 202; hostage taking, 76, 91, 160; Lucasville, 203–4; 1950s riots, 201; overcrowding, 94
prisons, regimentation in, 105
prison sentences, longer, 88–90
prison shirt stripes, 15
prison tours, 65
prison wardens, 95–102; demands on, 101; Ohio prison system, 96; political spoils